BLACK BRITISH DRAMA

Black British Drama: A Transnational Story looks afresh at the ways black theatre in Britain is connected to and informed by the spaces of Africa, the Caribbean and the USA.

Michael Pearce offers an exciting new approach to reading modern and contemporary black British drama, examining plays by a range of writers including Michael Abbensetts, Mustapha Matura, Caryl Phillips, Winsome Pinnock, Kwame Kwei-Armah, debbie tucker green, Roy Williams and Bola Agbaje. Chapters combine historical documentation and discussion with close analysis to provide an in-depth, absorbing account of post-war black British drama situated within global and transnational circuits.

A significant contribution to black British and black diaspora theatre studies, *Black British Drama* is a must-read for scholars and students in this evolving field.

Michael Pearce is a Lecturer in Socially Engaged Theatre at the University of Exeter, UK.

BLACK BRITISH DRAMA

A Transnational Story

Michael Pearce

Routledge
Taylor & Francis Group

LONDON AND NEW YORK

First published 2017
by Routledge
2 Park Square, Milton Park, Abingdon, Oxon OX14 4RN

and by Routledge
711 Third Avenue, New York, NY 10017

Routledge is an imprint of the Taylor & Francis Group, an informa business

British Library Cataloguing-in-Publication Data
A catalogue record for this book is available from the British Library

Library of Congress Cataloguing-in-Publication Data
Names: Pearce, Michael, 1977– author.
Title: Black British drama : a transnational story / Michael Pearce.
Description: New York : Routledge, 2017.
Identifiers: LCCN 2016051485| ISBN 9781138917859 (hardback) |
   ISBN 9781138917866 (pbk.) | ISBN 9781315688787 (ebook)
Subjects: LCSH: Black theater—Great Britain—History—20th century. |
   English drama—Black authors—History and criticism. | English
   drama—20th century—History and criticism.
Classification: LCC PN2595.13.B34 P43 2017 | DDC 792.089/
   960410904—dc23
LC record available at https://lccn.loc.gov/2016051485

ISBN: 978-1-138-91785-9 (hbk)
ISBN: 978-1-138-91786-6 (pbk)
ISBN: 978-1-315-68878-7 (ebk)

Typeset in Bembo
by Apex CoVantage, LLC

Printed and bound by CPI Group (UK) Ltd, Croydon, CR0 4YY

CONTENTS

PREFACE

I am writing this just a few months after Britain's decision to leave the EU and just before the Clinton versus Trump US election. In the background, the greatest refugee crisis since the Second World War. It is a time when politics in the West seems to be pulling at either the far left or far right sides of ideology.

I teach a course on twenty-first century black British drama at the University of Exeter. We discuss prominent black British playwrights who have been making waves over the last fifteen years. We contextualise their struggles and achievements in British and world history – slavery, colonisation, decolonisation, Civil Rights, Black Power, Brixton riots, the Stephen Lawrence murder, 9/11, 7/7. Black British theatre is a barometer for a changing Britain. It tracks this evolving landscape through its exploration of themes of migration, race, belonging and nation. It is also a model for understanding the changes occurring in our rapidly globalising world regardless of our cultural background or 'race' – whatever that word even means. In light of recent events, the issues embedded in the plays we discuss emerge more starkly than in previous years. It strengthens my belief that we are not studying works that speak to minority experiences. The plays speak to issues of global relevance that resonate with all individuals.

My own experiences of migration have nurtured an interest in the movement of people across national borders, the meeting of cultures and their effects. I was born in Zimbabwe, where I grew up and became a member of 'Over the Edge', the country's first professional multi-racial theatre company. Since then I have lived in South Africa, the USA, France and the UK. Approaching an analysis of late twentieth and early twenty-first century black British drama using a broader framework than the nation reflects the way in which I make sense of and have experienced the world. Having lived in South Africa during apartheid, I have also on many occasions seen first-hand the violence of racism and understood how racial difference is mobilised to divide and oppress. My career to date has been predicated on the belief that theatre can play a part in changing these belief systems and creating a better world.

This book draws on research for my PhD which was awarded in 2012. Since the PhD more scholarship has emerged that makes connections between black British drama, the nation and beyond. This still remains an under-researched area, however, with much work to be done. Since the PhD, I have published essays about contemporary black British playwrights, conducted a number of filmed interviews with theatre practitioners for the National Theatre's Black Plays Archive website and written a ten-part radio documentary about the history of black performance on the British stage and screen. The documentary was presented by Sir Lenny Henry and broadcast on BBC Radio 4 in late 2015. I learned a lot working with Lenny Henry who has been vocal about the lack of ethnic diversity in the media in all areas and levels of production. Institutional racism lies at the heart of this inequality. But if deep change is going to occur, it must happen at the level of education. If black British theatre history is not taught then our knowledge literally becomes whitewashed. How we understand the world and ourselves in it comes from what and how things are represented. It follows that to not tell is to forget, to make something un-happen, to render it invisible. Only once structures of oppression are made visible can we begin to dismantle them.

Exeter, October 2016

ACKNOWLEDGEMENTS

Thank you to Nicola Abram, Katie Beswick, Mary Brewer, Colin Chambers, Kate Edwards, Lynette Goddard, Graham Ley, Daniel Malamis, Jane Milling, Kate Newey, Deirdre Osborne, Dan Rebellato, Talia Rodgers, Kerrie Schaefer, Cathy Turner.

Thank you to the staff at the British Library, the George Padmore Institute, National Theatre Archive and the Victoria and Albert Museum.

A special thank you to the practitioners I interviewed for this book and over the course of my research in this area, including Mojisola Adebayo, Oladipo Agboluaje, Yvonne Brewster, Denton Chikura, Felix Cross, Inua Ellams, Arinze Kene, Kwame Kwei-Armah, Mustapha Matura, Courttia Newland, Roy Williams.

Special thanks to Gemma Birss, David Sabel and Christopher Stafford.

NOTES ON THE TEXT

Notes on terminology

In this book race is understood to be a socially constructed and contestable category. Throughout 'black' is spelt with a lower case 'b' indicating a non-essentialising term that refers to colour or racial identification. The upper case spelling – 'Black' – is used to connote an Afrocentric identity or articulate a political position of empowerment (e.g. Black Power). Race and ethnicity are not used interchangeably.

In the UK during the 1970s and 1980s the term 'Black' (adopted from the USA) signified a political identity used by people of African, Caribbean and South Asian descent in solidarity against the white majority. For example, the Indo-Trinidadian playwright Mustapha Matura identifies himself as Black. However, black was also used by the white majority as a blanket term which placed all non-white people into one homogeneous group. Today black tends to refer to people of African ancestry only.

In this book, reference to specific countries and cultures is balanced with the use of much broader terms 'Africa' and 'the Caribbean'. This usage responds to how some people self-identify with these continental/regional spaces. It also highlights how these vast and complex spaces become streamlined within the UK whereby, over time, intricate cultural differences and specific ethnic identifications become flattened out. Their usage also reflects how these terms are employed as organising categories in the UK at a popular (e.g. Caribbean carnival), political and cultural (e.g. the Africa Centre), and official level (e.g. in the Census).

Notes on referencing

When not included in the text, the year of a play's first production is provided in brackets when mentioned for the first time. Where this was in the UK the name of the theatre is provided where possible.

INTRODUCTION

Alvin: I can't live here, I can't live there. What am I supposed to do? What are we supposed to do? Live on a raft in the middle of the Atlantic at a point equidistant between Africa, the Caribbean and Britain?

(Phillips, C., 1981, pp. 98–99)

This outburst occurs at the end of Caryl Phillips' *Strange Fruit* [1980, Crucible Theatre]. British-born Alvin has returned from the (un-named) Caribbean island where his mother was born and grew up. Having left hopeful of forging a connection with his roots, he returns disillusioned by the poverty and corruption he encounters. As a young black man he feels unwelcome in Britain. Neither is he able to identify with his brother's Black Power-inspired 'back to Africa' politics. His declaration that 'the only people who can help me are either too busy playing white or too busy playing black' (Phillips, C., 1981, p. 88) marks his shift in understanding race as a constructed category and not something determined by nature. Ultimately, he rejects those who attempt to box him into an identity based on rigid notions of race, ethnicity or nation. Instead, Alvin begins to see himself, and his place in the world, in terms of process rather than fixity, defined by connection not separatism, at the junction of Africa, the Caribbean and Britain.

Black British Drama: A Transnational Story examines the ways in which black British plays are generated in, and speak to, multiple spatial, cultural, and political contexts. It proposes a number of transnational frameworks to trace the ways in which people, cultures and ideas from the USA and countries in Africa and the Caribbean have converged in the UK and how these find dramatic representation. That is not to suggest that black British drama is proof of a trend of global deterritorialisation. Taking as its starting point the 1970s, the space of the UK and the specificities of the British socio-political and cultural landscape remain central to this discussion of playwrights who mostly all live in Britain (specifically England) where their plays are regularly set (often in London). Nevertheless, the underlying contention of this book remains that a national paradigm alone is not capable of containing this complex and textured history or of providing the necessary analytic tools with which to discuss it.

The prioritisation of the nation as a framework in black British cultural historiography and discussions of post-war black British drama has been both politically responsive and urgent. Michael McMillan and SuAndi remind us that 'the experience of the black communities forms a cultural and political backdrop and mediates the discourse of black performance in theatre and representation in Britain' (2002, p. 122). In particular, the struggle to belong has powerfully shaped political and cultural agendas. Although mindful of talking about a monolithic 'black experience', social and political histories of post-war Britain, such as Paul Gilroy's provocatively titled *There Ain't No Black in the Union Jack* (1987), consistently highlight how because of their race black people in Britain were excluded from sharing in a sense of belonging to what Benedict Anderson describes as the nation's 'imaginary community' (1991, p. 6).

The immediate post-war period saw mass migration of non-white people to the UK. Although hostility towards immigrants was nothing new (for example, the experience of the Irish), the non-white presence in what had fundamentally been a racially homogenous island precipitated a crisis, as the 1958 race riots in Nottingham and London's Notting Hill testified. Black people did not fit in with the nation's sense of self and, despite being *in*, they were not regarded as *of* the nation. The association of blackness with non-Britishness ran much deeper than birthright, as was highlighted in the racist views of Conservative MP Enoch Powell's speech at the London Rotary Club at Eastbourne on 16 November 1968:

> The West Indian or Asian does not, by being born in England, become an Englishman. In law, he becomes a United Kingdom citizen by birth; in fact he is a West Indian or an Asian still.
>
> *(Powell, 1968b)*

Despite the implementation of Race Relations Acts in 1965, 1968 and 1976 (which also saw the establishment of the Commission for Racial Equality), institutional racism remained entrenched. Black people faced persistent discrimination, in particular from the police. The controversial 'sus' law, which gave the police stop and search powers, mainly targeted black male youth. Race-related riots in 1975 (Chapeltown), 1976 (Notting Hill Carnival), 1980 (St. Pauls), 1981 (Brixton, Peckham, Chapeltown, Handsworth, Moss Side, Toxteth) and again in 1985 (Brixton, Handsworth, Tottenham) made visible the level of indignation at being treated as second-class citizens. The situation reached boiling point with the maturation of a generation of black people who were born in Britain. The adoption of the term 'Black British' as a political signifier of solidarity among non-whites sent a message to the Establishment that black and Asian people were, to quote a slogan at the time, 'Here to Stay' (Owusu, 2000, p. 9).

Black British plays since the 1970s reflect this struggle to belong in their thematic enquiries. The struggle has also undoubtedly been one for the right to being produced. Naseem Khan's Arts Council sponsored report, *The Arts Britain Ignores: The Arts of Ethnic Minorities in Britain* (1976), was the first of its kind to draw attention to issues of lack of funding and visibility faced by ethnic minority artists. It also linked the peripheral status assigned to minority theatre practitioners by the state at the time to the perception that they and their art were not really 'British'. Despite a number of reports, events and funding initiatives to raise awareness of and encourage multiculturalism and diversity in the theatre since 1976, improvements to equality on and backstage have, arguably, been slow. It is telling that a quarter of a century after Khan's report, the Eclipse Theatre Conference, held at the Nottingham Playhouse in 2001, aimed to identify and implement solutions to systemic racial inequalities in the theatre industry.[1]

Nevertheless, the visibility of black drama in high-profile London venues, including the National Theatre and the Royal Court, in the 2000s has been noted (see Goddard, 2015; Osborne, 2006a). In 2003, Kwame Kwei-Armah's *Elmina's Kitchen* premiered at the National Theatre's Cottesloe Theatre (now the Dorfman), before transferring to the Garrick Theatre in 2005, where it became the first drama by a black British-born writer to be staged in the commercial West End. The mainstream success of Caribbean-origin playwrights such as Kwei-Armah, debbie tucker green and Roy Williams might suggest, as one theatre critic put it, that black British theatre has 'come of age' (Crompton, 2003).

Black British theatre scholarship is also increasing. However, it remains an underrepresented field of enquiry. Claire Cochrane notes the 'fragmented and inadequate published record, itself a product of marginalisation within the academy' (2011, p. 224). Alongside book chapters and journal articles, key books that deal specifically with black (sometimes incorporating Asian) British theatre have only recently emerged.[2] These include: Gabriele Griffin's *Contemporary Black and Asian Women Playwrights in Britain* (2003); Geoffrey Davis and Anne Fuchs' edited volume *Staging New Britain: Aspects of Black and South Asian Theatre Practice* (2006); Dimple Godiwala's edited volume *Alternatives within the Mainstream: British Black and Asian Theatres* (2006); Lynette Goddard's *Staging Black Feminisms: Identity, Politics, Performance* (2007); Colin Chambers' *Black and Asian Theatre in Britain: A History* (2011), Rodreguez King-Dorset's *Black British Theatre Pioneers: Yvonne Brewster and the First Generation of Actors, Playwrights and other Practitioners* (2014), Mary Brewer, Lynette Goddard and Deirdre Osborne's edited volume *Modern and Contemporary Black British Drama* (2015); and Lynette Goddard's *Contemporary Black British Playwrights: Margins to Mainstream* (2015).

Black British Drama engages with and responds to how the field has mainly been discussed to date, while introducing an accent on transnationalism. Playwrights and plays are privileged, with an implicit emphasis on the dramaturgy of scripts. Although primary sources do exist, archives are incomplete, records are scattered and perhaps crucially recordings of live productions are rare or difficult to access (Osborne, 2006b, p. 77).[3] As a result, criticism has had to be weighted in favour of playwrights and invariably relies upon a text-based approach when, as so often, viewing past performances is not possible. So while the analysis focuses on thematic enquiry, where possible performance forms and aesthetics have been included in the discussions of plays. Providing a historical record of productions remains important to the field. Throughout this book, therefore, attention is paid to listing plays and productions by individual playwrights and theatre companies.

If criticism has tended to focus on content rather than form, employing 'non-dramatic methodologies' to discuss themes (Peacock, 2015, p. 155), then in particular cultural studies have formed a key resource for discussions of black British drama. Prominent cultural theorists Stuart Hall, Paul Gilroy and Kobena Mercer have not written in any detail about black British theatre; however, their theorisation on black British culture and particularly their emphasis on representational discourses have resulted in their frequent inclusion in analyses of black British drama and historiography. This book is no different and draws extensively on their research. The pioneering work carried out by the Race and Politics Group of the Centre for Contemporary Cultural Studies (CCCS) at the University of Birmingham, led by Stuart Hall, is particularly pertinent to a discussion of post-war black British belonging (see Centre for Contemporary Cultural Studies, 1982). The CCCS explored the way in which British national identity was constructed through imperialism. In the context of the economic recession of the 1970s, their work demonstrated how racism operated through representational discourses that constructed black people as outsiders and a threat to Britishness. Issues such as lack of housing and jobs, low wages, school overcrowding and violence came to be blamed on immigration. Black people became the scapegoats for the economic and social failures of the nation whereby 'the "alien" cultures of the blacks are seen as either the cause or else the most visible symptom of the destruction of the "British way of life"' (Lawrence, 1982, p. 47). These scholars aimed to 'decouple' the notion of ethnicity 'from its equivalence with nationalism, imperialism, racism and the state' (Hall, 1988, p. 29). At the same time, they provided an historical revisionism, which demonstrated the closely intertwined relationship Britain had with the cultures of the people it had colonised and how they had shaped British culture in the process. The point of this revisionism was to unpack notions of Britishness from their automatic association with ethnic and racial purity. These cultural theorists, particularly Hall, have persuasively argued that the presence of non-white people in post-war Britain has expanded and re-defined Britishness. By drawing attention to the fact that white British people – more specifically white English people – are themselves ethnically located, a plethora of what Hall refers to as 'new ethnicities' (1988) have emerged, complicating essentialist assumptions of both blackness and Britishness. These post-structural critiques of race and nation and of how blackness has re-defined Britishness have been carried over into black British theatre scholarship.

The genealogy of post-war black British drama is typically discussed as having three 'generations'. The first generation of playwrights who immigrated to the UK between the 1950s and 1970s are understood to have retained strong connections with their countries of origin. Their plays were often entirely set in their homelands or, when set in the UK, focused on themes of alienation, (un)belonging, disillusionment with the 'Mother Land' and expressed a nostalgic yearning for home. Their British-born children (the 'early' second generation), writing in the 1980s and 1990s, focused on issues of identity wrought by their in-between status as both British-born and children of immigrants, yielding dominant themes of inter-generational culture-clash, (un)belonging and self-discovery. Themes of racial identity, racism and national belonging are highlighted as prominent during this period. Second-generation playwrights writing since the millennium have begun to represent the third generation, frequently urban youth who, in Hall's words, 'look as if they *own* the territory' (1987, p. 44). Following suit, some scholars argue that diasporic themes and associated issues of identity are less prevalent in contemporary black British plays than they were previously (see Goddard, 2015; Peacock, 2008, 2015). Terms now being used to describe black British theatre include 'indigenous' (Osborne, 2006a, p. 96) and some commentators, such as D. Keith Peacock, reflecting on the work of debbie tucker green, imagine a time in the not-too-distant future when 'the designation '*black* British drama' will no longer be relevant' (2008, p. 63). This 'three generations' narrative charts the journey from immigrant to indigenous – an echo of African American discourses which map the journey from slave to citizen. It is a journey, such scholarship argues, that is reflected as much in the themes of the texts themselves, as in black British theatre's position within the British theatre landscape as it moves from 'margins to mainstream'.[4]

The way in which migration has traditionally been understood as a linear process that results in acculturation over subsequent generations (Vertovec, 2009, p. 13) has further cemented the reliance of a national paradigm in black British theatre scholarship. This 'three generations' narrative is partly due to black British theatre scholarship focusing on Caribbean British playwrights. To some extent this can be accounted for by demographics – the majority of black immigrants came from the Caribbean in the immediate post-war period and the majority of twentieth century black British playwrights of profile have been of Caribbean heritage. However, it would not be unfair to say that African-origin playwrights in the UK have, until recently, been largely overlooked, a gap this book begins to redress.[5] The arrival of the *SS Empire Windrush* on the 22 June 1948 at Tilbury Docks in England carrying 492 Caribbean migrants (mainly Jamaican men) is cited as the starting point for a number of historical narratives of post-war black British theatre (see, for example, Goddard, 2007; Thomas, 2015). Mass migration from the Caribbean to Britain as part of the post-war reconstruction reached its peak in the 1960s 'and was effectively over by 1973' (Peach, 1996, p. 28). To some extent, therefore, the generational narrative holds in so far as it relates to the point of migration but not necessarily the thematic focus of the plays.

Experiences of racism in post-war Britain hindered acculturation and engendered strong ties with other global black communities with similar experiences of racial oppression. Gilroy argues that 'the assimilation of blacks is not a process of acculturation but of cultural syncretism [. . .] Accordingly, their self-definitions and cultural expressions draw on a plurality of black histories and politics. In the context of modern Britain this has produced a diaspora dimension to black life' (1987, pp. 155–156). This 'diaspora dimension', or the social, political and cultural relationships maintained with the homeland and forged between other black people of African origin outside of the UK, can also be traced in black British theatre, particularly through its plays. Questions of influence and tradition underwritten by race-based identification remain underexplored in relation to black British drama. As Bruce King points out, 'when a literature starts alluding to and building upon its predecessors there is a tradition' (2004, p. 7). But, it cannot be assumed that influences are necessarily inherited from previous generations or acquired from the immediate social and cultural milieu in which a writer is positioned. The issue at stake, as John McLeod argues in his discussion of black British literature, is that if we only regard black *British* art within the space of the nation, then there is the danger of 'falsifying the mechanics of black British creativity and tradition'; if analyses become 'spatially constricted', this will impact negatively upon the way an artist's work is 'mapped, remembered and read' (2006, p. 98). When one begins to examine plays through a broader lens than the nation, the explanatory power of generational taxonomies begins to weaken.

Some scholarship on works by first and 'early' second-generation playwrights has revealed how, through a dramatic text's thematic explorations and performance, black British theatre has the potential to challenge dominant discourses by staging alternative national and cultural identities. In her chapter on the subject, Mary Karen Dahl prefers to describe black British theatre as postcolonial as opposed to immigrant theatre, as it acknowledges the multiple cultural occupancies of black Britons yet does not erase the imperial past (1995, pp. 52–53). In a broader study on the performance of citizenship, May Joseph places movement at the heart of the black British plays under discussion which, she argues, challenge neatly bound notions of national belonging (1999, pp. 95–96). And, in her chapter 'Bodies outside the state: black British women playwrights and the limits of citizenship' (1998) Joseph also identifies transnational affiliations in Winsome Pinnock's *A Rock in Water* [1989, Royal Court Theatre] and Jacqueline Rudet's *Basin* [1985, Royal Court Theatre]. In her monograph, Griffin (2003) provides an in-depth study of the diasporic condition as expressed thematically through black and Asian women's drama. She explores how dramatists represent the effects of occupying an in-between or (borrowing Hélène Cixous' term) '*entre-deux*' cultural position between the (parental) homeland and Britain as host-land or birth place. However, scholarship that employs a poststructuralist theorising of diaspora or which draws on postcolonial criticism tends to be more concerned with cultural intermixture and instances of resistance and re-definition of dominant narratives within the host society than with the nationalistic characteristics of diaspora, such as a maintained connection with the homeland and transnational relationships with other members of the same diaspora. Despite the employment of frameworks that stretch beyond the nation, the idea that black British theatre contributes to the racial and cultural re-framing of Britain and the theatre landscape concludes these discussions, although the degree to which this has been achieved remains contentious.

The achievements of 'later' second-generation playwrights whose plays have been staged in mainstream venues in the 2000s (but who were also working in the 1990s) have been historicised by scholars through particular national events and crises. For instance, Meenakshi Ponnuswami (2015) contextualises arts funding initiatives and the rise to prominence of writers such as Roy Williams, Kwame Kwei-Armah and Winsome Pinnock against the race riots of the 1980s. Goddard (2015) links changes in arts funding policy and the mainstream visibility of neo-millennial playwrights such as Roy Williams (along with Bola Agbaje, Kwame Kwei-Armah and debbie tucker green) to 'major public traumas' (p. 7), specifically Stephen Lawrence's murder in 1993. The Macpherson Report (1999), which identified institutional racism in the Metropolitan Police Service's mishandling of the investigation of Stephen Lawrence's murder in 1993 and ushered in the Race Relations (Amendment) Act of 2000, bound public organisations by law to promote race equality, equal opportunity and eliminate discriminatory practices. The aims of the Eclipse Theatre Conference were explicitly linked to the Macpherson Report. Goddard highlights this conference and its recommendations published in the Arts Council's *Eclipse Report* (2002) as key to opening the door to the mainstream success enjoyed by a number of black playwrights in the 2000s (2015, p. 9).

Black British Drama adds to and extends studies of first and early second-generation playwrights by mapping the transnational affiliations in a significant number of plays produced in Britain since the 1970s in relation to the geo-cultural spaces of Africa, the Caribbean and the USA. This is carried out in three contextual chapters which begin each of the book's three sections. This book also seeks to situate contemporary black British drama more firmly within historical and contemporary global social, political and cultural currents. In order to do so, six playwrights working since the 2000s have been chosen as case studies. To this end this book responds to and extends some of the scholarship that has begun to reflect on the ways in which neo-millennial plays engage with wider concerns beyond the nation. In doing so *Black British*

Drama: A Transnational Story reiterates that plays by black British dramatists are testament to and an active agent in the changing British social, political and cultural landscape, *and* they speak to and are positioned in a variety of other social, cultural and political spaces.

The movement of people and products across national borders that the term transnational describes has stimulated the transfer, adoption and adaptation of cultures around the world. Although not a new phenomenon, this movement across and between nation states has been facilitated by technological advancements which have been closing the gap between places, knitting distances together to create what Marshall McLuhan famously termed the 'global village' (1962, p. 43). Globalisation – or the reduction in world-space and world-time (Steger, 2009, p. 22) – has resulted in the increasing interconnection of people and cultures as well as new ways of perceiving, or what Roland Robertson describes as 'global consciousness' (1992). One of these new ways of perceiving is transnationalism. Transnationalism has provided 'a new analytic optic which makes visible the increasing intensity and scope of circular flows of persons, goods, information and symbols triggered by international labour migration' (Caglar qtd in Vertovec, 2009, pp. 13–14). This book does not propose transnationalism as a theory but rather a way of considering, a lens which draws attention to the relationships that exist between black British playwrights and plays with other specific nations and broader geo-cultural spaces.

Migration remains intrinsic to discussions of black British playwriting. Arguably, the theme of migration has abated in plays by contemporary second generation Caribbean British writers. However, debbie tucker green, Kwame Kwei-Armah and Roy Williams have all set work in the Caribbean. Thinking about their plays through migration also sheds light onto their dramatic structuring.[6] In many of their plays, black British families and communities are represented as generationally stratified, whereby fundamental differences between characters are articulated through their proximity to the moment of migration. This is signified in the text and performance not just through age but also through a character's ethnicity, views, use of language and accent. Caution should be used in drawing conclusions about an entire group from a playwright's representation of a small set of characters; however, this suggests that the Caribbean remains a vital creative space for these playwrights. This corroborates existing social scientific research into the persistence of transnational relationships between second and third-generation black Britons and the Caribbean (see Goulbourne 2002; Goulbourne, Reynolds, Solomos and Zontini 2010; Reynolds 2006). Furthermore, the black population in Britain continues to be re-defined by the arrival of new immigrant communities. According to a comparison of ethnicity and national identity data collected in 2001 and 2011, the number of black people of Caribbean heritage has remained almost the same over the twenty-year period since the 1991 census. The black African population, on the other hand, has doubled since 2001 (Office for National Statistics, 2012). This increase is reflected in the theatre, which has seen a significant increase in plays produced by first and second-generation African British playwrights, mainly from Nigeria. Furthermore, whereas the number of black African and black Caribbean people who are British born is roughly the same (323K and 358K respectively), the non-UK born African population is nearly two-thirds bigger than the non-UK born Caribbean population (666K and 237K respectively) and double that of both the African and Caribbean UK-born populations (Office for National Statistics, 2015). Therefore, the majority of Britain's black population are first-generation immigrants. Thus, issues of migration, diaspora and identity remain pertinent for black British playwrights and audiences. In light of this, the term 'indigenous' as applied to describe black British practitioners demands scrutiny. The word's implication of irrefutable belonging has merit as an argument for black inclusion. However, the term is uncomfortably entwined with nationalist discourses. Invoked to differentiate those of the nation from the 'other', it ironically reinstates and repeats binaries of us/them that disallowed black people from being seen as British in the first place. Thus, the term's use to describe second and third-generation black Britons problematically distinguishes black people born here from those who were not, but who nevertheless have grown up in the UK. It gives British-born black people a measure of authenticity and a stronger claim to entitlement over new arrivals. Although the African presence in British theatre has a long history, emerging more confidently in the 1990s (as seen in Chapter 9), the inclusion and analysis of African British playwrights in studies of black British theatre has only just begun.

New technologies have enhanced transnational experiences and practices (Vertovec, 2009, pp. 14–16). In particular, recent plays by African British writers represent characters living – like some of their authors – between countries, with families scattered in cities such as London, New York and Lagos. In such instances the cosmopolitan experiences of the playwrights and the worlds they represent illustrate the turn towards the 'Afropolitan' (see Selasi, 2005 for a discussion of this term). The confident representation of intercultural modes and transnational lifestyles in plays by writers such as Nigerian British Bola Agbaje and Inua Ellams lends credence to the assertion that 'in many Western countries 25 years of identity politics . . . have created a context in which migrants feel much more at ease when publicly displaying their transnational connections' (Vertovec, 2009, p. 16). In comparison with many developing countries in Africa and the Caribbean, the UK during the latter half of the twentieth century has provided an economically stable, tolerant and democratic space which has drawn people in search of a better life (cf King, 2004, p. 5). For playwrights, the existence of a professional and subsidised theatre industry and the protection of free speech are added features that have made the UK an attractive place to settle. Arguably, in the context of multicultural Britain, maintaining ties to the homeland has become increasingly possible and even encouraged. Although multiculturalism has never been officially codified in Britain (unlike in Canada and Australia), as Anne Phillips notes, in the latter half of the twentieth century Britain has seen a process of 'multicultural drift', defined as 'a series of smallish adjustments and accommodations that added up to a quite substantial practice of multiculturalism' (2007, p. 5). A number of plays in this study reiterate how in this globalised environment identification with a single nation is rendered more tenuous. The intention is not to paint an overly optimistic picture. Since 9/11 and in the aftermath of subsequent terrorist attacks, critics of multiculturalism have become more vociferous. On 20 April 2008, Trevor Phillips, as chair of the Equality and Human Rights Commission (EHRC), gave a speech entitled 'Not a River of Blood, but a Tide of Hope: Managed Immigration, Active Integration'. In his speech, given forty years after Powell's 'Rivers of Blood' speech in 1968 and delivered from the same venue in Birmingham, Phillips highlighted the need to pursue 'a positive policy of active integration' in the fight against racism (Phillips, T., 2008).[7] Subsequently, David Cameron, then Prime Minister of the UK, gave a speech on 5 February 2011 in which he also criticised multicultural policy for encouraging separatism, and allowing 'the weakening of our collective identity' (2011). Increasingly, political rhetoric celebrates diversity on the one hand while insisting upon fidelity to the nation and adherence to certain British values on the other. This supports the observation that 'cultural diversity and transnational affiliations are seen to always harbour a danger of unruliness and political unreliability (Lindner, Mohring, Stein and Stroh, 2010, p. xxxii). These tensions and uncertainties register thematically in a number of plays in this study, particularly Agbaje's *Detaining Justice*. It should be noted that the UK's recent European Union referendum debate and its result has exposed racist and xenophobic beliefs and opinions and prompted aggressive acts, as documented by the media (see Boult, 2016; Dodd, 2016; Lusher, 2016). However, this occurred after any plays discussed in this book. A brief consideration of the future for black British drama and its study in light of the referendum result is offered in the conclusion.

One of the transnational analytical frameworks employed by this study is diaspora. In a narrow sense, diaspora describes the maintained relationship immigrants and their descendants have with their respective ancestral countries of origin (e.g. Nigerian diaspora). Used in this way it is, as Griffin's (2003) study demonstrates, a helpful trope to describe the experience of in-between-ness articulated by characters in a number of black British plays. However, Griffin's interpretation of diaspora as a condition defined by in-between-ness or the '*entre-deux*' can be further complicated. If we take into account the diasporic subject's relationship not only to their home and host-land, but with other members of the diaspora in different locations and what unites them, i.e. a common ancestral homeland, diaspora can be seen to encompass a triangular relationship or *entre-trois*. This 'triadic relationship' (Vertovec, 2009, p. 4) finds articulation in the notion of the African diaspora.

George Shepperson, basing his definition of the African diaspora on the classical model of the Jewish dispersion beyond Israel, defines traumatic dispersal (forced removal in the case of slavery and the flight from persecution under colonialism) and the sense of a shared original homeland as its key characteristics (1968, p. 152). Complex social networks and political movements based on shared experiences of racism and resistance have been forged between black people living in countries in Africa, Europe and the Americas since slavery. Shepperson's formulation and subsequent theorisations of the term have arisen in order to chart and comprehend these 'diverse and cross-fertilized black traditions of resistance and anticolonialism' (Edwards, 2004, pp. 14–15). The African diaspora (also referred to as the Black diaspora) pivots around the notion of blackness. White, Asian and other African minorities, for instance, are not included in its conceptualisation. For this reason the term often conveys essentialist and nationalist ideology.[8] This is especially in evidence in some Pan-African, Afrocentric and Black nationalistic rhetoric, discussed in the following chapter.

In contrast, in *The Black Atlantic* (1993) Gilroy proposes an anti-essentialist model of African diasporic interaction that should be perceived in terms of 'routes' and not 'roots' (p. 133). He attacks cultural and political discourses that emphasise the 'aspiration to acquire a supposedly authentic, natural, and stable 'rooted' identity' (p. 30), which he sees as a legacy of Euro-American nationalist ideology. Gilroy's study of relationships forged between black people in the diaspora allows one to conceptualise blackness in terms of solidarity forged historically through social, cultural and political interaction and exchange, without purveying essentialist and homogenous notions. Providing another nuanced perspective, Michelle Wright identifies black diasporic identity operating between two extremes: the 'hypercollective', essentialist position and the 'hyperindividual'. A convincing definition of an African or black diasporic identity requires negotiating diversity and individuality with commonality and connection (2004, p. 2). Although, in Wright's words, 'there is no one historical moment or cultural trope to which one can link all of the African diasporic communities now living in the West' (Wright, 2004, p. 3), belief in certain shared experiences still nourishes identification and linkages that impact artistic expression.

Wright's formulation offers this book a constructive organising principle for the analysis of black British drama. For many black British playwrights, the category 'black' still has relevance, despite some scepticism about the term. For instance, in an interview in 2009, playwright Roy Williams was happy to disregard the 'black playwright' label: 'I stopped worrying about labels long ago. Once there was a big thing about whether to be called a black playwright, and I thought, do what you like, just don't miss out the word playwright! If you want to worry about the label black, go ahead, but I'm not' (qtd in Sierz, 2009). This is a confident attitude, and might in part be related to the historical moment in which Williams was speaking. Not long before, 2003 had been described in the press as a 'boom time for black theatre' (Crompton, 2003) because a number of playwrights had had their work staged in the same year, including some in mainstream venues.[9] The comment might also reflect his assumption of a post-black identity. Elam and Jones describe post-black playwrights as artists whose work moves beyond traditional definitions of blackness (Elam and Jones, 2012, p. ix), and the capital 'B' black politics of the late 1960s and 1970s with its emphasis on the collective experience of racism, notions of a 'black community' and a 'black experience' that elided other factors that determine experience, such as class, gender, sexuality and ethnicity. However, following the 2010 UK general election where the Labour government was replaced by the Conservative-Liberal Democratic Coalition and in the context of economic austerity and plans to cut arts funding, Williams revised his position: 'I think we need that [black British] phrase more than ever . . . we need to do whatever we can to jump up and say we're here' (qtd in interview with Michael Pearce, 2010). It is clear that connotations of community and solidarity can accompany the label 'black' which offers a means to imagine and even organise collective resistance. This supports Stuart Hall's observation of two overlapping and co-existing moments in black cultural politics in Britain. Whilst the overarching notion of 'Blackness' has yielded to incorporate multiple subject positions or 'new ethnicities' in recognition of 'the extraordinary diversity of subjective positions, social experiences and cultural identities which compose the category 'black", the political importance of the project based upon a constructed collective identity nevertheless endures, so long as racism exists (Hall, 1988, p. 27). When examining black British drama one is confronted by a practice that is 'rooted' within and 'routed' through the nation (Gilroy, 1993). This is reflective of a wider experience whereby some black people in Britain claim the UK as 'a site of identity' while also embracing and retaining a number of cross-cultural and transnational affiliations (Petropoulos, 2006, p. 106). As 'black' does not refer to a homogenous group with a singular history and culture then, as Mark Stein suggests in his reading of black British literature, black cultural production should be understood in terms of 'plural alliances' (2004, p. 17). In this regard, borders should not be perceived as sites of separation but as sites of confluences and crossings.

The influence of the USA on black British theatre has not been explored in any detail. Although the USA has not meaningfully contributed to the black British demographic, when thinking of diaspora as a 'triadic relationship' it comes into focus as an important and influential space for black British drama. Similarity in experiences of being a minority suffering racial discrimination combined with the global visibility of black American politics and culture has meant that African America has provided a powerful point of comparison for black people in Britain. Apart from the number of African American politicians, actors, theatre directors and playwrights who have visited the UK or temporarily based themselves in Britain, the distribution of cultural products – 'African Americana' – has had a significant impact on black British identity and cultural production. Films, television shows, music and novels are frequently cited as influential on playwrights. Furthermore, the visible impact of African American culture on black British dramatists reminds us that transnational movement is not restricted to people. Neither is it the privy of cosmopolitan elites; in an increasingly mediatised world, transnational social and political formations can operate within and through physically rooted communities.

A key issue confronting scholars is finding appropriate critical frameworks with which to discuss black British drama. Referring to newspaper critics, Osborne finds that 'much of the neglectful reception of new black writing appears to stem from the lack of knowledge of the cultural networks and writing worlds in which these playwrights circulate and from where they draw their inspiration' (2006a, p. 98). Similarly, the 'methodological nationalism' (Albert, Bluhm, Helmig, Leutzsch and Walter, 2009, p. 13) of scholarship that relies on a national paradigm and narratives of belonging risks imposing what John Ball describes as a 'Eurocentric hermeneutics' by forcing a 'common agenda' upon a group of heterogeneous people and texts (2004, p. 12). A transnational perspective facilitates the identification and implementation of theoretical frameworks embedded in and which have emerged out of networks that exist between black people in the UK, the USA and countries in Africa and the Caribbean. Attempts to cultivate black or 'indigenous' (pre-colonial) aesthetics have been influenced by transnational political and cultural nationalist movements including anti-slavery, Pan-Africanism, the Harlem Renaissance, Negritude, anti-colonialism, decolonization, Civil Rights and Black Power. Despite operating within specific contexts, many of the conversations surrounding dramatic composition and aesthetic approaches are ideologically inter-connected. Attempts by black writers to recuperate and incorporate 'indigenous' African or African-origin/diasporic cultural practices, histories and myths occur in plays found across Africa, the Caribbean, the USA and in the UK. This book looks at black aesthetics and content from elsewhere in order to determine how they have impacted and shaped approaches to black British drama. By examining black British plays in relation to international examples and practices, the degree to which black British drama is influenced by, and how it articulates, a politics of race-based solidarity can also be assessed.[10]

The book is divided into three sections, focused on the USA, the Caribbean and Africa. Each section comprises three chapters. The first chapter in each section establishes a particular transnational process and mode of analysis: the USA section examines black British drama through the lens of 'African Americanisation', specifically in relation to Black Power and Afrocentrism, the Caribbean through 'creolisation' and Africa through the notion of 'diaspora'. These contextual chapters also apply these theories to a broad range of plays produced in the UK since the 1970s. This historical approach frames the discussion in order to contextualise the processes that have led to the emergence of various cross-cultural and political interactions and their impact on black plays and playwriting. The remaining two chapters in each section focus on a contemporary dramatist and a selection of their work.

Black British Drama is a study of plays by black and mixed-race people who were born in or who have lived for an extended period in the UK. The discussion takes the 1970s as its starting point, reflecting the beginnings of sustained black play writing activity in Britain. The research encompasses black theatre companies in so far as they play an important role in staging new writing. A number of plays are listed for their treatment of various themes and influences and while there is not the scope to provide detailed synopses or analyses, it is hoped this mapping will provide a launch pad for further interrogations.

The order of the sections is loosely chronological in terms of black British theatre history. The USA provided the UK with its first black actors of note and mainstream theatrical representations of black people. In the post-war period and latter half of the twentieth century black British theatre has had a distinct Caribbean influence, reflecting the origins of the majority of the black population at that time. The composition of the black population began to change significantly from the 1990s which saw increased emigration from Africa. The theatre has responded to these changes and the early twenty-first century has seen an increase in playwrights of African origin and the exploration of African-related themes and issues.

The USA

In the first chapter in this section, Chapter 1, the notion of 'African Americanisation' frames the discussion. It traces the influence of Black Power on black British theatre's formation, organisation and expression in the post-war period. Chapters 2 and 3 examine works by Kwame Kwei-Armah (British-born of Grenadian parentage) and Mojisola Adebayo (British-born to a black Nigerian father and a white Danish mother). Kwei-Armah's work is discussed in relation to African American political and artistic influences, particularly the writers of the Black Arts Movement and August Wilson. Ideas of legacy sit alongside a discussion of his dramatisation of the impact of the past on the present. The influence of black America is also traced in Adebayo's work. The chapter discusses two of her plays which weave autobiography with the life stories of African Americans Ellen Craft and Muhammad Ali respectively. Linking with the previous chapters, Adebayo's work is contextualised within an African diasporic tradition deeply inflected by black American politics and culture.

The Caribbean

The first chapter of the Caribbean section, Chapter 4, brings new perspectives to an already well-documented history of late twentieth century black British drama by reading it through the notion of creolisation. In Chapter 5, the process of border crossing and cultural mixing that the term creolisation understands frames the discussion of plays by Roy Williams (British-born of Jamaican parentage). Chapter 6 focuses on plays by Bola Agbaje (British-born of Nigerian parentage). It echoes and extends Chapter 5's discussion of the evolution of Britishness to consider the creolisation of black Britishness and black British drama.

Africa

Chapter 7 discusses the recent increase in migration of people from different parts of Africa to the UK since the 1990s. In order to provide a historical context and map the diversity of African British drama practitioners and their impact on black British drama, reference is made to playwrights and practitioners with backgrounds from Ghana, Nigeria, Sierra Leone, South Africa and Zimbabwe. However, the majority of African works discussed in this chapter (and throughout the book) are connected with Nigeria. The focus on plays by those of Nigerian origin reflects the dominance of this demographic among black African British playwrights.

Using diaspora as an analytic model, the chapter explores how African British playwrights negotiate themes of home and host-land in their work. The chapter also introduces the concept of the 1.5 generation to describe immigrants who arrived in the UK as adolescents and, therefore, spent formative years in both home and host-lands. Chapter 8 examines how the experience of being 1.5 generation finds theatrical representation in two plays by Inua Ellams (Nigerian-born). Chapter 9 follows with an exploration of plays by debbie tucker green (British-born of Jamaican parentage). Paying particular attention to three of her plays which feature/ explore Africa, this chapter expands the notion of diaspora as an experience of being in-between home and host-land evoked in the previous chapter to accommodate the political and cultural concept of the African diaspora. The notion of empathy guides the discussion of tucker green's work, probing how twenty-first century black diasporic solidarity finds theatrical representation.

The choice to discuss a mainstream and emergent playwright in each section intentionally brings less known artists to readers' attention. The decision to place playwrights in sections that do not necessarily reflect their heritage is also deliberate. For instance, Bola Agbaje is housed under the Caribbean section, tucker green under Africa and Adebayo and Kwei-Armah under the USA. A transnational perspective actively problematises assumptions that practitioners 'from a particular place by default situate their writing in an aesthetic tradition that derives foremost from their own or their parents' or their grandparents' birthplaces' (Stein, 2004, p. 16). The placement of each chapter provokes a consideration of that dramatist's work in relation to a particular geo-cultural space's history, culture and/or politics, the theoretical framework that underpins each section and the other playwright's work is considered in that section. It is a heuristic device which, by placing works in new and sometimes unexpected relationships and locations, enables new considerations. This placement is not meant to be fixed and definitive. A work analysed through the USA and Americanisation might yield very different results if placed under the Caribbean or Africa sections. For instance, Kwei-Armah's plays, currently in the USA section, could equally be read through the Caribbean and creolisation or Africa and diaspora. It is hoped that this book might prompt such alternative considerations of writers' work. It should also be noted that, for the most part, the playwrights and companies discussed in this book operate in England, and in London. There is clearly work to be done that focuses on less mainstream and regional black theatre activity in Britain. This particular book, however, has as its major aim the demonstration that black British drama not only merits a transnational approach, but is a transnational practice in and of itself.

Notes

1 For discussions of black British theatre in relation to Arts Council policy and funding, see, for example, Chambers (2011, pp. 180–182), Goddard (2015, pp. 7–9), Peacock (2015, pp. 147–153), Saunders (2015, pp. 78–102).

2 See, among others, chapters/sections in Bull (2016), Cochrane (2011), King (2004), Kritzer (2008), Lane (2010), Peacock (1999), Saunders (2015) and Tomlin (2015).

3 The Black Plays Archive is a recent initiative which aims to provide details of the first professional production in the UK of every African, Caribbean and black British play. For further information see the National Theatre Black Plays Archive website: blackplaysarchive.org.uk. This study contributes to and extends the archive's aims by including plays by African American playwrights to be premiere in the UK.

4 *From Margins to Mainstream: The Story of Black Theatre in Britain* is the title of a documentary film made by young people and produced by the Octavia Foundation and Nu Century Arts, Birmingham. It also forms part of the title of Goddard's (2015) book about contemporary black British playwrights. See also Eva Pirker, who highlights the preponderance of success over trauma narratives in dominant accounts of black British history, 'in which the collective protagonist, the black community, has undergone tribulation and tests but has eventually become established and successfully integrated into British society' (2012, p. 8).

5 For chapters on contemporary African British playwrights see, for example, Ekumah (2015) and Goddard (2015, pp. 155–172) on Bola Agbaje and Ukaegbu (2015) on Oladipo Agboluaje.

6 For discussions of migration using a transnational framework, see Glick-Schiller, Basch and Blanc-Szanton (1994, 1992), Hannerz (1996) and Nieswand (2011).

7 On 20 April 1968 Enoch Powell gave a speech to a Conservative Association
   meeting in Birmingham which has become known as his 'Rivers of Blood' speech
   (1968a). In the speech he argued that increased non-white immigration from
   the Commonwealth would result in violence and bloodshed similar to what was
   occurring in the USA at the time in the wake of the assassination of Martin Luther
   King Jr. on 4 April that year.
8 For discussions of the term diaspora and its application in an African context, see
   Edwards (2004), Harris (ed.) (1982), Kilson and Rotberg (eds.) (1976) and Zeleza
   (2008).
9 For a list of plays by black British playwrights staged in 2003 and 2004, see
   Osborne (2006a, pp. 82–83).
10 The ways in which this is achieved in relation to, or in spite of, differences in ethnicity, class, gender and sexuality is also of interest. Feminist approaches provide
   a useful and important precedent. For early discussions of black British women's
   theatre located within broader transnational feminist contexts, see Aston (2003),
   Brewer (1999), Goodman (1993) and Joseph (1998).

Works cited

Albert, M., Bluhm, G., Helmig, J., Leutzsch, A., and Walter, J. 2009. Introduction: The
communicative construction of transnational political spaces. In: Albert, M., Bluhm,
G., Helmig, J., Leutzsch, A., and Walter, J. eds., *Transnational political spaces: Agents,
structures, encounters*. Frankfurt: Campus Verlag, pp. 7–34.

Anderson, B. 1991. *Imagined communities: Reflections on the origin and spread of nationalism.*
Revised edition. London: Verso.

Arts Council England. 2002. Eclipse report: Developing strategies to combat racism
in theatre. [Accessed 3 March 2014]. Available from: http://www.artscouncil.org.
uk/media/uploads/documents/publications/308.pdf

Aston, E. 2003. *Feminist views on the English stage: Women playwrights, 1990–2000.*
Cambridge: Cambridge University Press.

Ball, J. 2004. *Imagining London: Postcolonial fiction and the transnational metropolis.* Toronto:
University of Toronto Press.

Basch, L. G., Glick-Schiller, N., and Blanc-Szanton, C. 1994. *Nations unbound: Transnational projects, postcolonial predicaments, and deterritorialized nation-states.* New York:
Gordon and Breach.

Boult, A. 2016. Steep rise in racist incidents after EU referendum cataloged by Worrying Signs Facebook group. *The Telegraph.* [Online]. 1 July. [Accessed 29 October
2016]. Available from: http://www.telegraph.co.uk/news/2016/07/01/steep-
rise-in-racist-incidents-after-eu-referendum-cataloged-by/

Brewer, M. F. 1999. *Race, sex and gender in contemporary women's theatre: The construction
of 'woman'.* Brighton, UK: Sussex Academic.

Brewer, M. F., Goddard, L., and Osborne, D. eds. 2015. *Modern and contemporary black
British drama.* London: Palgrave Macmillan.

Bull, J. 2016. *British theatre companies: 1965–1979.* London: Bloomsbury Methuen
Drama.

Cameron, D. 2011. Speech on radicalisation and Islamic extremism. [Online]. 5 February. Munich. [Accessed 24 October 2016]. Available from: http://www.newstatesman.com/blogs/the-staggers/2011/02/terrorism-islam-ideology

Centre for Contemporary Cultural Studies. ed. 1982. *The Empire strikes back: Race and racism in 70s Britain.* London: Hutchinson.

Chambers, C. 2011. *Black and Asian theatre in Britain: A history.* London: Routledge.

Cochrane, C. 2011. *Twentieth-century British theatre: Industry, art and empire.* Cambridge: Cambridge University Press.

Crompton, S. 2003. The arts column: Black British drama takes centre stage. *The Telegraph.* [Online]. 9 July. [Accessed 20 October 2016]. Available from: http://www.telegraph.co.uk/culture/theatre/3598232/The-arts-column-black-British-drama-takes-centre-stage.html

Dahl, M. K. 1995. Postcolonial British theatre: Black voices at the centre. In: Gainor, J. E. ed., *Imperialism and theatre: Essays on world theatre, drama and performance.* London: Routledge, pp. 38–55.

Davis, G., and Fuchs, A. eds. 2006. *Staging new Britain: Aspects of black and South Asian British theatre practice.* Brussels: P.I.E. Peter Lang.

Dodd, V. 2016. Police blame worst rise in recorded hate crime on EU referendum. *The Guardian.* [Online]. 11 July. [Accessed 29 October 2016]. Available from: https://www.theguardian.com/society/2016/jul/11/police-blame-worst-rise-in-recorded-hate-on-eu-referendum

Edwards, B. H. 2004. The uses of 'diaspora'. In: Benesch, K., and Fabre, G. eds., *African diasporas in the new and old worlds: Consciousness and imagination.* Amsterdam: Rodopi, pp. 3–38.

Ekumah, E. 2015. Bola Agbaje: Voicing a new Africa on the British stage. In: Brewer, M., Goddard, L., and Osborne, D. eds., *Modern and contemporary black British drama.* London: Palgrave Macmillan, pp. 178–193.

Elam, H. J., and Jones, D. A. 2012. Introduction. In: Elam, H. J., and Jones, D. A. eds., *The Methuen drama book of post-black plays.* London: Methuen Drama, pp. ix-xxxv.

Gilroy, P. 1987. *'There ain't no black in the Union Jack': The cultural politics of race and nation.* London: Hutchinson.

———. 1993. *The black Atlantic: Modernity and double consciousness.* London: Verso.

Glick-Schiller, N., Basch, L. G., and Blanc-Szanton, C. 1992. *Towards a transnational perspective on migration: Race, class, ethnicity, and nationalism reconsidered: Workshop Papers.* New York: New York Academy of Sciences.

———. 1994. *Nations unbound: Transnational projects, postcolonial predicaments, and deterritorialized nation-states.* New York: Gordon and Breach.

Goddard, L. 2007. *Staging black feminisms: Identity, politics, performance.* Basingstoke, UK: Palgrave Macmillan.

———. 2015. *Contemporary black British playwrights: Margins to mainstream.* Basingstoke, UK: Palgrave Macmillan.

Godiwala, D. 2006. *Alternatives within the mainstream: British black and Asian theatres.* Newcastle upon Tyne, UK: Cambridge Scholars Press.

Goodman, L. 1993. *Contemporary feminist theatres: To each her own.* London: Routledge.

Goulbourne, H. 2002. *Caribbean transnational experience.* London: Pluto.

Goulbourne, H., Reynolds, T., Solomos, J., and Zontini, E. 2010. *Transnational families: Ethnicities, identities and social capital.* London: Routledge.

Griffin, G. 2003. *Contemporary black and Asian women playwrights in Britain.* Cambridge: Cambridge University Press.

Hall, S. 1987. Minimal selves. In: Appignanesi, L. ed., *The real me: Post-modernism and the question of identity: ICA Documents 6.* London: Institute of Contemporary Arts, pp. 44–46.

————. 1988. New ethnicities. In: Mercer, K. ed., *Black film, British cinema: ICA documents 7.* London: Institute of Contemporary Arts, pp. 27–31.

Hannerz, U. 1996. *Transnational connections: Culture, people, places.* London: Routledge.

Harris, J. 1982. Introduction. In: Harris, J. E. ed., *Global dimensions of the African diaspora.* Washington, DC: Howard University Press, pp. 3–10.

Joseph, M. 1998. Bodies outside the state: Black British women playwrights and the limits of citizenship. In: Phelan, P., and Lane, J. eds., *The ends of performance.* New York: New York University Press, pp. 197–215.

————. 1999. *Nomadic identities: The performance of citizenship.* Minneapolis: University of Minnesota Press.

Khan, N. 1976. *The arts Britain ignores: The arts of ethnic minorities in Britain.* London: Arts Council of Great Britain.

Kilson, M., and Rotberg, R. eds. 1976. *The African diaspora: Interpretive essays.* Cambridge: Harvard University Press.

King, B. 2004. *The internationalization of English literature.* Oxford: Oxford University Press.

King-Dorset, R. 2014. *Black British theatre pioneers: Yvonne Brewster and the first generation of actors, playwrights and other practitioners.* Jefferson, NC: McFarland & Company.

Kritzer, A. H. 2008. *Political theatre in post-Thatcher Britain: New writing, 1995–2005.* Basingstoke, UK: Palgrave Macmillan.

Lane, D. 2010. *Contemporary British drama.* Edinburgh: Edinburgh University Press.

Lawrence, E. 1982. Just plain common sense: The 'roots' of racism. In: Centre for Contemporary Cultural Studies ed., *The Empire strikes back: Race and racism in 70s Britain.* London: Hutchinson, pp. 45–92.

Lindner, U., Mohring, M., Stein, M., and Stroh, S. 2010. Introduction. In: Lindner, U., Mohring, M., Stein, M., and Stroh, S. eds., *Hybrid cultures – nervous states: Britain and Germany in a (post)colonial world.* Amsterdam: Rodopi, pp. xi-xlvi.

Lusher, A. 2016. Racism unleashed: True extent of the 'explosion of blatant hate' that followed Brexit result revealed. *The Independent.* [Online]. 28 July. [Accessed 29 October 2016]. Available from: http://www.independent.co.uk/news/uk/politics/brexit-racism-uk-post-referendum-racism-hate-crime-eu-referendum-racism-unleashed-poland-racist-a7160786.html

McLeod, J. 2006. Fantasy relationships: Black British canons in a transnational world. In: Low, G., and Wynne-Davies, M. eds., *A black British canon?* Basingstoke, UK: Palgrave Macmillan, pp. 93–104.

McLuhan, M. 1962. *The Gutenberg Galaxy: The making of typographic man.* Toronto: University of Toronto Press.

McMillan, M., and SuAndi. 2002. Rebaptizing the world in our own terms: Black theatre and live arts in Britain. In: Harrison, P. C., Walker, V. L., II, and Edwards, G. eds., *Black theatre: Ritual performance in the African diaspora.* Philadelphia: Temple University Press, pp. 115–127.

Macpherson, W. 1999. *The Stephen Lawrence inquiry: Report of an inquiry by Sir William Macpherson of Cluny: Advised by Tom Cook, the Right Reverend Dr John Sentamu and Dr Richard Stone (Cm 4262–1).* London: HMSO.

Nieswand, B. 2011. *Theorising transnational migration: The status paradox of migration.* New York: Routledge.

Office for National Statistics. 2012. Ethnicity and national identity in England and Wales 2011. [Online]. [Accessed 24 February 2016]. Available from: http://www.ons.gov. uk/ons/rel/census/2011-census/key-statistics-for-local-authorities-in-england-and-wales/rpt-ethnicity.html–tab-Changing-picture-of-ethnicity-over-time

––––––. 2015. 2011 census analysis: Ethnicity and religion of the non-UK born population in England and Wales. [Online]. [Accessed 24 February 2016]. Available from: https://www.ons.gov.uk/peoplepopulationandcommunity/culturalidentity/ ethnicity/articles/2011censusanalysisethnicityandreligionofthenonukbornpopulat ioninenglandandwales/2015-06-18

Osborne, D. 2006a. The state of the nation: Contemporary black British theatre and the staging of the UK. In: Godiwala, D. ed., *Alternatives within the mainstream: British black and Asian theatres.* Newcastle upon Tyne, UK: Cambridge Scholars Press, pp. 82–100.

––––––. 2006b. Writing black back: An overview of black theatre and performance in Britain. In: Godiwala, D. ed., *Alternatives within the mainstream: British black and Asian theatres.* Newcastle upon Tyne, UK: Cambridge Scholars Press, pp. 61–81.

Owusu, K. 2000. Introduction: Charting the genealogy of black British cultural studies. In: Owusu, K. ed., *Black British culture and society: A text-reader.* London: Routledge, pp. 1–20.

Peach, C. 1996. Black-Caribbeans: Class, gender and geography. In: Peach, C. ed., *Ethnicity in the 1991 census: The ethnic minority populaitons of Great Britain.* Vol. 2. London: HMSO, pp. 25–43.

Peacock, D.K. 1999. *Thatcher's theatre: British theatre and drama in the eighties.* London: Greenwood Press.

––––––. 2008. Black British drama and the politics of identity. In: Holdsworth, N., and Luckhurst, M. eds., *A concise companion to contemporary British and Irish drama.* Oxford: Blackwell, pp. 48–65.

––––––. 2015. The social and political context of black British theatre: The 2000s. In: Brewer, M., Goddard, L., and Osborne, D. eds., *Modern and contemporary black British drama.* London: Palgrave Macmillan, pp. 147–160.

Petropoulos, J. 2006. Performing African Canadian identity: Diasporic reinvention in 'Africa Solo'. *Feminist Review.* 84(1), pp. 104–123.

Phillips, A. 2007. *Multiculturalism without culture.* Princeton, NJ: Princeton University Press.

Phillips, C. 1981. *Strange fruit.* Ambergate, UK: Amber Lane.

Phillips, T. 2008. Not a river of blood, but a tide of hope: Managed immigration, active integration. [Online]. [Accessed 20 April 2015]. Available from: http://www.equalityhumanrights.com/key-projects/race-in-britain/modern-multiculturism/not-a-river-of-blood-but-a-tide-of-hope/

Pirker, E. U. 2012. *Narrative projections of a black British history.* New York: Routledge.

Ponnuswami, M. 2015. The social and political context of black British theatre: 1980s–90s. In: Brewer, M., Goddard, L., and Osborne, D. eds., *Modern and contemporary black British drama.* London: Palgrave Macmillan, pp. 79–94.

Powell, E. 1968a. Rivers of blood. [Online]. 20 April, Conservative Association meeting in Birmingham. [Accessed 29 October 2016]. Available from: http://www.telegraph.co.uk/comment/3643823/Enoch-Powells-Rivers-of-Blood-speech.html

———. 1968b. Speech to London Rotary Club. [Online]. 16 November. [Accessed 29 October 2016]. Available from: http://www.enochpowell.net/fr-83.html

Reynolds, T. 2006. Caribbean families, social capital and young people's diasporic identities. *Ethnic and Racial Studies.* 29(6), pp. 1087–1103.

Robertson, R. 1992. *Globalization: Social theory and global culture.* London: Sage.

Saunders, G. 2015. *British theatre companies: 1980–1994.* London: Bloomsbury Methuen Drama.

Selasi, T. 2005. Bye-Bye Babar. *The LIP.* [Online]. 3 March. [Accessed 9 March 2016]. Available from: http://thelip.robertsharp.co.uk/?p=76

Shepperson, G. 1968. The African abroad or the African diaspora. In: Ranger, T. O. ed., *Emerging themes of African history: Proceedings of the International Congress of African Historians held at University College, Dar es Salaam, October 1965.* Nairobi: East African Publishing House, pp. 152–176.

Sierz, A. 2009. The arts desk Q&A: Playwright Roy Williams. *theartsdesk.com.* [Online]. 24 October. [Accessed 26 October 2016]. Available from: http://www.theartsdesk.com/theatre/theartsdesk-qa-playwright-roy-williams

Steger, M. 2009. *Globalization: A very short introduction.* 2nd edition. Oxford: Oxford University Press.

Stein, M. 2004. *Black British literature: Novels of transformation.* Columbus: Ohio State University Press.

Thomas, H. 2015. The social and political context of black British theatre: 1950s–80s. In: Brewer, M., Goddard, L., and Osborne, D. eds., *Modern and contemporary black British drama.* London: Palgrave Macmillan, pp. 17–31.

Tomlin, L. 2015. British theatre companies: 1995–2014. London: Bloomsbury Methuen Drama.

Ukaegbu, V. 2015. Witnessing to, in, and from the centre: Oladipo Agboluaje's theatre of dialogic centrism. In: Brewer, M., Goddard, L., and Osborne, D. eds., *Modern and contemporary black british drama.* London: Palgrave Macmillan, pp. 194–209.

Vertovec, S. 2009. *Transnationalism.* London: Routledge.

Wright, M. M. 2004. *Becoming black: Creating identity in the African diaspora.* Durham, NC: Duke University Press.

Zeleza, P. T. 2008. The challenges of studying the African diasporas. *African Sociological Review.* 12(2), pp. 4–21.

SECTION I
The USA

1

AFRICAN AMERICANISATION, BLACK POWER AND BLACK BRITISH DRAMA SINCE THE 1970S

In an increasingly globalised world, a recurring debate around cultural inter-actions focuses on 'the tension between cultural homogenization and cultural heterogenization' (Appadurai, 1990, p. 295). In the same way that Ameri-canisation can be viewed as a process that threatens to erode an authentic and indigenous British culture, the adoption of African American culture by black Britons – a process of African Americanisation – has similarly been attacked. Travel and fiction writer Ferdinand Dennis, for instance, per-ceives this process to be detrimental to indigenous cultural expression. He notes that 'the small population of people of African descent in Britain have become the victims of African-American cultural imperialism, mimicking styles and taking on concerns which sit uneasily in the British context, rather than engaging in the more difficult task of searching for a language to define the uniqueness of this situation' (2000, p. 44). Stuart Hall also notes the degree to which black British identity has been 'Americanized', particularly among youth cultures: 'Its ideal images, its stylistic references are very pow-erfully Black American. Even though the style may have been indigenized, given a British home-grown stamp, all the leads come from Afro-America' (2000, p. 129). Unlike Dennis, however, Hall perceives the process as less detrimental; vulnerable to local mediation and translation.

African American politics and culture have clearly had an impact on black British drama. As this chapter demonstrates, this is discernible across a large number of plays and is evident in their content and form. Yet, although

African American influences have been noted in scholarship this relationship has not been explored in any depth. Ironically, this may be because it is too apparent. When interviewing playwrights for this study, some of them had not noticed the influence of African America on their work. This unawareness points to the pervasiveness and resultant normativity of American culture, whereby its myths and icons have become dislodged and even obscured from their geo-cultural roots and entered into the global public domain. Attention, when paid, to the intersection of black British drama with black America tends to focus on issues of cultural imperialism. However, tracing black America in black British plays since the 1970s reveals a formative relationship characterised by inspiration and imitation, adoption and adaptation.

The global political and economic dominance enjoyed by the USA that began before the First World War but accelerated exponentially after the end of the Second has resulted in an indelible American cultural footprint cast across every continent. The assimilation of African American cultural forms into the American mainstream has meant that black America has enjoyed similar reach. African American musical forms in particular have defined the quintessential character of American sound: blues, jazz, soul, R&B and more recently rap/ hip-hop, with its attendant culture of language, dress and behaviour have been globally disseminated. Exceptional African American personalities in diverse fields such as politics, media, entertainment and sport have also developed as global icons. In terms of theatre, the post-war period elevated American dramas and musicals to the echelons of the highly esteemed. According to Richard Eyre and Nicholas Wright in *Changing Stages: A View of British Theatre in the Twentieth Century* (also a television series), American works injected new life into British theatre during the late 1940s and 1950s, emancipating it as an art form that had become 'drained of vigour, etiolated, bound up by class, public puritanism, hypocrisy, self-censorship and state censorship' (2000, p. 135). Celebrated American plays by the likes of Edward Albee, Sam Shepard, David Mamet and Tony Kushner, and their dramatisation of the rise and demise of the American Dream, have continued to capture the British audience's imagination.

The African American presence on the British stage has also enjoyed a long history. High-profile pre-war achievements include acclaimed African American actors Ira Aldridge in the nineteenth century and Paul Robeson during the interwar period.[1] Dimple Godiwala criticises Eyre and Wright for hardly referencing black or Asian British contributions in their history of British theatre (2006, p. 6). It is telling, however, that the authors devote relatively lengthy discussions to the importance to British theatre of African American music (particularly ragtime and jazz), African American representation by white playwrights and performers (minstrel shows, the antislavery play *Uncle Tom's Cabin* [1852], dramas about race such as Eugene O'Neill's *All God's Chillun Got Wings* [1924] and *The Emperor Jones* [1920], and African American penned dramas in the post-war period (including Lorraine Hansberry's *A Raisin in the Sun* [1959] and August Wilson's plays). Since the 1950s, a significant number of African American musicals and dramas have been staged in London's West End and across white-run subsidised venues.[2] In 2009, a hugely successful all-black production of Tennessee Williams' *Cat on a Hot Tin Roof* [1955] directed by Debbie Allen and starring James Earl Jones transferred from Broadway to the West End's Novello Theatre, demonstrating the pulling power of an American classic revamped with African American stars.[3]

The profile and popularity of African American actors and dramas in the UK has a long precedent and has been accompanied by anxiety from local industry professionals and critics alike. During the inter-war and immediate post-war period, the success of African American actors such as Paul Robeson frustrated the attempts of British-based colonial black actors to enter the industry. In 1947, actor Robert Adams (Guyana) wrote an article for Unity's magazine, *New Theatre*, in which he expressed his disillusionment at the British theatre scene, which, he felt, provided limited and stereotyped roles for non-white actors and fed the prevailing belief that, side-lining African and West Indian actors, 'only the American Negro artist had any talent' (qtd in Chambers, 2011, p. 106). The actor Orlando Martins (Nigeria) echoed Adams' sentiments in the same magazine a year later, extending his criticism to the dominance of plays about the black American experience in the British theatre: 'We are tired of such plays as *Emperor Jones*, *All God's Chillun*, *Little Foxes*, etc. What we really need is some new material written by British authors' (qtd in Chambers, 2011, p. 107). Surveying the theatre landscape in the first decade of the new millennium, Lynette Goddard raises similar concerns. She notes a tendency of commercial mainstream venues 'to promote popular African American classics over home-grown voices' (2015, p. 211). She cites the staging of plays by Lorraine Hansberry, Langston Hughes and James Baldwin as examples of some theatre's 'fill[ing] their culturally diverse quotas by staging commercially viable African-American plays' (Goddard, 2007, p. 37).

Black Power and the Black Arts Movement

During the late 1960s black America came to occupy a more prominent point of navigation for black British identity politics. When Stokely Carmichael used the phrase 'Black Power' in a speech made during the Meredith

'March against Fear' in Mississippi on 16 June 1966 it marked a turning point in American race politics. A year later when Carmichael spoke at the Dialectics of Liberation conference at London's Roundhouse it was a key moment for black British politics and art.[4] As Ashley Dawson notes, the Black Power ideology expounded by Carmichael 'offered his audience a transnational perspective that transformed them from an isolated and outnumbered national minority to an integral part of a militant global majority' (2007, p. 50).[5] Black Power, which rejected the principle that race equality should be negotiated, and instead demanded that it was a right, not a privilege, resonated with black people in Britain who were persistently defined as unwelcome immigrants. It chimed with Britain's former colonial non-white residents because the issues facing this small but growing minority were more closely aligned with those faced by African Americans than in the newly independent colonies (Gunning and Ward, 2009, p. 151). In the UK, Black Power ideology also allowed those of African, Caribbean *and* Asian heritage, and the very different ethnicities and experiences those broad identities entailed, to see themselves within Britain as a community, as politically 'Black' (Wild, 2008, p. 131). A 'Black' identity did not efface ethnic particularity; however, it provided a sense of intra and inter-national solidarity in the fight against oppression. Rosalind Wild highlights that in the British context, although Black Power's ideas pertaining to anti-colonialism and internationalism made it attractive, ultimately it was in the sphere of identity (culture, self-definition, history and pride) that brought about 'the most significant and enduring achievements' (2008, p. 5). These spheres of Black Power identity would become the central points of reference for the nascent black British theatre of the 1970s.

First-generation black playwrights living in Britain who had work produced in the 1950s and 1960s include Errol John (Trinidad) and Wole Soyinka (Nigeria). These dramatists were more concerned with depicting their homelands than the experience in the host-land. Plays about the black experience in Britain were few, often represented by white dramatists, such as Shelagh Delaney's *A Taste of Honey* [1958, Theatre Royal Stratford East], or white groups, in particular the Unity Theatre. Plays by black first-generation writers that engaged with life in Britain include Barry Reckord's *You in Your Small Corner* [1961, Royal Court Theatre] and *Skyvers* [1963, Royal Court Theatre] and Norman Beaton's musicals *Jack of Spades* [1965, Liverpool Everyman Theatre] and *Sit down Banna* [1968, Connaught Theatre]. Attempts to establish black theatre companies were also short-lived and struggled to operate professionally. A continuous tradition of black playwrights engaging directly with the black experience *in* Britain and the formation of sustainable black-led theatre companies began with the birth of the alternative theatre in the 1960s. Black Power politics and culture in particular played a key part in black British theatre's formation and expression.[6]

The revolutionary tone of the 1960s and accompanying anti-war, civil rights and student protests resulted in 'a flourishing international traffic in culture' predominantly through the 'Atlantic axis' (Kershaw, 2004, p. 357). For the embryonic black theatre scene in Britain the creation of the fringe may have provided the space, but it was American Black Power politics and the Black Arts Movement that provided the model for its development. The Black Arts Movement defined itself as 'the aesthetic and spiritual sister of the Black Power concept' (Neal, 1968, p. 29). For its members, inspired by the message of black political and cultural nationalism expounded by activists like Malcolm X and the anti-colonial writings of Franz Fanon, the imperative to create a theatre about, by, for, and near black people advocated by W. E. B. Du Bois in 1926 became its driving force (p. 134). The members of the Black Arts Movement rejected what they perceived to be a Western model of 'art for art's sake', embracing instead a theatre with a clear social function aimed first and foremost at black people: 'the Black Arts Movement believes that your ethics and your aesthetics are one. That the contradictions between ethics and aesthetics in western society is symptomatic of a dying culture' (Neal, 1968, p. 31). The quest for a 'Black aesthetic' became a central component of the movement's aims as its members strove to access 'a separate symbolism, mythology, critique, and iconology' which would provide 'a radical reordering of the western cultural aesthetic' (Neal, 1968, p. 29). The Black Arts Movement, with Amiri Baraka (formerly LeRoi Jones) and Ed Bullins at its vanguard, sought to confront the 'truth' about race in America presented through the lens of a black cultural idiom and value system. Their plays, whether directly political ('Black Revolutionary Theatre') or more concerned with depicting the lives and experiences of black Americans ('Theatre of Black Experience'), were distinctly urban, supplanting earlier and supposedly romantic depictions of the working class (perceived as having 'white' aspirations) or the folk in the south (perceived as pandering to white stereotypes that stretched back to minstrelsy) by the experience of inner-city living.[7] Their plays, written in African American vernacular, aimed to depict how 'real' urban black people spoke and used language as a weapon to attack the white Establishment and undermine and challenge the aspirations of the black bourgeoisie.

Black Power's influence on black British drama was specifically linked to the Black Arts Movement. This connection, ironically, was facilitated by a white British director, Roland Rees. In 1968, Rees had recently returned to the UK from living in the USA and began to stage works in London by Bullins and Baraka. The fact that, as a white man, Rees was given permission to stage such work was remarkable (Rees, 1992, p. 108). Black artistic autonomy that the members of the Black Arts Movement were advocating was not possible in Britain. Black theatre in the British case was, and still is, very much dependent on support from white industry professionals and audiences. Between 1968 and 1970, Rees directed five British premieres of Ed Bullins' plays for American Ed Berman's Ambiance Lunch Hour Theatre Club at the Ambiance restaurant in Queensway.[8] *The Electronic Nigger* [1968], *A Minor Scene* [1966] and *It Has No Choice* [1966] were staged in 1968 and *The Gentleman Caller* [1969] and *How Do you Do* [1965] in 1969. Rees was drawn to the 'political acumen' in the writing that he found 'totally lacking' in British playwriting (qtd in Coveney, 1973a). It was something he was keen to nurture (Rees, 1992, p. 101). When Berman decided to stage a 'Black and White Power Season' of American plays, Rees convinced him that the season should have a black British presence to accompany the African American perspective. In 1970 at the Institute of Contemporary Arts (ICA), staged alongside the world premiere of Bullins' *It Bees Dat Way* and the UK premieres of *Clara's Ole Man* [1965] and Baraka's *The Baptism* [1964], Mustapha Matura made his début with a series of short vignettes entitled *Black Pieces*.

Matura is the most well known of the first-generation black British playwrights. He was born in Trinidad in 1939 and immigrated to Britain in the early 1960s. Matura cites 1968 as a watershed year in terms of him becoming a playwright. During that year in the USA there were large-scale protests against the Vietnam War, race riots and both Robert F. Kennedy and Martin Luther King, Jr. were assassinated. It was also the year Tommie Smith and John Carlos gave a Black Power salute when they were awarded their medals at the Olympic Games in Mexico City. In the UK there were violent anti-Vietnam War protests in London, Enoch Powell delivered his 'Rivers of Blood' speech, James Earl Ray, the man who shot Martin Luther King, Jr., was apprehended in London, a new Race Relations Act was passed and censorship in the British theatre was abolished. Matura felt he needed to respond to the political moment:

> Information and knowledge about my life and history was arriving at breakneck speed, the effects of which were so dramatic and inspiring I felt an urge, a need to speak, to tell it like it is, to pass it on, to confirm.
> *(1992, p. ix)*

Inspired by the Nation of Islam and trend among some African Americans to denounce their 'slave names', Matura changed his first name from the European 'Noel' to Mustapha. (His surname was actually 'Mathura' but became Matura by accident: it was a misspelling in the *Black Pieces* programme which Matura felt had a better sound to it (Rees, 1992, p. 103)). Initially, Matura put aside exploring the politics of his native land – although this would become his primary area of focus later in his career with plays such as *Play Mas* [1974, Royal Court Theatre] and *The Coup* [1991, National Theatre]. Like the playwrights of the Black Arts Movement who accused their predecessors of pandering to white Western values and dramatic traditions, the new generation of Caribbean playwrights in Britain rejected writers such as Errol John and his play *Moon on a Rainbow Shawl* [1958, Royal Court Theatre] for presenting backward and romantic depictions of life in the Caribbean: 'In the heat of the cultural and political explosion of the 1960s, we all thought he [Errol John] was an 'Uncle Tom" (Matura qtd in McMillan, 2000, p. 259). Matura and his contemporaries sought instead to portray the urban, 'front-line' black British experience. The changes occurring in the USA in the late 1960s and filtering across the Atlantic provided potent political and artistic fertilizer that would nurture the voice of the new generation of black playwrights in Britain.

Matura's *Black Pieces* comprises four short works: *Dialogue, Indian, Party* and *My Enemy*. *Dialogue* features three men watching television and is constructed around the lesson that white consumer culture erodes and impinges on the development of black consciousness and self-determination. *Indian* portrays a group of men whose lust after a white woman gets in the way of finding food. *Party*, the longest of the pieces, satirises white bohemian fetishisation of black men and stresses the need for black people to overcome this white liberal milieu which limits their political possibilities. *My Enemy* is about an interview between Mustapha Black, the self-styled Prime Minster of the Black Nation of Britain and a journalist whose daughter is having a relationship with Black. The piece exposes how easily racism erupts when the relationship between black and white people becomes personal.[9] The short vignettes are remarkable for depicting urban black youth experiences in London at the time and for being written in dialect. According to D. Keith Peacock, 'for the first time, Matura reproduced the authentic voice of the working-class, black West Indians who were attempting to settle in Britain' (1999, p. 174). Matura's plays are not only remarkable for depicting the black experience in Britain, they are also strikingly similar in theme, style and tone to the Black Arts Movement plays that Rees had imported.[10] *Black Pieces'* representation of issues and themes about black self-consciousness, latent racism of white liberals and white women as threats to black self-determination, ally the plays with the style and content of Baraka and Bullins' work. Like Baraka's and Bullins' plays, *Black Pieces* were didactic in tone, naturalist with a touch of absurdity in style and were written in a black urban vernacular.

Matura continued to explore the theme of authentic blackness in his next and first full-length work *As Time Goes By* [1971, Traverse Theatre]. The satirically drawn protagonist is a spiritual guru named Ram who, through his pandering to his white hippie clients, is exposed as living an inauthentic existence. Matura describes the piece as being about Ram 'escaping from the realities of being a black man [. . .] how he's pretending and not being himself, not being black, not being his own true identity (qtd in Coveney, 1973b, p. 29). Matura's use of language in *As Time Goes By* is the principal way of communicating the play's theme of authenticity. Ram's linguistic imitation of his white clients' repetitive and vapid speech underlines his denial of his true self. His faux English contrasts sharply with his wife's natural Trinidadian dialect and the other Caribbean characters' use of patois. Matura highlights this as 'a conscious political act' and that 'there was a very, very strong motto or rap going on at the time – 'Tell it like it is!' And that is what I thought I was doing' (qtd in Rees, 1992, p. 107). Representing this Caribbean-in-London linguistic idiom in order to explore the themes of authentic black identity was, following the Black Arts Movement, an attempt to assert an 'auditory' aesthetic, reflective of the black urban 'truth'.

Matura's *Black Slaves – White Chains* [1975, Royal Court Theatre] echoes the Black Arts Movement most. It is a symbolic meditation on the history of black oppression as well as a parable of resistance. The play depicts three black men chained together who are watched over by a guard who they think is asleep but who is actually dead. In their attempts to escape, they experience sexual temptation from a white woman, a white priest offering salvation and a hailstorm of Western epistemology symbolised by books being thrown onto the stage. The play ends with the arrival of a judge who offers the men work in exchange for housing and food but no money. The offer is accepted by two of the men and rejected by the third who refuses to be co-opted. Although the play ends with the third man alone, he defiantly eats the dead guard. A year later Matura provided a scathing critique of the struggles facing black playwrights in a white-dominated and racist industry in *Bread*, which was produced by the National Theatre but staged at the Young Vic in 1976. On the whole, Matura's work lacked the 'savage intensity' of the Black Arts Movement playwrights (Coveney, 1973b, p. 28); his work, by contextual necessity, was tempered. The hostile and aggressive tone of some of the Black Arts Movement's plays were untenable within the British context where a discreet black theatre and/or audience did not exist.

Nevertheless, Matura's plays represent a shift in focus and tone found in earlier plays by first-generation black playwrights. Barry Reckord (Jamaica) had had four plays produced at the Royal Court by the time Matura made his début in 1970. His first play set in Britain, *You in Your Small Corner,* was first staged in 1961. (In 1962 the play was broadcast on television). Set in Brixton, the play features a middle-class family who have moved to England from the Caribbean and is about a matriarch's disapproval of her son Dave's relationship with a working-class white woman. The representation of a black middle-class family and an intellectual protagonist (Dave is going to Cambridge University) contrasts with much of the urban and working-class depictions found in black British plays by male authors that emerged in the 1970s and which persist in the contemporary. Although representations of middle-class lives in plays occur – for instance Jimi Rand's *Sherry and Wine* [1976, Hampstead Theatre] – working-class urban experiences have come to dominate. Arguably, this shift occurred as playwrights sought to represent the situation for the majority of black people in Britain more accurately. The prevalence of these representations could also be reflective of the perceptions and assumptions of white (mainly male) commissioners and programmers. While a combination of factors is most likely, the point in time at which this shift happens is also very specific and is indicative of the USA's growing influence on black British youth culture which playwrights sought to reflect and of which they were/a part.

Matura's plays provided a model for future British-based playwrights to articulate themes of black consciousness and activism. Alfred Fagon's involvement as an actor in Matura's *Black Pieces* and *As Time Goes By* inspired him to become a playwright (Rees, 1992, p. 109). Alfred Fagon's first play, *11 Josephine House* [1972, Almost Free Theatre], is set in Bristol and focuses on the experience of Caribbean immigrants adjusting to life in England. However, his subsequent plays, *No Soldiers in St Paul's* [1974, Metro Club], the surreal *The Death of a Black Man* [1975, Hampstead Theatre], the symbolic one-act *Four Hundred Pounds* [1982, Royal Court Theatre], and *Lonely Cowboy* [1985, Tricycle Theatre], focus on younger generations of black people in Britain and engage with themes of self-determination and authenticity. Other 'Revolutionary'-style plays which depart from social realist conventions, are less linear and/or convey a message of solidarity against the white Establishment include Linton Kwesi Johnson's performed poem *Voices of the Living and the Dead* [1973, Keskidee], Michael McMillan's *On Duty* [1983, Carlton Centre] and *Brother to Brother* [1996, the Greenroom]. These and other plays such as Jimi Rand's *Say Hallelujah* [1977, Keskidee], Michael McMillan's *The School Leaver* [1978, Royal Court Theatre], Caryl Phillips' *Strange Fruit* [1980, Crucible Theatre], Michael Ellis' *Chameleon* [1985, Oval House Theatre], Kwame Kwei-Armah's *A Bitter Herb* [2001, Bristol Old Vic] and Courttia Newland's *B is for Black* [2003, Oval House Theatre] feature (and critique) Black Power characters and individuals battling against a white Western construction of identity. They frequently stage a conflict between those who have achieved consciousness versus 'uncle Toms'. Plays by women writers such as Jackie Kay's *Chiaroscuro* [1986, Soho Poly], Winsome Pinnock's *Talking in Tongues* [1991, Royal Court Theatre] and Zindika's *Leonora's Dance* [1993, Cockpit Theatre] reveal the painful internalisation of white conceptions of beauty and feature protagonists who must discover, to echo a Black Power slogan, that 'Black is Beautiful'. It is also common to find playwrights, including Kwame Kwei-Armah whose work is discussed in the following chapter, who weave 'education' with 'entertainment' in their works resulting in a distinctly didactic tone in line with the Black Art's Movements aesthetic aspirations.

Black Power's imperatives of self-determination and collective opposition fuelled the creation of a number of black arts organisations and theatre companies, for which black nationalism provided an ideological foundation. Jeffrey Ogbar defines black nationalism as a 'group consciousness among black people and the belief that they, independent of whites, can achieve liberation by the creation and maintenance of black institutions to serve the best interests of black people' (2004, p. 3). However, these groups were short lived and struggled to operate professionally.[11] In 1969 The Dark and Light theatre company, established by Jamaican Frank Cousins, set its sights on becoming Britain's first professional multi-racial theatre company (qtd in Chambers, 2011, p. 140). But as the 1970s progressed, black theatre, fuelled by Black Power rhetoric, would become increasingly separatist in reaction to the lack of representation in, and access to, the white-run mainstream. The emergence of the Keskidee Theatre Workshop (est. 1971 by Guyanese Oscar Abrams), The Radical Alliance of Poets and Players (RAPP) (est. 1972 by Guyanese Jamal Ali,[12] Temba (est. 1972 by South African Alton Kumalo and Trinidadian Oscar James) and the Drum Arts Centre (est. 1974 by Guyanese Cy Grant and Zimbabwean John Mapondera) heralded a proliferation of fringe theatre companies and organisations committed to community development and raising consciousness through art. By 1975, Cousins' Dark and Light theatre company found itself out of sync with the radical mood among black youth. He was replaced by Norman Beaton (Guyana), Jamal Ali (Guyana), and Rufus Collins (USA) who changed the company's name to the Black Theatre of Brixton. The new title was significant. The term 'Black' was indicative of the widespread adoption of the American term as a marker of identity among non-white people in political solidarity against racial oppression, a fact reflected in the company's multi-ethnic leadership. The incorporation of 'Brixton', a multi-ethnic area of London with a large population of people of African and Caribbean descent, into the name highlighted the company's community-oriented approach aimed at the grass-roots level, or what African American activists called 'the front-line' (Chambers, 2001, p. 143). The late 1970s and the 1980s continued to see the emergence of organisations dedicated to developing black arts and culture and building a black audience: Staunch Poets and Players, formed by Don Kinch in 1975; the Black Theatre Co-operative (BTC), formed by Matura and white director Charlie Hanson in 1978, and re-named Nitro in 1999; Carib Theatre, formed by Anton Phillips and Yvonne Brewster in 1980; Theatre of Black Women, formed by Bernadine Evaristo, Patricia Hilaire, and Paulette Randall in 1982; Umoja, formed by Gloria Hamilton in 1983; Imani-Faith, founded by Jacqueline Rudet in 1983; the Black Theatre Forum, a collective of black and Asian companies that delivered six annual Black Theatre Seasons in London between 1983–1990; Double Edge, formed by Derrick Blackwood and Clarence Smith in 1984; Black Mime Theatre, formed in 1984 by Sarah Cahn and David Boxer; and Talawa, formed by Yvonne Brewster with Inigo Espejel, Mona Hammond and Carmen Munroe in 1985.

The frequent programming of African American plays by black theatre companies since the 1970s attests to the importance attributed to the African American experience, and its capacity to illuminate the black British situation. For instance, Dark and Light produced the UK premieres of Baraka's *The Slave* [1964] in 1972 and Lonne Elder III's *Ceremonies in Dark Old Men* [1969] in 1974. In 1974 Temba staged a revival of *Dutchman* [1964] (the latter received its British premiere in 1967 at the Hampstead Theatre).[13] In 1985 Black Theatre Co-operative staged a revival of Lorraine Hansberry's *A Raisin in the Sun* [1959] at the Tricycle. In 1987 Carib Theatre Company staged a revival of Baldwin's *The Amen Corner* [1954], directed by Anton Phillips, also at the Tricycle. It then transferred to the Lyric Theatre, becoming the first play by a black British theatre company to be staged in the West End.

African American expatriates also contributed to bringing black American voices to the British stage. Rufus Collins moved from New York to

London in the 1970s and worked as an actor and director for Black Theatre of Brixton and the Keskidee Centre. He brought with him his experience of working for the experimental Living Theatre as well as a Black Power political awareness fostered in Harlem during the 1960s. Collins directed a number of British premieres of African American plays, including Steve Carter's *Eden* [1976] in 1978 at the Keskidee Centre, and *Nevis Mountain Dew* [1978] in 1983 at the Arts Theatre.

More recently Collective Artists, under Chuck Mike's artistic direction, has brought an African American presence to the British stage via Nigeria. (Mike grew up in the USA but immigrated to Nigeria in 1976 where he originally formed Collective Artistes in 1988). The company now operates in the UK (established in 2002) and Mike's native USA. Productions by African American playwrights staged in the UK include Carlyle Brown's *The African Company Presents Richard III* [1993] in 2009 at the Greenwich Theatre, and Jeff Stetson's *The Meeting* [1987], which stages an imaginary meeting between Martin Luther King and Malcolm X, in 2010 at the Pleasance Theatre in London.

African American-inspired Afrocentrism

The view of African American and African Caribbean people as a diaspora who share a common origin and cultural similarity with continental Africa emerged as an important ideological accompaniment to black political and cultural discourses that sought to highlight essential differences between black and white people in reaction to white racism. Perceiving Africa as an ancestral homeland which informs a political rhetoric of solidarity has a long precedent among diasporic black activists and artists. Afrocentric ideology emerges in political movements such as Pan-Africanism in the early twentieth century and cultural movements such as the Harlem Renaissance in the 1920s and, most forcefully, in the Francophone Négritude literary movement of the 1930s. In the 1960s and 1970s, Black Power reinvigorated these notions. As Tunde Adeleke shows, a key aspect of Carmichael's Black Power rhetoric was the view that knowledge about African history and culture was a necessary part of the emancipatory process from white subordination (2009, p. 80). Afrocentrism has broad interpretations. Adeleke defines it as a racially essentialist ideology that uses Africa in order 'to advance a monolithic and homogeneous history, culture, and identity for all blacks, regardless of geographical location' (2009, pp. 0–11). Stephen

Howe highlights its less extreme interpretations that place 'an emphasis on shared African origins among all "black" people, taking a pride in those origins and an interest in African history and culture – or those aspects of New World cultures seen as representing African "survivals" – and a belief that Eurocentric bias has blocked or distorted knowledge of Africans and their cultures' (1998, p. 1). Varying degrees along the Afrocentric spectrum began to be represented on the stage, impacting theme, dramaturgy and aesthetics. Kimberly Benston notes a shift in African American theatre in the 1970s from realistic drama with an emphasis on education to drama that encompasses ritual, 'embracing the audience in collective affirmation of certain values, styles, and goals' (1980, p. 77). Africa and its pre-Western oral traditions and rituals provided an important cultural seam which could be mined in an attempt to further differentiate a 'Black' approach.[14] Ritual practices that emphasised circularity and folk forms (particularly music and especially drumming, myth and storytelling), which encoded and communicated 'African' values of community preservation, were woven into the Euro-American dramatic template.

Pan-African politics and Afrocentric aesthetics found regular airings on the British stage in American Edgar Nkosi White' plays. (White was born in Montserrat in 1947 but grew up in New York City). The world premiere of White's *Masada*, directed by Rufus Collins, was staged in 1978 at the Keskidee before it transferred to Royal Court.[15] White later moved to London in 1981 where a number of his plays received their world premiere, including *Man and Soul* [1982, Riverside Studios],[16] *The Nine Night* [1983, Bush Theatre], *Redemption Song* [1984, Riverside Studios], *The Boot Dance* [1984, Tricycle Theatre] and *The Moon Dance Night* [1987, Arts Theatre]. All of these were produced by Black Theatre Co-operative except *The Boot Dance* which was produced by Temba and *The Moon Dance Night* which was directed by Yvonne Brewster at the Arts Theatre as part of the Black Theatre Forum's 1987 Black Theatre Season. White's plays, set in, and sometimes between, the Caribbean, the USA and the UK, explore issues of cultural heritage, migration and exile, refracted through his Afrocentric beliefs and pre-empt a number of second-generation black British playwrights who treat similar themes.[17]

A number of plays incorporate and draw attention to African elements retained in African American and Caribbean cultural practices, known as 'survivals'. Utilising 'survivals' for aesthetic purposes and formal innovations embeds a cultural and symbolic connection to continental Africa in a play's architecture. African American cultural discourses have been particularly influential in this regard. The belief in, and act of, tracing survivals emphasises the importance of historical and cultural recuperation. Alex Haley's Pulitzer Prize-winning novel *Roots: The Saga of an American Family* (1976) and its adaptation into a miniseries for television in 1977 is arguably the definitive example of the representation of Afrocentric ideology. *Roots* tells the story of how a young man named Kunta Kinte was captured by slave traders from his village in what is now the Gambia. The story charts his journey across the Middle Passage, life as a slave in Virginia and the lives of his descendants who retained the story of how Kinte was once a free man. *Roots'* popularity brought Afrocentrism into the mainstream (Howe, 1998, p. 108). The story was, according to Haley, based upon fact. In the book Haley claimed that through his mother's line he traced his family tree back to the Gambia and that the link was confirmed by a *griot* (West African historian, storyteller, musician), who named Kinte as Haley's ancestor.[18] Howe claims that

> since it is often difficult, if not impossible, especially in the United States, to identify Afro-American cultural traits as deriving from particular African peoples, it has become politically important for some intellectuals to emphasize that distinctions between those peoples were essentially insignificant, so that descent from a generalized 'Africa' becomes more meaningful.
>
> *(1998, p. 103)*

Complex intercultural processes occurred throughout the Americas and the Caribbean during the Atlantic slave trade; however, the USA, in particular, has contributed much to the way in which Afrocentric discourses have been represented. In particular, essentialist ideas and images of Africa have been globally transmitted and find themselves re-represented on the British stage. The visibility of *Roots* and other African American popular cultural forms that encode Afrocentrism has influenced a number of black British playwrights. The *sine qua non* of Afrocentric drama is the presence of a 'griot' – a figure which *Roots* introduced to the mainstream (Hale, 1998, p. 247). Griots appear in a number of African American and black British dramas, occupying the position of mystic and signifying the performance's ritual element and link to Africa (see Chapters 2 and 3). In black British dramas that draw attention to survivals the so-called African elements represented tend to be non-specific and homogenous, distinguishing 'Africa' as a symbolic, imaginary space. Indeed, when black diasporic themes are explored and represented in black British plays, they tend to signify the USA rather than specific African cultures.

A number of black British women playwrights take inspiration from African American Afrocentric-inspired approaches to aesthetics and dramatic composition. Echoing the male-dominated Black Arts Movement, black British theatre was until relatively recently monopolised by men. Furthermore, aside from Una Marson's *At What A Price* [1932], staged in London in 1933 at the YWCA for one night followed by a three-day run at the Scala Theatre in 1934, plays by black women before the 1980s came mainly from the USA.[19] Black British women playwrights, directors and women-led theatre companies emerged in the 1980s. However, African American women writers have remained popular programming choices. To date a third of the plays by women produced by Black Theatre Co-operative/Nitro and Talawa have been by Americans.[20] Lorraine Hansberry's *A Raisin in the Sun* remains the only play by a black woman to be staged in the West End. During the 1960s, Adrienne Kennedy's plays provided an important counterpoint to the imported Black Arts Movement plays. Kennedy spent time in England between 1966 and 1969, where her plays *Funnyhouse of a Negro* [1964] and *A Lesson in Dead Language* [1964] were produced at the Royal Court Theatre in 1968 and *A Rat's Mass* [1966] in 1970, also at the Royal Court. In 1968 the Royal Court commissioned *Sun*, a tribute to Malcolm X. Kolin identifies *Sun* as a choreopoem – defined as 'a poem written to be staged with an emphasis on music, drama, lighting, spectacle, and the fluidity of performance' – which anticipates Ntozake Shange's *for colored girls who have considered suicide/when the rainbow is enuf* [1975] (2005, p. 149). In 1968 the one act play *The Lennon Play: In His Own Write* was staged at the National Theatre (then at the Old Vic). The piece, also credited to John Lennon and the director Victor Spinetti, is probably the first example of a play by a black woman to be performed at the National Theatre.[21] The next time a play by a black woman was performed at the National Theatre was probably in 1995 with a revival of Winsome Pinnock's *Leave Taking* [1987, Liverpool Playhouse] which was staged in the Cottesloe space. Despite Kennedy's relative visibility, her surreal and heavily symbolic style made little impact on the black British theatre scene of the 1970s, which was dominated by men who tended towards a social realist mode.

The Afrocentric influence of black American women playwrights (and novelists) on plays by black British women is particularly visible at the level of content and form. Although Kennedy seems to have faded into obscurity, her pioneering style re-emerges through Ntozake Shange's influence on a number of black British women playwrights who cite Shange as an inspiration.[22] In 1979 Shange's *for colored girls who have considered suicide/when the rainbow is enuf* premiered in the UK at the Royalty Theatre. Although the piece has not been staged often in Britain, it has had a significant impact.[23]

Along with Mojisola Adebayo and Valerie Mason-John, Jackie Kay acknowledges the influence of Shange on her play *Chiaroscuro* [1986, Soho Poly] and admits to being 'impressed with the way she [Shange] made poetry work as theatre' (1987, p. 83). In literary criticism, Gabriele Griffin also finds similarity between *for coloured girls* and later black British women's writing, such as Trish Cooke's *Running Dream* [1993, Theatre Royal Stratford East]. Elaine Aston, who describes tucker green as a 'black British *griotte* (female storyteller)' (2011, p. 183) also draws attention to Shange as one of tucker green's inspirations.

Shange's theatre provides a model against which the feminist potential of black British women's drama is often measured (see Goddard, 2007; Griffin, 2003). However, the implications of the interaction with the African American tradition remain underexplored. For instance, Goddard draws attention to the thematic and aesthetic similarity between Kay's *Chiaroscuro* and *for colored girls*, which both examine 'black women coming into sexual awareness and maturity' (2007, p. 123). In defining the choreopoem Goddard, quoting Neal Lester, describes it as: 'a theatrical expression that combines poetry, prose, song, dance, and music [. . .] to arouse an emotional response in an audience (Lester, 1995, p. 3)', which is located within a black ritual theatrical style that 'emerges from an African tradition of storytelling, rhythm, physical movement, and emotional catharsis' (3) (Goddard, 2007, p. 123).

However, Goddard does not include in this quotation that part of Lester's critical summary that points to 'those elements that, according to Shange, outline a distinctly African American heritage' (1995, p. 3). And as a result, the choreopoem becomes located seemingly solely within 'African traditions'. In so doing, however, we lose the important ways in which ideas of 'a black ritual theatrical style' and fantasies about Africa, which emerged in the USA during the 1960s Black Power movement, are mediated through African America. Kay's use of the choreopoem does not connect her to any specific African traditions or theatrical style but rather to imagined generic ones filtered through an African American ideological prism. Kay's work, therefore, and other black British writers who employ similar techniques, are much more closely connected to African American traditions.

African 'Americana'

The culture, icons and myths of black America have provided potent inspiration for black British dramatists. The adoption of African American culture in the British context draws attention to the global dissemination of

Americana and its hegemony. It also points to how black British experiences of racism have fostered identification with other black cultures and histories. For a number of black British dramatists, black America is a model, a resource and a means by which to articulate political and cultural solidarity. In terms of popular culture, African American accoutrements from fashion to slang have travelled across the Atlantic. The Black Arts Movement's playwrights tapped into urban cultural codes as a means of depicting the 'front line' and moving away from what they perceived to be hackneyed representations of black rural life. A direct legacy of this is how the ghetto and its cultural and linguistic codes have come to be seen by some as markers of blackness and representative of 'the black experience'. This is critiqued in Alfred Fagon's *Lonely Cowboy* [1985, Tricycle Theatre]. The play, set in Brixton, is populated by British-born black youth whose 'Afro' or 'Rasta' hairstyles and 'army fatigues' hint at 1980s black 'street' fashion influenced by African American and Rasta styles. The play is about a young couple opening a new café in Brixton who are determined to disassociate themselves from the 'front line', characterised by youth who interpret resistant politics as a justification for a life of crime and drugs. As Flight, the 28 year-old co-owner of the Lonely Cowboy café makes clear, there will be no 'back to Africa politics' in his café (1999, p. 154). The image of Brixton as a lawless place akin to the Wild West evoked by the play's title suggests a critique of the Americanisation of black British youth culture. The melodramatic ending, which sees the mass death of the characters seems to borrow from, and critique, the Blaxploitation genre that emerged in the USA in the 1970s.

British-born Tunde Ikoli's (black Nigerian and white British parentage) depiction of London's underworld in several of his plays reveals his debt to Blaxploitation and mafia films and his adaptation of the genre to a British setting. Before writing his first play, at the age of seventeen Ikoli wrote, directed and starred in his film, *Tunde's Film* (1973). The film focuses on the lives of a group of black youth in London's East End and depicts their struggle to find work, their friction with the police and an attempted robbery. One reviewer described it as an 'an East End version of *Superfly*, with shades of *Shaft* and *The Godfather*' (PHS, 1973). Ikoli's second play, *On the Out* [1978, Bush Theatre], continues this thematic and stylistic trajectory. It is set in Whitechapel, and revolves around a newly released convict Zoltan who must decide whether to take part in a crime after his release or to change the direction of his life.[24]

The urban portrayal of black life in the films of Spike Lee in the 1990s have also proven influential. Arinze Kene cites Lee's 1994 film *Crooklyn* as significant and draws parallels between Lee finding inspiration in Brooklyn with his own representations of Hackney in his play *Estate Walls* [2010, Oval House Theatre]. He also cites African American hip-hop artists Mos Def and Pharoahe Monch as influential in terms of their musical styles and messages of black consciousness on his writing style and plots (in interview with Pearce, 2013). Hip-hop's linguistic and cultural codes have all had a visible impact on British youth culture, black and white. As a result of hip-hop's uptake into mainstream popular culture, its function as a form created in resistance to white racism is today often ambiguous. Hip-hop culture has been blamed for glamorising the ghetto. The 'street' emerges in a number of twenty-first century black British plays. Plays by Bola Agbaje, Kwame Kwei-Armah and Roy Williams which depict black youth in urban settings with a focus on themes of crime and violence are discussed in detail in subsequent chapters.

Homage to African American singers and music appears in a number of guises. It features in a play's soundtrack, such as Felix Cross and Paulette Randall's *Up Against the Wall* [1999, Tricycle Theatre], a tribute to the funk, soul and disco music of the 1970s Blaxploitation films. African American music references also appear in plays' titles which borrow from songs, such as Caryl Phillips' *Strange Fruit*, named after the song made famous by Billie Holiday, and Kwei-Armah's *Let There Be Love* [2008, Tricycle Theatre], after the Nat King Cole version. Femi Elufowoju Jr. uses Sammy Davis Jr.'s biography in his play *Sammy* [2002, Theatre Royal Stratford East] as a means to draw attention to the challenges facing black people in the performing arts. More recently Roy Williams' *Soul* [2016, Royal & Derngate] depicts Motown superstar Marvin Gaye's final days. For debbie tucker green, the influence of African American music occurs at the level of writing: she attributes singer/songwriters Lauryn Hill and Jill Scott as influences on her poetic style (Gardner, 2005).

The formative influence of black American icons on young people also emerges, such as Muhammad Ali in Mojisola Adebayo's play, *Muhammad Ali and Me* [2008, Oval House Theatre], discussed in Chapter 3. Black British identification with African American boxers also appears in Roy Williams' *Sucker Punch* [2010, Royal Court Theatre]. In *Sucker Punch* Williams taps into the long tradition of aligning boxing with race relations. Set against the 'sus' law and race riots of the 1980s, Williams pastiches the myths which surround both black British and American boxing. When protagonist Leon fights and defeats Tommy, the white British champion, Williams draws on the now mythic 1908 fight between African American Jack Johnson and white Canadian Tommy Burns, which led to Burns' defeat and the search for a white champion to take the title from Johnson. The fight, first dramatised in Howard Sackler's *The Great White Hope* [1967], has come to symbolise black achievement over white supremacy and provides a fertile launch pad for Williams' exploration of British racism.[25] The second half of the play pits Leon against his old school friend, Troy, who moved to the USA. Troy, now a naturalised American, has embraced Black Power ideology and scorns Leon for having a white manager and being in love with a white woman. When Troy accuses Leon of being an Uncle Tom, Leon's identity crisis echoes the antagonism between Frank Bruno and Lennox Lewis before the 'Battle of Britain' in 1993. When Bruno questioned Lewis' 'Britishness' because he had grown up in and fought for Canada, Lewis responded by calling Bruno an Uncle Tom. By staging battles of Britishness and blackness, and through allusion to historic boxing fights and boxing icons, Williams plumbs the continuum of racial struggle, how it has been played out within the boxing ring in the USA and Britain, and ultimately draws attention to how these spaces are discursively entwined.

The division between separatist and integrationist camps that Malcolm X and Martin Luther King have come to represent can be traced in a number of plays that focus on themes of intra-racial hostility and/or which stage debates around black identity. John McLeod identifies Phillips' exploration and critique of African American political discourses as a dominant theme in his work (2009, p. 191). In his analysis of Caryl Phillips' *Rough Crossings* [2007, Birmingham Rep], about black Loyalists who fought on the British side during the American War of Independence and their 'repatriation' to Sierra Leone, adapted from Simon Schama's history with the same title, McLeod argues that the play's two black protagonists, David George and Thomas Peters, are represented as 'hagiographical' characters that reflect the political choices of King and X (2009, p. 191). The same ideological conflict defines the relationship between the brothers in Phillips' *Strange Fruit* and surfaces in a number of character relationships in black British dramas, such as Kwei-Armah's *Statement of Regret* [2007, National Theatre] and Newland's *B is for Black*. The continued importance placed on African American political figures as role models is highlighted by David Levi Addai's play for young people *I have a Dream* [2011, Polka Theatre], about Martin Luther King, Jr. and Kwei-Armah's *Seize the Day* [2009, Tricycle Theatre] which, inspired by Barack Obama's election victory, imagines a black mayor of London.

A number of black British dramatists have sought to highlight the black British/American connection through their plays, which can be described as recuperations of history. Works such as these bring to light forgotten stories and people and retrace the routes of connection that link black people in Britain politically and culturally with African America. Mojisola Ade-bayo's *Desert Boy* [2010, Albany Theatre] like Phillips' *Rough Crossings*, draws attention to the history of slaves in America who fought on the side of the British during the American Revolutionary War. Not only did these men win their freedom, they also became British citizens, becoming, in a way, the 'first' black Britons. Michael McMillan's *Master Juba* [2006, Luton Library Theatre] chronicles the life of William Henry Lane who toured to England in 1848 with the American blackface minstrel troupe the Ethiopian Serenad-ers. Lane, credited with creating modern tap dance by fusing Irish folk and African American forms, found fame in London when he danced for Queen Victoria. The play highlights the important contribution made by African American performers to British culture, especially in music and dance. It also draws attention to the trans-Atlantic circulation of racial stereotypes, which emphasised black people as musical buffoons and objects of patronising fas-cination.[26] Winsome Pinnock's *A Rock in Water* [1989, Royal Court Theatre] traces the life of Trinidadian-born, American-raised Claudia Jones, a Civil Rights activist, journalist and member of the American Communist Party who was eventually deported to Britain in 1955 where, in 1958, she founded and edited the first black weekly newspaper, *The West Indian Gazette*. Pinnock's play dramatises the important political connections between black people in America and the UK in the post-war period and highlights how Jones' skills and political acumen fostered in the US were applied to the particular needs of the UK's Caribbean community. In a number of plays, particularly those more oriented towards performance poetry, the names of famous black icons from around the world are listed as a means of emphasising the genealogy of global black achievement and solidarity. The names of African Americans are prominent, underlining the degree to which African America has captured black British imaginations. Names invoked in plays such as Sol B River's *Moor Masterpieces* [1994, West Yorkshire Playhouse], SuAndi's *This is all I've got to Say* [1993, ICA] and Valerie Mason-John's *Brown Girl in the Ring* [1998, Lyric Hammersmith] include, among others, Martin Luther King, Jr., Malcolm X, Muhammad Ali, Ira Aldridge, Paul Robeson, James Baldwin, Booker T. Washington and W. E. B. Du Bois.

Black Power imperatives of self-definition, cultural and historical recu-peration and pride have had a considerable impact on black British theatre's development, particularly in terms of the focus on community and the formation of theatre companies. In terms of drama, although much of the thematic exploration and representation of characters in plays reflects a writ-er's particular heritage and location, links with the USA regularly emerge.

In particular, the consciousness raising aims of Black Power, the Black Arts Movement and Afrocentrism have provided a vocabulary and aesthetic with which to articulate and represent black British experiences, locating them in and through a wider diasporic history. The influence of the Black Arts Movement's approach that melded aesthetics with ethics has also channelled a didactic style that registers across a number of twentieth-century plays. In many contemporary plays consciousness raising remains a priority even when this information is more subtly woven into the text and stage directions. Likewise, depictions of the 'front line' and plays written in an urban vernacular persist, another legacy of the Black Arts Movement. Indeed, African America is a nodal point in the nexus of transnational relationships that complicates black British identities/identifications; disturbing parochial notions of the nation as the primary/singular site of cultural formation and of diaspora as an over-simplified hybrid model comprising duel influences of home and host-land cultures.

Notes

1 For a dramatisation of events surrounding Aldridge in the title role of *Othello* at the Theatre Royal, Covent Garden in 1833, see Lolita Chakrabarti's *Red Velvet* [2012, Tricycle Theatre] which starred Adrian Lester as Aldridge.

2 African American plays staged in London's West End between the 1950s and the 1970s include: Langston Hughes and David Martin's musical *Simply Heavenly* [1957] at the Adelphi in 1958. (Also staged in 2003 at the Young Vic, directed by Josette Bushell-Mingo, transferring to the Trafalgar Studios in 2004); Hughes' *Black Nativity* [1961] at the Criterion in 1962 and at the Vaudeville 1964; Lorraine Hansberry's *A Raisin in the Sun* at the Adelphi in 1959. (Also staged in 1985 at the Tricycle Theatre in a Black Theatre Co-operative production, directed by Yvonne Brewster; in 2001 and 2005 at the Young Vic; in 2010 at the Manchester Exchange, directed by Michael Buffong; and in 2016 at the Crucible Theatre in an Eclipse Theatre production directed by Dawn Walton); James Baldwin's *Blues for Mister Charlie* [1964] at the Aldwych in 1965. (Also staged by Talawa in 2004 at the New Wolsey and Tricycle Theatre, directed by Paulette Randall); Baldwin's *The Amen Corner* [1954] at the Saville in 1965. (Also staged in 1987 by Carib Theatre Company at the Tricycle Theatre before transferring to the Lyric Theatre in the West End, directed by Anton Phillips; and in 2013 at the National Theatre).

3 For the London production Adrian Lester played the role of Brick. The production won an Olivier Award for Best Revival of a Play in 2010.

4 For accounts of political and cultural networks forged among black radicals in the USA, the UK, the Caribbean and Africa in the early twentieth century through Pan-Africanism, see, for example, Dawson (2009), Geiss (1974) amd Walters (1993).

5 For a transcript of the speech, see Carmichael (1968). See also Carmichael and Hamilton's manifesto, *Black Power: The Politics of Liberation in America* (1967). For a discussion of the global impact of Black Power and black revolutionary politics, see West, Martin and Wilkins (eds.) (2009). On the African American influence

on black politics in Britain, see Kelley and Tuck (2015), Malchow (2011), Shukra (1998), Thomlinson (2016) and Wild (2008, 2015).

6 Black Power politics and playwriting were directly linked through Nigerian Obi Egbuna. The Black Power activist Egbuna, who became leader of the Universal Coloured People's Association (UCPA) in 1967, was also a poet and playwright. In 1968 he spent six months in Brixton prison charged with conspiring to incite murder. He captured his experience of incarceration in a play entitled *The Agony* which was performed by Unity Theatre in 1970. No script for *The Agony* has been located. Egbuna's other stage plays include *Wind Versus Polygamy* [1966] and *The Anthill* [1965]. Egbuna's personal account of British Black Power is captured in his book *Destroy this Temple: The Voice of Black Power in Britain* (1971).

7 In the special 'Black Theatre' edition of *The Drama Review* (1968) the editor, Ed Bullins, grouped the Black Arts Movement's plays as being either 'Black Revolutionary Theatre' or 'Theatre of Black Experience'.

8 Ambience was part of American expatriate Ed Berman's Inter-Action theatre, an umbrella organisation under which a number of theatre and performance groups operated. For further information see the Unfinished Histories website: www. unfinishedhistories.com

9 The publication of these plays under the title *As Time Goes By; and, Black Pieces* (1972) includes *My Enemy* as part of *Black Pieces*; however, it is not clear if the piece was ever produced.

10 Matura's *Bakerloo Line* [1972, Almost Free Theatre] develops the theme of *Party*. The play's titular reference to the London underground and focus on the relationship between a black man and a white woman are reminiscent of Baraka's *Dutchman* [1964] whose black male and white female protagonists meet on the New York subway. However, the theme of racial relationships is told through Matura's trademark satirical style. (No script for *Bakerloo Line* has been located. The plot has been gleaned from reviews).

11 Examples of early attempts at organising black theatre companies include the Negro Theatre Company (initiated by Edric Connor in 1948), the West Indian Drama Group and the Ira Aldridge Players (formed in 1956 and 1961 and initiated by white directors, Joan Clarke and Herbert Marshall respectively), the New Day Theatre Company and The New Negro Theatre Company (both established in 1960 by Lloyd Reckord and Clifton Jones respectively) and the Negro Theatre Workshop (formed by Edric and Pearl Connor which ran from 1961–1968). For details of the activities of these early companies, see Chambers (2011, pp. 111–116 and 125–133).

12 For further details about Jamal Ali's work, see Shaw (2014).

13 *Dutchman* was presented on a double bill with *Neighbours* by James Saunders (white British). *Neighbours* echoed *Dutchman* in its exploration of race issues through an antagonistic relationship between a white woman and a black man.

14 See Paul Carter Harrison's *The Drama Of Nommo* (1972) in which he sets out a framework for a black theatre aesthetic and practice based upon African retentions in African American culture.

15 Collins also directed *Les Femmes Noires (Black Women)* [1974] and *Lament for Rastafari* [1975] in 1977 at the Keskidee.

16 *Man and Soul* is one of three short plays produced under the collective title, *Trinity: The Long and Cheerful Road to Slavery*. The other plays, *The Case of Dr. Kola* and *That*

Generation, were also produced in 1982 at the Riverside Studios by Black Theatre Co-operative.

17 For a discussion of White's work and details of his productions staged in the UK, see Stone (1994, pp. 161–167) and Chambers (2011, pp. 147–148, 178 and 187).

18 The veracity of Haley's claims are highly questionable. Nevertheless, *Roots* continues to have a significant impact. The miniseries was remade in 2016.

19 *At What A Price* was produced by the League of Coloured Peoples (LCP). It is about a woman living in the Jamaican countryside who moves to Kingston where she has an affair with her white boss and falls pregnant. Marson's play *London Calling* [1937], a comedy about an African prince moving in British high society, has never been performed in Britain (Chambers, 2011, pp. 99–101). For a biography of Marson, see Jarrett-Macauley (1998).

20 Black Theatre Co-operative/Nitro staged *A Raisin in the Sun* in 1985 at the Tricycle Theatre, directed by Yvonne Brewster, white American Ruth Dunlap Bartlett's (aka Helena Stevens) *The Cocoa Party* [1975, Unity Theatre] in 1987 at the Drill Hall and British-based Bonnie Greer's *Dancing on Black Water* in 1994, directed by Joan-Ann Maynard. Talawa produced Ntozake Shange's *The Love Space Demands* in 1992, Endesha Ida Mae Holland's *From The Mississippi Delta* [1987] in 1993 at the Cochrane Theatre – the play received its British premiere at the Young Vic in 1989, directed by Annie Castledine – and Pearl Cleage's *Flyin' West* [1992] in 1997 at the Drill Hall. Other plays by African American women staged in the UK include Alice Childress' *Trouble in Mind* [1955] and *Wine in the Wilderness* [1969] staged in 1992 and 2000 at the Tricycle – the latter was staged in double bill with Winsome Pinnock's *Water*, written as a response to Childress' play. The Royal Court premiered Anna Deavere Smith's *Fires in the Mirror* [1992] in 1993, Suzan Lori-Parks' *Topdog/Underdog* [2001] in 2003 and *Father Comes Home From The Wars (Parts 1, 2 & 3)* [2014] in 2016. Lori-Parks' *In The Blood* [1999] was staged in 2010 at the Finborough. Lynn Nottage's *Fabulation, or the Re-Education of Undine* [2004] was staged in 2006 at the Tricycle, *Ruined* [2007] in 2010 at the Almeida and *Intimate Apparel* [2003] in 2014 at the Theatre Royal Bath before transferring to London's Park Theatre; Katori Hall's *The Mountaintop* received its world premiere at the fringe London venue Theatre 503 in 2009 before transferring to the Trafalgar Studios where it went on to win the Olivier Award for Best New Play.

21 Kennedy had had the idea to write a play adapted from John Lennon's books *In His Own Write* and *A Spaniard in the Works*. A workshop version was presented on 3 December 1967 by the National Theatre under the title *Scene Three Act One*.

22 Osborne makes a connection between the thematic and formal explorations in Valerie Mason-John's *Brown Girl in the Ring* [1998, Lyric Hammersmith] and Mojisola Adebayo's *Moj of the Antarctic* [2006, Lyric Hammersmith] with Kennedy (Osborne, 2009, p. 7). See Bonnie Greer's *Munda Negra* which also recalls *Funnyhouse of a Negro*.

23 *For colored girls who have considered suicide/when the rainbow is enuf* was revived in 1983 at the New End Theatre. It was later staged by Siren Theatre at the BAC in 1990 and (by the same company now re-named the Daughters of Oshun) the Albany Empire in 1991, both directed by Paulette Randall. Shange's *Spell #7* [1979] was staged by the Women's Playhouse Trust at the Donmar in 1985, and

The Love Space Demands [1992] was staged by Talawa at the Cochrane in 1992 and directed by Yvonne Brewster. It was the company's first play by a woman writer.
24 Ikoli's plays include his début, *Short Sleeves in Summer* [1977, Royal Court Theatre], *Sink or Swim* [1982, Tricycle Theatre]; *Sleeping Policemen* [1983, Royal Court Theatre], co-written with Howard Brenton; *Week In, Week Out* [1985, Hoxton Hall]; *The Lower Depths* [1986, Tricycle Theatre]; and *Banged Up* [1986, Young Vic], a double bill comprising *Soul Night* and *Please and Thank You*. The latter six plays were produced by Roland Rees' company, Foco Novo.
25 Howard Sackler's *The Great White Hope* received its British premiere in 1985 at the Tricycle Theatre.
26 For a discussion on the transatlantic circulation of blackface minstrelsy, see Nowatzki (2010). For an overview of minstrelsy in the British theatre and a list of key sources on the subject, see Chambers (2011, pp. 52–56 and 214).

Works cited

Adeleke, T. 2009. *The case against Afrocentrism*. Jackson, MS: University Press of Mississippi.

Appadurai, A. 1990. Disjuncture and difference in the global cultural economy. *Theory, Culture & Society*. 7(2), pp. 295–310.

Aston, E. 2011. debbie tucker green. In: Middeke, M., Schnierer, P., and Sierz, A. eds., *The Methuen drama guide to contemporary British playwrights*. London: Methuen Drama, pp. 183–202.

Benston, K. 1980. The aesthetic of modern black drama: From *mimesis* to *methexis*. In: Hill, E. ed., *The theatre of black Americans: A collection of critical essays*. New York: Applause, pp. 61–78.

Bullins, E. ed. 1968. The Drama Reivew: TDR. 12(4), pp. 1–193.

Carmichael, S. 1968. Black Power. In: Cooper, D. ed., *The dialectics of liberation*. Harmondsworth, UK: Penguin, pp. 150–174.

Carmichael, S., and Hamilton, C. 1967. *Black Power: The politics of liberation in America*. New York: Random House.

Chambers, C. 2011. *Black and Asian theatre in Britain: A history*. London: Routledge.

Coveney, M. 1973a. All messed up and nowhere to go: Michael Coveney describes a crisis in the careers of five young directors. *Plays and Players*. 20(239), pp. 34–38.

———. 1973b. Getting on nicely. *Plays and Players*. 20(12), pp. 28–31.

Dawson, A. 2007. *Mongrel nation: Diasporic culture and the making of postcolonial Britain*. Ann Arbor: University of Michigan Press.

———. 2009. The rise of the black internationale: Anti-imperialist activism and aesthetics in Britain during the 1930s. *Atlantic Studies: Literary, Cultural and Historical Perspectives*. 6(2), pp. 159–174.

Dennis, F. 2000. Journey without maps. In: Dennis, F., and Khan, N. eds., *Voices of the crossing: The impact of Britain on writers from Asia, the Caribbean and Africa*. London: Serpent's Tail, pp. 39–50.

Du Bois, W. E. B. 1926. Krigwa players little negro theatre. *The Crisis*. 32, pp. 134–136.

Egbuna, O. 1971. *Destroy this temple: The voice of Black Power in Britain*. London: Mac-Gibbon & Kee.

Eyre, R., and Wright, N. 2000. *Changing stages: A view of British theatre in the twentieth century*. London: Bloomsbury.

Fagon, A. 1999. Lonely cowboy. *Alfred Fagon: Plays*. London: Oberon, pp. 149–209.

Gardner, L. 2005. 'I was messing about'. *The Guardian*. [Online]. 30 March. [Accessed 18 July 2011]. Available from: https://www.theguardian.com/stage/2005/mar/30/theatre

Geiss, I. 1974. *The Pan-African movement: A history of Pan-Africanism in America, Europe, and Africa*. London: Methuen.

Goddard, L. 2007. *Staging black feminisms: Identity, politics, performance*. Basingstoke, UK: Palgrave Macmillan.

———. 2015. *Contemporary black British playwrights: Margins to mainstream*. Basingstoke, UK: Palgrave Macmillan.

Godiwala, D. 2006. Introduction. In: Godiwala, D. ed., *Alternatives within the mainstream: British black and Asian theatres*. Newcastle upon Tyne, UK: Cambridge Scholars Press, pp. 1–19.

Griffin, G. 2003. *Contemporary black and Asian women playwrights in Britain*. Cambridge: Cambridge University Press.

Gunning, D., and Ward, A. 2009. Tracing black America in black British culture. *Atlantic Studies: Literary, Cultural and Historical Perspectives on Europe, Africa and the Americas*. 6(2), pp. 149–158.

Hale, T. A. 1998. *Griots and griottes: Masters of words and music*. Bloomington: Indiana University Press.

Haley, A. 1976. *Roots: The saga of an American family*. New York: Doubleday.

Hall, S. 2000. Frontlines and backyards: The terms of change. In: Owusu, K. ed., *Black British culture and society: A text-reader*. London: Routledge, pp. 127–130.

Harrison, P. C. 1972. *The drama of Nommo*. New York: Grove Press.

Howe, S. 1998. *Afrocentrism: Mythical pasts and imagined homes*. London: Verso.

Jarrett-Macauley, D. 1998. *The life of Una Marson, 1905–65*. Manchester: Manchester University Press.

Kay, J. 1987. Chiaroscuro. In: Davis, J. ed., *Lesbian plays*. London: Methuen, pp. 58–83.

Kelley, R., and Tuck, S. eds. 2015. *The other special relationship: Race, rights, and riots in Britain and the United States*. New York: Palgrave.

Kershaw, B. 2004. Alternative theatres, 1946–2000. In: Kershaw, B. ed., *The Cambridge history of British theatre: Since 1895*. Vol. 3. Cambridge: Cambridge University Press, pp. 349–376.

Kolin, P. 2005. *Understanding Adrienne Kennedy*. Columbia: University of South Carolina Press.

Lester, N. 1995. *Ntozake Shange: A critical study of the plays*. New York: Garland.

McLeod, J. 2009. British freedoms: Caryl Phillips's transatlanticism and the staging of *Rough Crossings*. *Atlantic studies: Literary, cultural and historical perspectives on Europe, Africa and the Americas*. 6(2), pp. 191–206.

McMillan, M. 2000. Ter speak in yer mudda tongue: An interview with playwright Mustapha Matura. In: Owusu, K. ed., *Black British culture and society: A text reader*. London: Routledge, pp. 255–264.

Malchow, H. 2011. *Special relations: The Americanization of Britain?* Stanford, CA: Stanford University Press.

Matura, M. 1992. Introduction. In: Matura, M. ed., *Matura: Six plays*. London: Methuen Drama, pp. ix-x.

Neal, L. 1968. The black arts movement. *The Drama Review*. 12(4), pp. 29–39.

Nowatzki, R. 2010. *Representing African Americans in transatlantic abolitionism and blackface minstrelsy*. Baton Rouge: Louisiana State University Press.

Ogbar, J. 2004. *Black Power: Radical politics and African American identity*. Baltimore: Johns Hopkins University Press.

Osborne, D. 2009. 'No straight answers': Writing in the margins, finding lost heroes: Mojisola Adebayo and Valerie Mason-John in conversation with Deirdre Osborne. *New Theatre Quarterly*. 25(1), pp. 6–21.

Peacock, D.K. 1999. *Thatcher's theatre: British theatre and drama in the eighties*. London: Greenwood Press.

PHS. 1973. Black thriller. *The Times*. 20 August. p. 12.

Rees, R. 1992. *Fringe first: Pioneers of fringe theatre on record*. London: Oberon.

Shaw, S. 2014. *'But where on earth is home?' – A social and cultural history of black Britain in 1970s film and television*. Portsmouth. Ph.D. thesis, University of Portsmouth.

Shukra, K. 1998. *The changing pattern of black politics in Britain*. London: Pluto Press.

Stone, J. 1994. *Studies in West Indian literature: Theatre*. London: Macmillan.

Thomlinson, N. 2016. *Race, ethnicity and the women's movement in England, 1968–1993*. Basingstoke, UK: Palgrave Macmillan.

Tunde's film. 1973. [Film]. Maggie Pinhorn and Tunde Ikoli dir. UK: Basement Films Project Group.

Walters, R. W. 1993. *Pan Africanism in the African diaspora: An analysis of modern Afrocentric political movements*. Detroit, MI: Wayne State University Press.

West, M., Martin, W., and Wilkins, F. C. eds. 2009. *From Toussaint to Tupac: The black international since the age of revolution*. Chapel Hill: University of North Carolina Press.

Wild, R. 2008. *'Black was the colour of our fight.' Black Power in Britain, 1955–1976*. Sheffield Ph.D. thesis, University of Sheffied.

———. 2015. 'Black was the colour of our fight': The transnational roots of British Black Power. In: Kelley, R. D. G., and Tuck, S. eds., *The other special relationship: Race, rights, and riots in Britain and the United States*. New York: Palgrave Macmillan, pp. 25–46.

2

BLACK POWER LEGACIES IN KWAME KWEI-ARMAH'S *ELMINA'S KITCHEN, FIX UP* AND *STATEMENT OF REGRET*[1]

Kwame Kwei-Armah (b. 1967), formerly Ian Roberts, was born in England to Grenadian parents and grew up in Southall, London. Whilst growing up, Kwei-Armah felt disconnected from his parents' Caribbean culture and struggled to find his place in Britain. Looking back at his youth, Kwei-Armah expresses a profound sense of dislocation:

> When I was young I never had a home. I used to call myself at sixteen famously a 'universal alien'. When I walked out on the streets in London, they'd say 'Go back home, you black bastard.' When I went to the West Indies they'd say, 'You're English.' When I go to Africa, they say 'Go home. Look at you, Bob Marley.' I'd never had a home until I discovered that I was an African and that actually I was a diasporic African.
>
> *(qtd in Davis, 2006, p. 247)*

For a number of black people growing up in Britain during the 1960s and 1970s, the paucity of black role models, lack of a mainstream black British cultural presence, no precedent of a critical mass of British-born black people and a racist environment meant that youths had to look elsewhere for their cultural and political reference points. This, combined with widespread assumptions that black people born in Britain were not really 'British', opened the door to African American identification, particularly among activists and artists, and coincided with the ascendancy of black American popular culture in the USA and its global dissemination. This chapter examines the ways in which Black Power politics inflects Kwei-Armah's writing approach and how Afrocentric ideology finds aesthetic representation in his works. It highlights in particular how Kwei-Armah's plays interrogate the uniqueness of black British experiences but also speak to works by August Wilson, thereby reiterating the depth of the political and cultural influence black America has had on Kwei-Armah's identity and work.

Two African American writers played a decisive role in Kwei-Armah's life: Alex Haley, whose books *Roots: The Saga of an American Family* (1976) and *The Autobiography of Malcolm X* (1965) re-configured Kwei-Armah's identity and honed his political consciousness, and August Wilson, whose work inspired Kwei-Armah to become a playwright and whose style has highly influenced his dramaturgy. It was through Haley's Pulitzer Prize-winning novel *Roots* that Kwei-Armah literally 'discovered' Africa and decided to change his name. When the television series of *Roots* was broadcast in the UK, it had a profound influence on the young Kwei-Armah (then Ian Roberts): 'It was on when I was 11 and I changed my path. It inspired me to start connecting myself with Africa and to find my true identity' (qtd in West, 2008). In his twenties, the then Ian Roberts went to Ghana where he traced his family genealogy and, on his return, changed his name to Kwame Kwei-Armah.

Kwei-Armah sees himself as a 'diasporic African' occupying an interstitial position between three cultures that define his identity: 'I call myself tri-cultural: I'm African, Caribbean and British. And each one of those has an equal part to play and I can be one or all at the same time depending on what it is' (qtd in Davis, 2006, p. 240). Kwei-Armah's plays exhibit a deep awareness of Caribbean and British cultures and their staging draws attention to the unique ways in which these spaces intersect, giving rise to new cultural hybrids and histories. Kwei-Armah does not explicitly identify with African America. Arguably, however, his sense of self- and political consciousness as a 'diasporic African' is not refracted through the third space of Africa but rather through black America. His identification with Afrocentric ideology was the result of his experiences of racism and marginalisation growing up in the UK in the 1970s and 1980s; but crucially, his exposure and understanding of it was accessed through African American popular culture (e.g. *Roots*). His Pan-African, Afrocentric politics stems in the main from African American cultural nationalist thinkers. On the political influences that have shaped his work, he states:

> My work comes from a cultural perspective that is supported by my
> Pan-Africanist politics . . . My politics is a diasporic, black politics

influenced by the philosophies of Marcus Garvey and Malcolm X and the writings of James Baldwin and Amiri Baraka. It is non-apologetic politics.

(qtd in Osborne, 2007, p. 253)

The above mixture of activists and writers are all African American, apart from Garvey who nevertheless spent a substantial time in the USA. It is in black America that we see the dominant influences that have shaped Kwei-Armah's identity, politics and art.

Kwei-Armah's début play, *A Bitter Herb,* was written in 1999 but only produced in 2001, at the Bristol Old Vic. In 1999 two of his musicals were produced: *Big Nose,* based on Rostand's Cyrano de Bergerac and co-written with Chris Monks, which opened at the Belgrade Theatre in Coventry and *Blues Brother, Soul Sister.* The latter also toured nationally under the title *Hold On* in 2001. In 2003, *Elmina's Kitchen* premiered at the National Theatre in the Cottesloe before transferring to the Garrick Theatre in 2005, becoming the first drama by a black British-born writer to be staged in the commercial West End. *Elmina's Kitchen* was also performed in Baltimore and Chicago, making it one of a handful of black British plays to have crossed the Atlantic.[2] Kwei-Armah followed *Elmina's Kitchen* with two new plays, both of which also premiered at the National Theatre in the Cottesloe: *Fix Up* in 2004 and *Statement of Regret* in 2007. Together these three plays comprise what Kwei-Armah refers to as his 'triptych'. After *Statement of Regret* followed *Let There Be Love* in 2008 and *Seize the Day* in 2009, which both premiered at London's Tricycle Theatre and were directed by Kwei-Armah. In 2011, Kwei-Armah relocated to the USA where he became Artistic Director of Center Stage Theater in Baltimore. Despite this shift in his career, Kwei-Armah continues to write. *Beneatha's Place* opened at Centre Stage in 2013, playing in rep with Bruce Norris' *Clybourne Park* [2010]. Like Norris' play, *Beneatha's Place* is also inspired by Lorraine Hansberry's *A Raisin in the Sun*; but, *Beneatha's Place* also responds to *Clybourne Park* in its structure and often shockingly open and humorous debate about race. Most recently Kwei-Armah wrote the book for and directed a bio-musical about Bob Marley entitled *Marley* which opened at Centre Stage in 2015. Prior to *Beneatha's Place*, Kwei-Armah's plays were mainly set in contemporary London, demonstrating his commitment to representing the contemporary metropolitan black British experience. Nevertheless, Kwei-Armah's relocation to the USA follows a long infatuation with African American politics and culture.

In a number of his plays, the African American experience provides the starting point for Kwei-Armah's engagement with black issues in Britain: The title of *Let There Be Love* is taken from Nat King Cole's version of the song and uses its message of harmony and compassion in a plea against prejudice and intolerance of minorities in Britain; *Seize the Day* revolves around a candidate in the running to become London's first black mayor and was inspired by the election of Barack Obama in 2008; *Fix Up* was inspired by a book of African American slave narratives that Kwei-Armah received as a gift on the opening night of *Elmina's Kitchen*; and in *Statement of Regret*, Kwei-Armah bases the play's central exploration of the continuing impact of slavery on black peoples' experiences on African American social scientist Dr Joy DeGruy-Leary's theory of 'post traumatic slave syndrome'. In *Post Traumatic Slave Syndrome* (2005), DeGruy-Leary argues that the trauma of slavery continues to impact upon the psychological development of black Americans. The Caribbean experience of racial segregation under colonialism and the hostile and racist treatment of black people in Britain in the post-war period have had, in Kwei-Armah's opinion, a similarly damaging effect on black people as the USA's history of slavery and segregation/Jim Crow laws: 'Even though a lot of people say it's not the same in this country as in America, technically with colonialism, we are running in direct parallel' (2007).

August Wilson's chronicling of African American history in his plays provided Kwei-Armah with potent inspiration. In 1990, Kwei-Armah attended his first August Wilson play. It was *Joe Turner's Come and Gone* [1986] at London's Tricycle Theatre where Kwei-Armah admits he became a devotee of Wilson: 'I really got turned on to August in a big, bad way. I was smitten by its spirituality, by its haunting refrain to Africa, its exploration of the pain of the diaspora' (qtd in Edwardes, 2006).[3] In Wilson, Kwei-Armah would find a powerful role model. Kwei-Armah's triptych reveals a debt to Wilson's plays in their style, thematic exploration and underlying political belief system. Indeed, it is through Wilson's influence that one can trace the fundamental impression black America has had on Kwei-Armah's dramatic style.

Kwei-Armah's inspiration for his triptych of plays was a production of Wilson's *King Hedley II* [1999], which he saw while in Washington, D.C. in 2001. In an interview about *Elmina's Kitchen*, Kwei-Armah recounts: 'I was so touched by the magnitude of this man and his commitment to talk of and chronicle the African-American experience through the art form [. . .] I went back to my hotel room that night and said, "O.K., I now know what I want to do; I want to chronicle the black British experience"' (qtd in Wolf,

2005). For the Cycle, Wilson wrote ten plays, each set in Pittsburgh and each representative of a decade in the twentieth century. Kwei-Armah's triptych are not historical is this way. They are all set in London in the 2000s and are divided according to class: *Elmina's Kitchen* – the underclass, *Fix Up* – the working class and *Statement of Regret* – the middle class.

In *Elmina's Kitchen*, the action takes place in a fast-food takeaway called Elmina's Kitchen in Hackney's notorious 'murder mile'.[4] The play examines the failed attempts of restaurant owner Deli to keep his son Ashley from entering into a life of gangs and crime. Brother Kiyi's black-consciousness bookshop provides the setting for *Fix Up*. In the play, Brother Kiyi's struggle to keep his shop afloat is undermined by his lodger Kwesi, who plans to take over the premises and turn it into a black hair products shop. The conflict yields a debate centred on whether black self-determination is best won through intellectual or economic means. When Brother Kiyi's mixed-race daughter arrives, looking for the father who gave her up for adoption and for an explanation as to the whereabouts of her mother, a concurrent theme emerges around identity and the importance of historical knowledge and truth if individual and collective freedom is to be achieved. *Statement of Regret* is set in a black political think-tank. The play explores the role of black politics in contemporary British society and the differing generational and ethnic approaches taken by the think-tank's black British, Caribbean and African employees. At the play's core lies an examination of the continued legacy of slavery and its impact upon the black psyche.

Themes of inter-generational conflict and the struggle against racial oppression and for racial identity are as central to Kwei-Armah's work as they are to Wilson's. This has led a number of reviewers to comment on echoes of Wilson's work in Kwei-Armah's plays. For instance, one reviewer wrote of *Statement of Regret*:

> For all that the suited black British characters exist an ocean apart – and an economic class or two above – the black milieu unforgettably chronicled in the US by the late August Wilson, *Statement of Regret* seems in numerous ways to want to answer many of Wilson's ongoing concerns, adapting them for a UK audience. The result makes for an intriguing theatrical case of call-and-response, whereby one feels very directly the cultural and thematic baton being passed from one important dramatist to another.
>
> *(Wolf, n.d.)*

A number of thematic and situational similarities exist between Kwei-Armah's triptych and Wilson's ten-play cycle. In *Elmina's Kitchen*, Deli, an ex-boxer and reformed criminal, is determined to reform his and his son's life. The relationship is reminiscent of Wilson's *Fences* [1985]. In *Fences*, Troy, the play's protagonist, like Deli, is an ex-convict and ex-sportsman whose dreams never came true and who struggles in his job to provide enough money for his family. However, the relationship between father and son in *Fences* is reversed in *Elmina's Kitchen*. In *Fences*, Troy's jealousy prevents his son going to college on a football scholarship. In *Elmina's Kitchen*, Deli is desperate to remove his son from a world of gangs and violence and his motives are entirely altruistic. Nevertheless, the father and son relationship is destroyed in both plays. The similarity lies in both works' exploration of the themes of failed ambitions, the inability of the father to prevent history repeating itself and of death. When *Elmina's Kitchen* was produced by Center Stage in Baltimore, the reviewer for The Washington Post could not help but draw a comparison between Kwei-Armah and Wilson: "'Elmina's Kitchen" clearly owes a debt to, among other dramatists, Wilson; the play's setting – a funky diner in a marginal black neighbourhood is practically interchangeable with that of Wilson's "Two Trains Running"' (Marks, 2005).

However, while the setting may be familiar, the themes of *Two Trains Running* [1990] more closely resemble the issues explored in *Fix Up*. The setting of *Two Trains Running* in the declining neighbourhood of the Hill District in the 1960s, which was once a politically and culturally vibrant black area, resembles Brother Kiyi's struggling black-consciousness bookshop. In both plays, the setting (the restaurant in *Two Trains Running* and Brother Kiyi's bookshop in *Fix Up*) provides the locus for the exploration of a generational and gendered debate on approaches to black political activism and the routes to self-determination. *Fix Up*, like *Two Trains Running*, stages an ideological debate through the conflicting viewpoints of its central characters. In *Fix Up*, Brother Kiyi's political stance is based on the belief that historical knowledge should be sought to bring about emancipation from 'mental slavery', whereas Kwesi views economic power as the best means by which to achieve self-determination. Through the mixed-race character of Alice, Kwei-Armah brings a critical voice to the Black Nationalist debate. Alice's arguments, for example her summation of Claude McKay's poem 'If We Must Die' as 'sexist' because in it 'he only talks about the race by imagining the aspirations of men' (2009, p. 126), highlight the hypocrisy of black men who critique white oppression yet continue to oppress black women. In *Two Trains Running*, it is the character of Risa who fulfils this similar function. However, Kwei-Armah complicates the debate by making Alice mixed-race. As mixed-race or, as she points out, a woman of 'dual heritage' (Kwei-Armah, 2009, p. 130), her presence in the play not only exposes the male-centricity of black intellectual and political leaders but also her exclusion from black discourses of belonging as a mixed-race woman. She is treated with contempt by Kwesi who accuses mixed-race people of choosing their allegiance to black people only when it suits them:

Kwesi: I don't trust you type of people. I see you coming in here trying to be down, so when the white man thinks he's choosing one of us you're there shouting, 'Hey, I'm black.' But you ain't.

(Kwei-Armah, 2009, p. 134)

Alice's search to find her father and learn the truth about her birth mother's identity echoes broader political debates raised in the play around racial belonging and highlights how Britain's growing mixed-race population poses a challenge to assumptions of how blackness and whiteness are defined and experienced. Yet, by portraying Alice as 'beautiful but troubled' (p. 100) Kwei-Armah arguably perpetuates stereotypes that equate being mixed-race or of dual heritage with experiences of un-belonging and, at worst, psychosis.

In the same way that a triptych describes three individual yet correlated pieces of art intended to be appreciated together, *Elmina's Kitchen*, *Fix Up* and *Statement of Regret* are linked by a common thematic thread: despite differences in age, gender, birthplace, sexuality and ethnicity, Kwei-Armah asserts that black commonality may be found in a legacy of oppression which began with slavery and continues to manifest itself in the present. The most striking echo between Kwei-Armah's triptych and Wilson's Pittsburgh Cycle is the treatment of the impact of the past on the lives of the characters.[5] The interplay between past and present is a hallmark of Wilson's work and defining element of his dramaturgy. In plays such as *Joe Turner's Come and Gone*, *The Piano Lesson* [1987] and *Gem of the Ocean* [2003], Wilson inserts moments which pull apart the unities of time and place and force the characters into a space in which they must confront not only their specific pasts but the collective past of African Americans. It is only by going through this terrifying process that historical injustices can begin to heal.

Wilson encases his explorations of the relationship between the past and present within a dramaturgy that melds realism with ritual, and which allows the time and space of the present to be collapsed with that of the past. This unique style is achieved through a combination of music, African American folk traditions, mythology and ritual re-enactment. In *The Past as Present in the Drama of August Wilson*, Harry Elam writes: 'Wilson (w)rights history by invoking rites that connect the spiritual, the cultural, the social, and the political, not simply to correct the past but to interpret it in ways that powerfully impact the present. In a space and time outside of time, within the liminal dimensions of theater, Wilson (w)rights history' (Elam, 2004, p. 4). In the same way, Kwei-Armah's plays attempt to access a larger cosmos. Although the settings of a café (*Elmina's Kitchen*), a book shop (*Fix Up*) and a small, floundering think-tank (*Statement of Regret*) are parochial, Kwei-Armah inserts devices that link the ordinary people of his plays with the larger historical events of the trans-Atlantic slave trade and colonialism. The plays' themes in common (inter-generational conflict, the struggle against racial oppression and the search for identity) are placed within a broader continuum of black experiences. In *Elmina's Kitchen*, contemporary Hackney is firmly planted on the foundations of slavery. Elmina's Kitchen, named after Deli's mother, is also a reference to Elmina Castle, built in Ghana by the Portuguese in 1482, which later became a key slave trading post in the early seventeenth century. The reference to the Atlantic slave trade suggests, as Wilson does throughout his plays, that the origins of intra-racial violence lie in the violent historical treatment of black people by whites. Although the references to slavery point to an underlying cause of the intra-racial violence in the play, Kwei-Armah is also at pains to highlight that it is through knowledge of the history of black suffering and a connection with one's cultural and spiritual roots in Africa that black people in the diaspora can find healing.

Kwei-Armah also adds a griot figure into *Elmina's Kitchen* who appears as a man in the prologue to Act One, and as a woman at the start of Act Two. Their inclusion symbolises the play's connection to Africa as the ancestral homeland. They anchor the play and its characters within the space and history of the African diaspora formed during the Atlantic slave trade. The diaspora, this suggests, are direct inheritors of Africa's cultural and spiritual traditions. The stage directions for the prologue situate the play in this historical and ritualised time/space:

> The stage is in darkness. A single spotlight slowly reveals a costumed man, standing absolutely still with a gurkel (a one-string African guitar famed for possessing the power to draw out spirits) in his hands [. . .] The music starts. It is a slow lament-sounding concoction of American blues and traditional African music. The man then covers the length and breadth of the stage flicking handfuls of powder on to the playing area.
>
> *(p. 5)*

Traditionally, the West African *gurkel* is an instrument associated with exorcising malevolent spirits and the sprinkling of powder implies that the space is being consecrated and that a healing is about to take place. Although there is no interaction between the 'African' figure and the characters in the play, his appearance signifies the presence of the ancestral past in the present and suggests that the play is a ritual re-enactment that will bring about a healing by providing a bridge to the liberating space of collective memory.

In *Fix Up*, the melding of past and present is echoed in the set. The stage directions describe a space full of books as well as 'African statues and carvings of giraffes . . . Ashanti stools, sculptured walking sticks etc.' (p. 101). In the National Theatre production, bookshelves encased the performance space. The towers of books drew attention to the substantial contribution of black intellectuals and artists, reinforcing the idea that the play's setting within a black-consciousness bookshop is a space that harbours the thoughts, dreams and creativity of the past contained within the tomes. However, the general way in which the bookshop's ornaments and objects are described and jumbled together (and, by extension, the version of black consciousness articulated by Kiyi) seem to signify 'Africa' as a cultural free-for-all.

The volume of slave narratives that Brother Kiyi has recently purchased provide the catalyst for Alice's self-discovery. Alone in the shop, Alice begins to read an account by a slave named Mary Gould living on a plantation in Grenada. Mary Gould tells the story of a mixed-race woman who was raped by the white plantation master and bore his children. When the children identified the master as their father, the master's wife had their mother whipped and the children sold. The description highlights how mixed-race people in slave society occupied a social positioning between the black slaves and their white slave owners. The stage directions stipulate that as Alice reads, 'the lights reduce to a spotlight on her. We are in her head. She takes on the voice of the story-teller' (p. 132). Taking on Mary Gould's language, the extract collapses past and present, plunging Alice into an aspect of her history that had otherwise been unavailable to her growing up with white foster parents in Somerset. The moment confronts the audience with a horrific account of racist brutality and the point at which a character establishes a connection with their individual and collective identity. Moments such as these are a feature of Wilson's dramas. A prime example is during *Joe Turner's Come and Gone* when Herald Loomis, who, like Alice, is also looking for his family, is freed by Bynum's song to articulate his experiences of slavery (see Tyndall, 2011). Alice's connection with her past is both intellectual and physical. The act of storytelling (signifying African oral traditions) and her embodiment of Mary

Gould through voice is akin to a possession. In this moment the spirit of the past speaks through Alice, allowing her to begin the process of coming to terms with her present.

Kwei-Armah's plays draw on a plethora of cultural and linguistic forms so as to represent the complex cultural heritage of Britain's black communities. Kwei-Armah acknowledges Wilson as an inspiration for this approach:

> What he was doing with the African–American community, with his own community in Pittsburgh, inspired me to create what I perceive as the theatre of my front room. Validating your language, giving equal cultural status to the syntax, to the rhythm in which your own people speak: this is cultural equality.
>
> *(qtd in Edwardes, 2006)*

Kwei-Armah does this deftly through his use of Caribbean and black London vernacular, calypso and his representation of multiple generations with different cultural backgrounds. Kwei-Armah's 'theatre of my front room' presents a transnational hub through which diverse cultures move, meet and form anew. Through his plays' depiction of multiple generations and ethnicities, we are presented with the genealogical diversity of the black population, which encompasses different histories, cultures and geographies. The specific stage directions, indicating the characters' accents, reveal his acute awareness of language as a primary marker of such complex identities. In *Elmina's Kitchen*, 'Digger's accent swings from his native Grenadian to hard-core Jamaican to authentic black London' (p. 6), Anastasia, who is black British, is able to use 'authentic, full-attitude Jamaican at the drop of a hat' (p. 17) and Clifton, who is from Trinidad, 'uses his eastern Caribbean accent to full effect when storytelling' (p. 34). Identity is further complicated in *Fix Up* through Alice, who is mixed-race but was brought up in an all white environment, and whose physical appearance is in conflict with social assumptions. At one point, she remarks: 'Cos I'm brown, everybody expects me to somehow know everything black. And I'm like, 'Hey, how am I suppose to know what . . . raaasclaat means, I'm from Somerset' (p. 128). The inclusion of multiple generations fulfils Kwei-Armah's aim to chronicle black British experiences. The plays are also grounded within the remembered history of colonisation, migration of the Windrush generation and the contemporary phenomenon of large-scale African migration to the UK.

Kwei-Armah's approach to aesthetics is one that combines an educational aspect, demonstrative of his commitment to using theatre as a means to raise the self-awareness of his audience. When asked if he agreed with Linton Kwesi Johnson that 'no black writer working in England today can afford "art for art's sake"', Kwei-Armah responds: 'Correct, and I believe in that. Let's not mince words here, my work is political work' (qtd in Osborne, 2007, p. 253). The impact of Wilson on Kwei-Armah's playwriting, alongside cited influences such as Baraka and Baldwin, places Kwei-Armah as an inheritor of the USA's 1960s Black Arts Movement. Black Power cultural politics distinctly informs the aesthetic in Kwei-Armah's triptych. His plays are written with a black audience foremost in mind. The absence of white characters in all three plays signals Kwei-Armah's reluctance to enter into a discussion of racism or protest art that centres white people as the principal subjects by attacking them:

> I'm not interested in talking about race. What I'm interested in is presenting stories from my cultural lens that are about my humanity [. . .] What I'm saying is, we must not define ourselves purely in relation to racism.
>
> *(qtd in Newland, Norfolk and Kwei-Armah, 2003)*

Intrinsic to the Black Arts Movement's notion of the Black aesthetic was the social role art should play in helping the black community on its path to self-determination and self-consciousness. In accordance, the BAM rejected what they perceived to be a Western model of 'art for arts sake', embracing instead a theatre with a clear social function aimed first and foremost at black people:

> The Black Arts Movement believes that your ethics and your aesthetics are one. That the contradictions between ethics and aesthetics in western society is symptomatic of a dying culture.
>
> *(Neal, 1968, p. 31)*

This belief channelled a didacticism in their work: the more militant dramas often taught a lesson and advocated the need to overhaul the self and community if self-determination and black consciousness were to be achieved. Similarly, Kwei-Armah's aesthetic aligns ideological didacticism with black cultural forms in order to provide a vehicle for black-consciousness and self-determination. Like Anastasia's collection of self-help books that she passes on to Deli in *Elmina's Kitchen*, the principle of self-help informs the message of Kwei-Armah's plays, which explain their multiple references to black intellectual, political and cultural icons. In *Fix Up*, the space of the bookshop offers such a resource for the play's characters. In the dramatis personae Kwei-Armah lists three 'non-present characters': Marcus Garvey, James Baldwin and Claude McKay. Reiterating the theme of the impact of the past on the present, the play is haunted by their presence. Their legacy is voiced through the play's characters. For instance, Brother Kiyi plays a tape of one of Garvey's speeches in his bookshop, he cites Baldwin in his conversations and Carl reads McKay's poem, 'If We Must Die'. Norma comments that Brother Kiyi has taught her to love herself: 'you love Black. And all of my life I have been taught to fear it, hate it. That ain't right!' (p. 119). Through references and quotations, the intellectual, political and cultural life of these seminal black icons imbues the piece with their legacy and provides intellectual and spiritual nourishment to the characters and audience.

Kwei-Armah's authorial voice is clearly of the opinion that black improvement lies in historical recuperation. For those that embrace it, such as Deli, there is hope; for those that do not, there is despair, plainly demonstrated with Ashley's death at the end of *Elmina's Kitchen*. The need to know yourself, your roots and your people rings throughout the three works. For Kwei-Armah, pride in one's history is as important as coming to terms with the painful experience of the collective past. His plays provide a wealth of examples of extraordinary black achievement. As he states in an interview: 'Art is there solely to reflect ourselves. And it is only in that reflection that we are able to be self-critical and able to improve and remove some of the subconscious inferiority that has been placed in us since slavery' (qtd in Davis, 2006, p. 243). Running in parallel with Kwei-Armah's depiction of characters struggling in life is a strong seam of positivity to bolster and nourish the audience and characters if they choose to see it. For instance, in *Fix Up*, which takes place in October during Black History month, the discussions between characters convey historical information about Caribbean culture and how it was shaped by slavery, from people's names to the food they eat and the ways in which they style their hair.

The didactic elements in Kwei-Armah's work operate on the level of character as well as dialogue. Kwei-Armah creates characters grounded in African mythology as a means to root his plays in an African cosmology, and, presumably therefore, to access a collective culture and memory shared between continental Africans and the diaspora. For example, in *Elmina's Kitchen*, Anastasia arrives unexpectedly carrying a home-made macaroni pie and looking for a job. Her superior cooking secures her the job, and she quickly becomes a major force of change in the play. She convinces Deli to clean up the image his restaurant is projecting by getting rid of patrons like Digger, whose presence Anastasia describes as giving off 'the stench of death' (p. 45). She also helps Deli to give the restaurant a fresh image, a new name, and exposes him to self-help books. Her positivity strengthens Deli's resolve to extricate Ashley from mixing with gangs. As a character, she is almost too good to be true. There is something artificial about her, leaving the impression that she is more archetype than a three-dimensional representation. The macaroni pie, a traditional southern American 'soul food', hints at her more supernatural purpose. The power of food is not underestimated, as Digger comments before Deli takes a bite: 'Mind she obea you, boy!' (p. 18). Yet from his first taste of the food, Deli's life begins to change for the better and Anastasia secures a place in his life. Paul Carter Harrison writes that 'Black Theatre is not merely the social inscription of victimization arrested in the lens of social realism' (2002, p. 5). Its critical engagement, he argues, requires an understanding of African diasporic cultural traditions: 'It is not uncommon to discover in the ritual forms of Black Theatre characters that are more representative archetypes than individuated, full-dimensioned characters located in the conventions of realism. Characters configured as archetypes serve a universe that allows both the living and the dead to drive the actions of a dramatic event' (p. 5). The stage directions describe Anastasia in such a way that supports this idea: 'we can see that she has the kind of body that most men of colour fantasize about. Big hips and butt, slim waist and full, full breasts' (p. 17). The description that stresses her African physicality renders Anastasia as representative of an African 'Earth Mother Goddess' archetype. Anastasia has come to save Deli and his family. Yet for all the positive change she brings, her influence is destroyed by the jealous Clifton, who sees her as a threat to his ambitions for his son's attention and financial assistance. Clifton seduces her and then threatens to expose her unless she leaves Deli. Here, Kwei-Armah critiques a male-dominated culture that has lost respect for its women and any spiritual connection to their goddesses. Osborne criticises this particular stage direction as one among other examples of 'sexual denigration' of women within the play (2006, p. 92). Kwei-Armah's intentions, however, seen through a non-Western value system, are in fact the reverse. Yet, as Osborne's critique reveals, the stage direction exposes the heterosexist and patriarchal values of a traditional Afrocentric perspective and of the Black Power movement. The play, therefore, reflects a conservative world-view by dint of it being rooted in 1960s Black radical politics. An American reviewer noted that the play dealt with themes that may be new to a British audience, but to an American one, it trod upon familiar territory pioneered by writers such as Langston Hughes and Wilson (Marks, 2005). The play's success in a British context draws attention to both the limited exposure mainstream British audiences have had to these themes and the limited space given to playwright to explore such issues.

Soby is another archetypal figure in *Statement of Regret*. When Kwaku is desperate for money to keep the business afloat, Soby offers to help him on the condition that he reject his African name and take on his Caribbean birth name, Derek. Soby also forces Kwaku to take a stand against his African colleagues and to assert Caribbean superiority, an approach which ends up destroying the organisation with Kwaku losing everything. It is only at the end of the play that we discover Soby is the ghost of Kwaku's father. Soby's function is to demonstrate the dangers of separatist political approaches. Had Kwaku not been tempted into following a path of ethnic particularism but instead embraced one of Black solidarity, and instilled these values in his organisation, then, Kwei-Armah suggests, the think-tank might have survived. Kwei-Armah provides two possible endings for the piece. In the first (the ending staged at the National Theatre), Kwaku is left alone and confused and unsure of what he has done. However, the alternate ending (used in his radio adaptation) provides redemption. Lola, his wife, comes back to him and they are reconciled:

Lola: The battle has changed, Kwaku. Maybe it's time we rest. Maybe it's
         time we let the young ones make their mistakes.
Kwaku: Maybe. Take me home, Lola.

(p. 255)

In the first ending, Kwaku remains deceived and his life is in shreds. In the second ending, Soby brings about an eventual self-awareness. Although the latter ends on a note of hope, both versions convey Kwei-Armah's message to his black audience: united we stand, divided we fall.

The inclusion of archetypal characters is in line with Kwei-Armah's approach, which seeks to root his triptych beyond the purely social and place them within a larger mythological cosmos of the African diaspora. However, Kwei-Armah's route to these African cultural practices is mediated through African America. This explains the almost romantic and non-specific employment of African forms. Although it is possible that Kwei-Armah sourced these archetypes from West African culture directly, as he does not reference writers from Africa, it is plausible, as seen with his other depictions of Africa such as the griot/gurkel player, that he has accessed such knowledge from

African America. It is this cultural and political resource, not Africa, which informs his aesthetic.

The notion of black America as Kwei-Armah's source for his plays' African diasporic politics and aesthetic is particularly striking through the use of music in the plays. The blues features prominently in *Elmina's Kitchen* and in *Fix Up*. In the prologue to *Elmina's Kitchen*, the stage directions stipulate that the African griot is accompanied musically by 'a slow lament-sounding concoction of American blues and traditional African music' (p. 5). The mixture of American blues and African music traces in sound the movement of slaves from Africa to the USA. As the scene is meant to contextualise the action of the rest of the play, set in Hackney, the mélange of musical styles seems oddly placed. The music of the blues is used a second time at the opening of the second act during the funeral of Deli's brother, when the cast sing 'You Gotta Move'. Kwei-Armah also uses the blues in *Fix Up*. At the end of the play, Brother Kiyi cuts off his dreadlocks and sings the blues slave chant 'Adam in the Garden'. Tellingly, Kwei-Armah signifies slavery and its impact on contemporary black Britishness in such a way that does not yield identification with African Caribbean experiences but rather locates this in an African American context.

The blues does not just provide a soundtrack to Kwei-Armah's works, it permeates their tone. The plays in Kwei-Armah's triptych end on a melancholic note: *Elmina's Kitchen* ends with Deli covering the body of his dead son; in *Fix Up* Brother Kiyi is forced to leave his shop and has been exposed as a father who abandoned his daughter; and in *Statement of Regret* the positive work of the think-tank hangs in the balance after Kwaku's nervous breakdown. Nevertheless, juxtaposed with these endings the plays balance moments of light-heartedness, songs and comic relief. The result is a bittersweet tone that epitomises the blues. Although this tradition has nothing to do with Africa or the Caribbean, it seems Kwei-Armah uses the blues not to signify cultural specificity, but rather as a means to evoke an atmosphere of shared history. In this way, its use can be seen as a 'call and response' with not only a musical form, but with African American dramatists such as Baldwin, Baraka and Wilson, who are renowned for infusing their work with the spirit of the blues. Kwei-Armah's plays may document the black British experience and its links to the Caribbean and Africa; however, thematically, dramaturgically and aesthetically, they demonstrate the important impact of African American artists, thinkers and popular culture on his experience and work.

Notes

1 An earlier version of this chapter was published as 'Kwame Kwei-Armah's African American inspired triptych' in Brewer, M., Goddard, L., and Osborne, D. eds., 2014. *Modern and contemporary black British drama*. London: Palgrave Macmillan, pp. 128–144. Previously used sections have been reprinted with kind permission from Palgrave.

2 A handful of plays by black British-born playwrights have been staged in the USA. They include Winsome Pinnock's *Mules* [1996, Royal Court Theatre] at the Magic Theatre, San Francisco in 1998, Kwei-Armah's *Let There be Love* at Center Stage in 2010, debbie tucker green's *born bad* [2003, Hampstead Theatre] and *generations* [2007, Young Vic] at the off-Broadway Soho Rep in New York in 2011 and 2014, Roy Williams' *Sucker Punch* at the Studio Theatre, Washington D.C. in 2012 and *Loneliness of the Long Distance Runner* [2012, York Theatre Royal], adapted from the short story by Alan Sillitoe (1959), at Atlantic Stage 2, New York City in 2014.

3 *Ma Rainey's Black Bottom* [1984] was staged at the National Theatre in 1989 (and again in 2016). In 2004 is was staged at the Liverpool Playhouse and in 2006 at the Royal Exchange Theatre, Manchester. *Joe Turner's Come and Gone* [1986] was staged at the Tricycle in 1990 and at the Young Vic in 2010. *Fences* [1985], directed by Alby James, was staged at the Liverpool Playhouse in 1990 before transferring to the Garrick Theatre in London's West End. In 2013, a production directed by Paulette Randall opened at the Theatre Royal, Bath before transferring to the Duchess in London's West End. This marked the first time a play in the West End was directed by a black British woman. *The Piano Lesson* [1987] and *Two Trains Running* [1990] were staged at the Tricycle in 1993 and 1996 respectively, both directed by Paulette Randall. *Jitney* [1982] received its British premiere at the National Theatre in 2001, winning the Lawrence Olivier Award for Best New Play. *King Hedley II* [1999], *Gem of the Ocean* [2003] and *Radio Golf* [2005] were staged at the Tricycle in 2002, 2006 and 2008 respectively, all directed by Paulette Randall.

4 The Upper and Lower Clapton Roads in Hackney earned the nickname at the start of the 2000s. See the article in *The Independent*, 'Eight men shot dead in two years. Welcome to Britain's Murder Mile' (Mendick and Johnson, 2002).

5 See Goddard (2011) and Kasule (2006), who both highlight this aspect of Kwei-Armah's dramaturgy.

Works cited

Davis, G. 2006. 'This is a cultural renaissance': An interview with Kwame Kwei-Armah. In: Davis, G., and Fuchs, A. eds., *Staging new Britain: Aspects of black and South Asian British theatre practice*. Brussels: P.I.E.- Peter Lang, pp. 239–252.

DeGruy-Leary, J. D. 2005. *Post traumatic slave syndrome: America's legacy of enduring injury and healing*. Milwaukie, WI: Uptone Press.

Edwardes, J. 2006. Racing through history. *Time Out*. 4 January. p. 120.

Elam, H. J. 2004. *The past as present in the drama of August Wilson*. Ann Arbor: University of Michigan Press.

Goddard, L. 2011. Kwame Kwei-Armah. In: Middeke, M., Schnierer, P., and Sierz, A. eds., *The Methuen drama guide to contemporary British playwrights*. London: Methuen Drama, pp. 323–342.

Haley, A. 1976. *Roots: The saga of an American family.* New York: Doubleday.

Haley, A., and Malcolm, X. 1965. *The autobiography of Malcolm X.* New York: Grove Press.

Harrison, P. C. 2002. Praise/word. In: Harrison, P. C., Walker, V. L., II, and Edwards, G. eds., *Black theatre: Ritual performance in the African diaspora.* Philadelphia: Temple University Press, pp. 1–10.

Kasule, S. 2006. Aspects of madness and theatricality in Kwame Kwei-Armah's drama. In: Godiwala, D. ed., *Alternatives within the mainstream: British black and Asian theatres.* Newcastle upon Tyne, UK: Cambridge Scholars Press, pp. 314–328.

Kwei-Armah, K. 2007. *Statement of regret, interview with Dr Joy De Gruy Leary.* [Production programme]. (RNT/PP/1/4/275). London: National Theatre Archive.

———. 2009. *Kwame Kwei-Armah plays 1: Elmina's Kitchen; Fix Up; Statement of Regret; Let There Be Love.* London: Methuen.

Marks, P. 2005. Melting pot stew; hearty ingredients of 'Elmina's Kitchen'. *The Washington Post.* 6 January. p. C01.

Mendick, R., and Johnson, A. 2002. Eight men shot dead in two years: Welcome to Britain's murder mile. *The Independent.* [Online]. 6 January. [Accessed 21 October 2016]. Available from: http://www.independent.co.uk/news/uk/this-britain/eight-men-shot-dead-in-two-years-welcome-to-britains-murder-mile-662314.html

Neal, L. 1968. The black arts movement. *The Drama Review.* 12(4), pp. 29–39.

Newland, C., Norfolk, M., and Kwei-Armah, K. 2003. 'Our job is to write about what is in our hearts': Black British theatre is on a high: Three young writers look at where it's headed. *The Guardian.* 6 October. [Accessed 21 October 2016]. Available from: https://www.theguardian.com/stage/2003/oct/06/theatre.race

Osborne, D. 2006. The state of the nation: Contemporary black British theatre and the staging of the UK. In: Godiwala, D. ed., *Alternatives within the mainstream: British black and Asian theatres.* Newcastle upon Tyne, UK: Cambridge Scholars Press, pp. 82–100.

———. 2007. Know whence you came: Dramatic art and black British identity. *New Theatre Quarterly.* 23(3), pp. 253–263.

Sillitoe, A. 1959. *The loneliness of the long distance runner.* London: W. H. Allen.

Tyndall, P. 2011. Using black rage to elucidate African and African American identity in August Wilson's Joe Turner's Come and Gone (1911). In: Williams, D. A., and Shannon, S. G. eds., *August Wilson and black aesthetics.* Basingstoke, UK: Palgrave Macmillan, pp. 159–174.

West, N. 2008. The world of Kwame Kwei-Armah. *The Telegraph.* [Online]. 19 January. [Accessed 20 October 2016]. Available from: http://www.telegraph.co.uk/culture/theatre/3670618/The-world-of-Kwame-Kwei-Armah.html

Wolf, M. 2005. He talks of black Britain, and the West End listens. *New York Times.* [Online]. 1 June. [Accessed 20 October 2016]. Available from: http://www.nytimes.com/2005/06/01/theater/newsandfeatures/he-talks-of-black-britain-and-the-west-end-listens.html?_r=0

———. n.d. Tear down the wall. *Theatre News Online.* [Online]. [Accessed 20 October 2016]. Available from: http://theaternewsonline.com/LondonTheatreReviews/TEARDOWNTHEWALL.cfm

3

AFRICAN AMERICAN MYTHS, MUSIC, ICONS IN MOJISOLA ADEBAYO'S *MOJ OF THE ANTARCTIC* AND *MUHAMMAD ALI AND ME*

Mojisola Adebayo (b. 1971) identifies as black; however, she acknowledges that having a white mother has led to being treated differently by both black and white people:

> My mother is white Danish, but my experience of living in Britain is as a black woman [. . .] as a mixed-heritage person I have been and will be treated differently. I have been privy to racist comments on the basis that my mother is white, and the door has been opened to me more, as though somehow I'm not really black, that my mum has given me a passport out. I know I may be treated differently, but in terms of how I feel, I feel black.
>
> *(qtd in Goddard, 2008, p. 148)*

British-born with a Nigerian father, Adebayo's experience growing up in Britain during the 1970s and 1980s was shaped by outspoken as well as institutional racism. A particularly formative experience was the time she spent in white foster care as a child. Adebayo describes this period as providing herself with the 'tools' to navigate a 'white institution' an experience which equips one with the knowledge of 'how to be white' (qtd in Osborne, 2009, p. 14). This notion of having 'insider information' (p. 14) into whiteness, coupled with a sense of being alienated from one's blackness, of having 'to learn how to be black' (p. 14) has profoundly shaped Adebayo's thematic concerns and approach to performance. Whereas Kwei-Armah's work resonates the blues aesthetic of the Black Arts Movement's realist theatre of experience, Adebayo's work, like Ntozake Shange's which has been described as transferring 'the dissonance and syncopation of jazz rhythm into language creating a poetic, yet spontaneous vernacular' (Taumann, 1999, p. 57), is more aligned with the form and rhythm of jazz. This chapter examines the lines of narrative and performance influences that can be traced back to black America in Adebayo's work, highlighting in particular her adoption and adaptation of African American culture, icons and myths.

Adebayo's plays register the pain of being raised in an all-white environment and the search for, and reclamation of, a denied black identity. Both plays discussed in detail here – *Moj of the Antarctic* and *Muhammad Ali and Me* – were written and performed by Adebayo and contain elements of autobiography.[1] In both plays, the protagonists (Moj in *Moj of the Antarctic* and Mojitola in *Muhammad Ali and Me*) are mixed-race lesbians and share a similar first name with the author. *Moj of the Antarctic*'s depiction of a black/mixed-race woman's escape from slavery by dressing up as a white man and her journey to the Antarctic – 'into the heart of whiteness' (Adebayo, 2008, p. 178) – can be read as a metaphorical reflection of Adebayo's experience growing up in white foster care and its psychological implications: 'The autobiographical stuff for me [. . .] was about my own history of being a black kid brought up by white people' (qtd in Osborne, 2009, p. 14).[2] *Muhammad Ali and Me*, 'inspired by real life experiences' (Adebayo, 2011, p. 70), confronts Adebayo's experience in foster care more directly. Set in London during the 1970s, the play depicts the imaginary friendship between a mixed-race girl named Mojitola and Muhammad Ali. It traces the experiences of Mojitola growing up in a foster home and charts the development of her black consciousness through her imaginary relationship with Muhammad Ali. In this sense, the play, in contrast to *Moj of the Antarctic*, presents a journey into blackness.

The plays are characterised by their epic quality: unities of place and time yield to stories which cover extended periods and are set in multiple locations. This geographic scope is indicative of the stories, histories and cultures that inform Adebayo's thematic and aesthetic explorations. Her writing approach which blends fact and fiction can also be placed in dialogue with African American women writers. Borrowing from Audre Lourde's term 'biomythography' used to describe her memoir *Zami* (1982), Goddard describes Adebayo's style as 'auto-bio-mythography' (2008, p. 147). According to Katie King, biomythography describes an approach that employs 'a variety of generic strategies in the construction of gay and lesbian identity in the USA' (1988, p. 331). King goes on to identify a range of genres through which biomythographies are produced, including historical monographs, oral histories, novels and poems. Osborne notes the combination of genres as a feature of Adebayo's solo piece *Moj of the Antarctic* which she describes as a 'monodrama' and draws attention to how Adebayo's works, along with works by fellow black British poet and performer SuAndi, 'centralise polyphonic and transgeneric techniques to articulate mixed experiences' (2013, p. 54). In Adebayo's pieces, 'factional' narratives are encased within a poetic style of writing, presented using a physical theatre performance technique (influenced by her work with Denise Wong and the Black Mime Theatre Company[3]), and use of multi-media. These combinations create highly textured pieces with multiple resonances, which are, nevertheless, grounded in a more or less linear, yet symbolic, realism. Her works also incorporate Brechtian 'alienation' devices which draw attention to her productions' performed elements through use of projection/montage, anachronism and audience-actor participation/interruption. The effect is didactic; drawing attention to the ways in which discourses of race operate and representing strategies that resist their totalising impulses.

In both *Moj of the Antarctic* and *Muhammad Ali and Me* Adebayo explores the self through two African American figures. Echoing Kwei-Armah, Adebayo's identification with black America emerges from a sense of un-belonging. As Adebayo confirms, 'the experience of being black in Britain is a microcosm of homelessness, of being displaced, estranged, a foreigner in your own country (qtd in Osborne, 2009, p. 14). For Adebayo, the African diaspora becomes a space/community from which to draw inspiration and support. This finds theatrical representation in her plays in which blackness and black diasporic history retain central positions. Despite giving voice to a number of marginalised positionalities, particularly with regard to gender and sexuality, this, as she makes clear, is not her focus:

> I think my work is most definitely feminist [. . .] It's within lesbian history, but something in me says, I don't know if the feminists need me, I don't know if the lesbians need me. Maybe they do? I don't know. But I for sure know I need blackness. I need the African diaspora. I need Africa, I need and want, crave, will fight for, my place within my family – I mean my immediate family, the Adebayo family, as well as the wider family.
>
> *(qtd in Osborne, 2009, pp. 19–20)*

Like Kwei-Armah, Adebayo's understanding and representation of African diasporic history, politics, and aesthetics have been importantly shaped by black America. These strong empathetic links attest to how black British notions of the African diaspora are deeply informed by an African American cultural imaginary. The notion of cultural imaginary, as articulated by Graham Dawson, refers to 'those vast networks of interlinking discursive themes, images, motifs and narrative forms that are publicly available within a culture at any one time, and articulate its psychic and social dimensions' (1994, p. 48). Engaging with this cultural imaginary can be seen as an act of what Henry Louis Gates, Jr. refers to as 'Signifyin(g)'. Akin to intertextuality, Signifyin(g) is a process whereby African American writers build on and affirm work by their predecessors ('unmotivated signifying') or adapt and rework tropes to create new meaning ('motivated signifying') (Gates Jr., 1988, p. 122). Gates argues that these chartable relationships of Signifyin(g) which find their roots in vernacular traditions render an African American literary tradition: 'Whatever is black about black American literature is to be found in this identifiable black Signifyin(g) difference' (p. xxiv). When black British dramatists such as Adebayo engage with African American texts or 'talk back' to an African American tradition, complex transnational race-based identification and Signifyin(g) relationships emerge.

Moj of the Antarctic: An African Odyssey

Moj of the Antarctic: An African Odyssey premiered at the Lyric Hammersmith in 2006 and was followed by a reworked production in 2007 at the Oval House Theatre.[4] It is described by the author as 'a one woman play performed with photography, video, poetry, light, dance, movement, music, storytelling and song' (Adebayo, 2008, p. 149) and is dedicated to Ellen Craft as well as 'all our Afri-Queer Ancestors' (p. 149). For the production at the Oval House Theatre, directed by Sheron Wray, the set was made up of moveable pieces comprising a bookcase, a globe, a telescope and a platform. At the back of the stage photographs and videos were projected onto a screen.

Set in the nineteenth century, *Moj of the Antarctic* depicts the epic journey of Moj, a mixed-race house slave, who escapes from slavery by dressing up as a white man and fleeing to Boston and then to England. Once in London she finds work on a whaling ship and journeys to the Antarctic. Adebayo plays a number of characters in the play, including the titular Moj, a griot, Moj's slave lover named May, a male slave owner who is also Moj's father and a Scottish cross-dressing sailor. The play was inspired by the true story of William and

Ellen Craft who escaped from slavery in 1848. They escaped by Ellen, who was mixed-race and phenotypically white, dressing up as a white man with her darker-skinned husband pretending to be her slave. The couple fled from Georgia to Boston before journeying to England in 1851. While in England, William Craft published *Running a Thousand Miles for Freedom; or, The escape of William and Ellen Craft from Slavery* in 1860 (1969), which documented the couple's experiences. They lived in England for nearly two decades before returning to the USA in the late 1860s.

In *Moj of the Antarctic*, Adebayo pastiches the eighteenth century African American slave narrative. The main thrust of the plot for the first half of the play is taken from *Running a Thousand Miles for Freedom*. However, Adebayo also interweaves quotations from, among others, Frederick Douglass' 1845 *Narrative of the Life of Frederick Douglass, An American Slave* (1999), Harriet E. Wilson's 1859 *Our Nig* (1983) and Harriet Jacobs' 1861 *Incidents in the Life of a Slave Girl* (2001). Adebayo does not attempt to present an historical 'docu-drama'. Instead, she uses the Crafts' experience as a basic framework to construct a fantasy 'herstory'. Adebayo excises the figure of William Craft and gives the protagonist, re-named Moj, a female lover named May. When Moj's master (and father) discovers that May has taught Moj to read and write, May is whipped to death. The moment harrowingly highlights how at the time it was illegal for slaves to learn to read and write. This enabled their masters to maintain complete control of their access to information about the world and their ability to communicate with others beyond their immediate environment. The incident precipitates Moj's flight to Boston and then to England by dressing up as a white man. In London, Moj, still disguised but now as a black man, finds work on a whaling ship, which sets sail for the Southern Ocean. During the voyage she is involved in hunting a whale, performs a black-face minstrel show for the crew, and becomes the first black woman to set foot in Antarctica. Although the latter half of the play moves away from the slave narrative, its basic arc as a journey to emancipation (or, in this case, consciousness) remains intact.

In the second half of the play, Moj is plunged into a world of whiteness. During this section, the text incorporates quotations from mainly white Euro-American canonical works, including Shakespeare's *The Tempest,* Marx and Engels' *Communist Manifesto*, Darwin's *On the Origin of Species* and Melville's *Moby-Dick*. Their words highlight the effects these works have had in shaping art, economics, philosophy, politics, science and, of course, discourses about race. In this section, the majority of which is set on a whaling ship in the Antarctic, Melville's *Moby-Dick* and its representation of whiteness is used as a key source text. Moj's voyage to the Antarctic (represented by projected images of Adebayo's research trip to the region during the stage production at the Oval House Theatre) externalises her struggle to emancipate herself from the bondage of 'mental' and 'discursive' enslavement: to extricate herself from the role of 'Other' imposed on non-white people since – and despite – the so-called Age of the Enlightenment, ironically referred to in the play as the 'Enwhitenment' (p. 151).

In *Moj of the Antarctic*, Adebayo simultaneously draws attention to the conditions of slavery and treatment of black people, as well as their representation in literature and on stage. As a result, reference to books and literary allusions within the play carry significant weight. In the first scene when we are introduced to Moj (the play begins with a prologue presented by a griot) she is cleaning her master's/father's library:

Moj: One day/When I'm truly free/I'll read books by Negroes!/I'll read [. . .] Ignatius Sancho! Francis Harper,/Harriet Wilson, Harriet Jacobs, Phillis Wheatley! [. . .] But in the Greenwich meantime/I'll say these books are mine/By rights my 'inheritance'/And with this knowledge I'll make a recompense/A small 'reparation'/For the rape of my mother-nation.

(pp. 159–160)

The setting of the library and initial image of Moj reading from a book underlines the link between knowledge and power. Adebayo, echoing sentiments expressed in Douglass' slave narrative, draws attention to the importance of literacy as the slave's primary route to individual and collective freedom. When the master discovers that Moj has learnt to read and write he whips May to death, sparing Moj only because she is his illegitimate child. It is at this point that Moj, realising that 'the only creatures to walk truly free upon on [sic] the earth were men. White men' (p. 167), decides to disguise herself as a white man and flee to Boston.

Adebayo's focus on the importance of reading and books brings to mind Gates' notion of 'the trope of the Talking Book' which he identifies as the 'ur-trope of the Anglo-African tradition' (1988, p. 131). Gates traces this motif back to eighteenth century slave narratives and highlights how in the earliest works black slaves describe their first encounter with books as objects that can talk and impart knowledge to white people. Equating literacy with whiteness and whiteness with freedom, mastering the ability to read and write, therefore, brings with it the possibility of discursive freedom; a means by which black slaves can articulate their humanity (1988, pp. 127–169). Moj's decision to appropriate the knowledge of the white texts 'and with this knowledge . . . make a recompense . . . for the rape of my mother-nation' (Adebayo, 2008, pp. 159–160) echoes this desire to use 'white' knowledge for emanicpatory ends. In other words, literacy becomes a way in which to negotiate and resist the master discourse. This theme is supported stylistically by Adebayo's incorporation into her text of quotations from the mainly nineteenth century white Euro-American canon. At one point in the play, Moj reflects on her journey to Antarctica as a voyage 'into the heart of whiteness' (p. 178) – a clear reply to Joseph Conrad's 1899 novella, *Heart of Darkness*. Adebayo's engagement with these texts is, therefore, a self-conscious attempt to enter into conversation with the Euro-American canon, to undermine and critique its authority and draw attention to its contribution to the historical construction of race. When asked about her inclusion of white male writers into the play, Adebayo acknowledges that she intentionally sought to create a dialogue between (mainly) nineteenth century influential white male figures with the forgotten black male and female voices of the same period: 'in a sense, I'm Africanising the European literary voice (qtd in Goddard, 2008, p. 145). This act of 'canonical counter-discourse' or 'writing back' (Ashcroft, Griffiths and Tiffin, 1989), chimes with Gates' identification of the Talking Book trope. According to Gates the trope coincides with Bakhtin's notion of 'double-voiced discourse' through which a tradition emerges of 'making the white written text speak with a black voice' (1988, p. 131). Adebayo is writing back to the white canon *and* Signifyin(g) on African American slave narratives. However, by re-working the trope of the Talking Book she places herself within and extends this tradition. In *Moj of the Antarctic* it is Moj's lover May who teaches her to read. Moj's education is prompted by a combination of desire for emancipation and her desire for May. In other words, May is the embodiment of the 'Talking Book' and Moj's literacy becomes framed as both intellectual and sexual. By removing William Craft from the story and changing Ellen's sexuality and name to reflect her own, Adebayo inserts herself into history by critiquing and revising the heterosexual, male authorial voice of the slave narrative.

Osborne argues that Lisa Anderson's observation that African American women theatre makers employ 'imagined histories' in their works can equally be applied to the British context (2009, p. 6). This method, Anderson notes, provides artists with a means by which 'to fill in the gaps in the histories of black women, particularly black lesbians, gay men, and other black 'queers', whose histories have been left out' (qtd in Osborne, 2009, p. 6). The fictional additions to the Craft's story, in other words, allow Adebayo ownership of a past which has failed to provide representation:

> I chose a female lover for her because I'm acknowledging that there are many stories of female lovers in our history that I will never discover because they have never been written down and have never been acknowledged.
>
> *(qtd in Goddard, 2008, p. 144)*

According to Cook and Tatum, Douglass' *Narrative of the Life of Frederick Douglass, an American Slave* became 'the allegorical master narrative of later African American texts as varied as *Black Boy, The Street, Invisible Man, The Color Purple*, and *Beloved*' which 'reproduce the pattern he devised' by highlighting 'the symbiotic relationship between literacy and liberation in African American literature' (2010, p. 53). Adebayo follows in the footsteps of African American women writers such as Alice Walker (*The Colour Purple*) and Toni Morrison (*Beloved*) who have also signified on the trope of the Talking Book by bringing gender, and in some cases sexuality, to bear on the slave narrative tradition. Adebayo cites both writers as important influences: 'and where would I be without Toni Morrison, Alice Walker, all of those great black writers?' (qtd in Osborne, 2009, p. 9). Adebayo, who identifies with Alice Walker's notion of 'the role of the writer as a kind of medium' (qtd in Osborne, 2009, p. 10) perceives her incorporation of quotations from eighteenth century writers into her text as akin to a sort of possession, a call-and-response with other writers and traditions.

Adebayo's writing process indicates clear associations with canonical African American literary texts. However, as a piece of theatre, signifyin(g) occurs on a thematic and aesthetic level. Another way of thinking through how Adebayo's works signify on African American dramatic traditions is through the notion of call-and-response:

> Call-and-response is the alternation of voice (call) and refrain (response). It is the verbal and non-verbal interaction between speaker and hearer in which the speaker's statements are punctuated by responses. While rooted in African music, vernacular traditions, and black religious services, its genealogy can also be traced to slave life.
>
> *(Krasner, 2002, pp. 49–50)*

The notion of call-and-response lies at the heart of African American cultural discourses that highlight the links between black American and African cultures. Tracing African survivals in black American cultural forms and practices highlights continuity with the ancestral homeland. The belief in, and act of tracing, African survivals moves beyond objective anthropological study to embrace a distinct politicised ideology of recuperation. It gives a displaced people a sense of origin as well as justifying a cultural differentiation between black and white people along ethno-geographic lines. Studies tracing the retention and transformation of African cultural practices in the USA have highlighted their existence across a range of areas including folk tales and their telling, music and religious worship (see Holloway, 2005). Call-and-response is identified in practices which emphasise audience participation (e.g. storytelling), circular movements (e.g. religious circle dances), syncopation and improvisation (e.g. jazz). The project of a number of African American dramatists has been to harness these African informed folk forms for dramaturgical purposes, in order to articulate a theatre practice that is culturally and ideologically distinct from Euro-American theatre forms and the values embedded in its architecture. When black British dramatists emulate African American artists and work they inherit this ideology and the way in which it has informed aesthetic and structural choices.

Adebayo describes her style as rooted 'within an African diasporic aesthetic', exemplified by her use of audience interaction/call-and-response and her melding of speech with song (qtd in Osborne, 2009, pp. 11–12). Commenting on form, Adebayo states:

> I have never really related to the form of Western drama. I enjoy it, it can satisfy me – I love Synge, for example – but there's nothing like that kind of truth in how Shange and others like Suzan-Lori Parks write. Thought is so broken down, interactions are so fragmented, and one moment crosses another in a way that I really believe in.
>
> *(qtd in Osborne, 2009, p. 9)*

In fact, the stage directions for *Moj of the Antarctic* explain the style of the piece through direct comparison with Shange's "choreo-poem' style' (Adebayo, 2008, p. 151). Like Shange's, Adebayo's works incorporate a poetic text, fluid form, and combine elements of ritual, song, and movement. They too are informed by an aesthetic rooted in African American Afrocentric ideology. *Moj of the Antarctic* begins with a griot character (also played by Adebayo) addressing the audience. This immediately locates the piece within an oral tradition of story-telling. The stage directions for the griot (named The Ancient) state:

> A West-African female griot (storyteller, historian, singer, mystic), enacts a ritual: she sings, circles the space in a shuffle, speaks in tongues and sprinkles libation.
>
> *(p. 151)*

The Ancient's actions closely resemble the griot figure in Kwei-Armah's *Elmina's Kitchen*. Similarly, in *Moj of the Antarctic*, the figure's function as a mediator between the past and the present, the living and the dead, and as the embodiment of the Middle Passage, positions the play within an African American diasporic historical and cultural continuum. The generalised description of the griot, like the one found in *Elmina's Kitchen*, underlines the routes of its appropriation as a romantic ideal of pre-colonial Africa rooted in 1970s African American Afrocentrism.

The griot character in *Moj of the Antarctic* serves two complimentary purposes: to locate the work in the shared experience of the African diaspora and to frame the European literary text-based dramatic tradition within an African derived tradition of orality. In doing so, the form and performance of the piece reinforce the theme of historical recuperation and position it within an alternative, Afrocentric cultural value system that melds ethics with aesthetics. The circling of the space, speaking in tongues and sprinkling of libation contextualises *Moj of the Antarctic* within the framework of a ritual possession and the implication that a healing through consciousness raising will take place. During the opening section, Adebayo establishes the play's thematic exploration of binaries and introduces her use of audience participation as a style:

> *The Ancient:* If the world is a globe/Then there is no above/No below/ No North or South/No heaven or hell/No white or . . . (*She prompt audience to respond*) black/No male or . . . (*She prompt audience to respond*) female/No God or . . . (*She prompt audience to respond*) Devil.
>
> *(p. 155)*

This moment of call-and-response at the start of the play brings the speaker/performer and listener/audience together and compliments the anti-binary polemic and educational tone.

Following the formula of African American slave narratives, *Moj of the Antarctic* is a journey of self-discovery modelled upon the literacy/liberation relationship and the 'queering' of this tradition, which is as much about transgressing the borders of gender and race as it is about genre. Ellen Craft's act of dressing up as a white man as a survival strategy resonates with Adebayo's personal experience of being raised in white foster care during the 1970s. The fact the journey of self-discovery is based on American experiences, not Nigerian, Danish or British ones further compounds the sense of displacement. Craft's 'race-change' provides Adebayo with the starting point to explore a journey into whiteness. Susan Gubar uses the term 'racechange' to connote 'the traversing of race boundaries, racial imitation or impersonation, cross-racial mimicry or mutability, white posing as black or black passing as white, pan-racial mutuality' and as a way in which to understand and challenge 'racial parameters' (1997, p. 5). In one sense, the play becomes an affirmation of the in-between-ness of being mixed-race and its ability to challenge the static framework of black and white racial discourses. Throughout the play, Adebayo draws parallels between the bondage/confines of slavery with binary categories that thrive upon the 'Other' to maintain their own definition:

> I see what Ellen Craft did as a wonderfully queer thing, part of a queer history and legacy. It's nothing to do with her sexuality, but is about her transgressing the boundaries of gender.
>
> *(qtd in Goddard, 2008, p. 144)*

However, the piece focuses less on the elimination of binaries and more on Moj/Adebayo locating and excavating her blackness in an environment dominated by whiteness as an act of psychological healing. It is in Antarctica that she feels a sense of belonging on discovering the black Antarctic rock that is covered by white snow: 'And under all this white/Antarctica is a broken rock as Black as my great-grandfather' (Adebayo, 2008, p. 185). This recalls the way in which mixed-race people have had to navigate stringent racial categorisations, imposed by white and black people. Anne Wilson argues, writing in the late 1980s, that mixed-race British children were likely to 'consider themselves full members of the black community, since any attempt to adopt a white identity is likely to bring conflict and rejection' (1987, p. 1). Tizard and Phoenix highlight the important contribution that the 1960s American Black Power movement made to 'raising black self-esteem' in Britain; however, they also draw attention to its totalising discourse:

> paradoxically, the rise of the black consciousness movement led to a renewed insistence on the 'one drop of black blood makes a person black' rule, this time on the part of black people. They argued strongly that pride in being a person of colour should lead people of mixed parentage to regard themselves, and be regarded by others, as black. Any other identity was seen as a betrayal, a rejection of their black ancestry.
>
> *(2002, p. 4)*

By combining the Craft's story, quotes from slave narratives and canonical writers, and reworking them within her language and experience, Adebayo writes and performs herself 'into being' as black British in an act of myth-making that becomes, as Gates states, 'an act of rhetorical self-definition' (1988, p. 122).

Muhammad Ali and Me

Muhammad Ali and Me was first performed in 2008 at the Oval House Theatre by a cast of three. In the Oval House production, directed by Sheron Wray, Adebayo played the roles of Mojitola and Muhammad Ali with a male actor, Charlie Folorunsho playing all the other characters, including Mojitola's father. The third performer, Jacqui Beckford, a British Sign Language (BSL) interpreter, was incorporated into the action. The fictional text integrates speeches made by Ali. This documentary element was enhanced by film footage which was projected onto the set which resembled a boxing ring. The film footage was also played through 1970s-style television sets that were built into the boxing ring set.

Muhammad Ali and Me draws on Adebayo's experiences of being raised in foster care. The play begins with the forty-year-old Mojitola telling the audience that 'Muhammad Ali/And me/Have only one thing/In common./We were Black,/in the seventies' (Adebayo, 2011, p. 72). The play then proceeds to disprove this initial assertion by weaving together seminal moments in Mojitola's and Ali's lives. By the end of the play the impression is that it is precisely this commonality of being 'Black', during what is portrayed as the racist seventies in both Britain and America, that connects Mojitola's and Ali's otherwise very different experiences. After the opening statement, the narrative flashes back to 1970s London, to when Mojitola's father decides to return to

Nigeria, leaving her in the care of Mummy Angie. (Mojitola's mother is never seen; however, we are made aware that she was physically abused by her husband). Before the character of Ali is introduced, the play establishes Mojitola's struggles in foster care where she experiences both racism and sexual abuse. It is after a harrowing scene in which the seven-year-old Mojitola is sexually abused by her foster mother's son that Muhammad Ali appears in Mojitola's life.

Initially, Ali is invoked by a griot character who appears to Mojitola to tell her a bedtime story. Delivered in the style of an epic poem, the griot recounts Ali's (then Cassius Clay) early life growing up in Kentucky under Jim Crow segregation. The speech contextualises Ali's decision to become a boxer through his upbringing in the racist South; essentially tracing his journey to self-determination along similar lines found in the slave narrative: from 'slave ship to citizenship' (Gilroy, 1993, p. 31). Framing Ali's biography as a bedtime story told by a griot underlines two things. Firstly, that Ali's life, told within the didactic frame of the storytelling event, is a lesson of courage and self-pride for the young Mojitola (and the audience). Secondly, that Ali's story is accessible to and forms part of the repertoire and shared experience of the black/African diaspora. The moment in which the griot invokes Ali is not performed as a religious ceremony; yet, the griot's function of creating communion with others remains consistent except, in this case, it is not with the dead but with the geographically disparate.

After the griot's introduction of Ali's early life story, the narrative interweaves scenes of Mojitola's and Ali's lives. As Adebayo deftly switches between playing each character, scenes alternate between depicting seminal points in Ali's life – his rise to fame as a boxer, political radicalisation as a member of the Nation of Islam, key fights of his career, and refusal to fight in the Vietnam War – with Mojitola's coming of age. As opposed to depicting two distinct and isolated biographies, Ali is portrayed as Mojitola's imaginary friend with whom she interacts. Throughout the play, the performance draws comparisons between Ali and Mojitola's struggles. For instance, many people refused to acknowledge that after joining the Nation of Islam Ali had changed his name from Cassius Clay – what he referred to as his 'slave name'. In the opposite direction, the name Susan is forced upon Mojitola. The moment recalls how under colonialism, in symbolic acts of disempowerment and control, local people and places were frequently given names that reflected and asserted the culture of the coloniser (Gilbert and Tompkins, 1996, p. 165). In one scene when Mojitola is fighting a school bully who has been taunting her about her name, the fight between Ali and Ernie Terrell is simultaneously projected in which Ali repeatedly shouts 'What's my name?' (Adebayo, 2011, p. 106). Mojitola's recourse to African American icons and culture is played out against a white-washed 1970s Britain 'full of Teddy Boys, British Bull Dogs, National Front, Skin Heads . . . Thatcher Thatcher milk snatcher . . . all sorts of monsters' (p. 96). Her identification with Ali draws attention to the lack of black role models available to her – an experience that is shared and documented by a number of black British playwrights growing up in the 1970s, including Kwame Kwei-Armah. In addition, Mojitola's isolation from black culture is exacerbated by her father's abandonment. She is left 'to grow up Black, in Britain, alone' (p. 126). Without access to her father's Nigerian cultural heritage, Mojitola's exposure to positive and nourishing representations of blackness is accessed through America.

The representation of Ali in the play can also be read as an example of the trope of the Talking Book, albeit in a significantly reconfigured form. The book, as conduit of knowledge, is, by the 1970s, the television. Adebayo draws attention to both the ritual of watching television as a family and television as a cultural resource for children who imitate television shows. The importance of television finds aesthetic representation with footage of Ali's fights projected onto the stage. The use of projection adds a third, inter-medial space to the theatrical event by juxtaposing the present of the performance with snippets of the captured past in the images/films. The use of multimedia disrupts the linear narrative, allowing movement in time and place. This provides an aesthetic echo of the play's theme of memory and gives form to the transnational circuits along which Mojitola's identification operates.

Whereas in *Moj of the Antarctic* Moj approaches literacy and knowledge through a negotiation of whiteness which is then re-articulated for her own needs, in *Muhammad Ali and Me* the Talking Book/Ali figure provides the map for Mojitola's journey into blackness. In other words, Ali is the route through which she is able to locate a positive sense of self. Ali's presence, advice and example help Mojitola cope with her experiences of abuse and racial discrimination. Ultimately, he provides her with a template to facilitate her growing self-awareness and her decision to embrace a 'Black' identity. Her relationship with Ali also introduces her to other inspirational African American political activists, such as Malcolm X. The play, however, does not solely focus on overcoming racism. Mojitola's experience of sexual abuse, rejection by some of her black peers at school and subsequent feeling of un-belonging as neither white nor black, her homosexuality and abandonment by her father are equally important oppressions she faces. For the young Mojitola, Ali's example teaches her vital lessons in both self-assertion and self-consciousness. At the end of the play, when Mojitola meets her father for the first time since he abandoned her, she repeats verbatim the statement Ali made when he declared his conversion to Islam following his victory over

Sonny Liston in 1964:'I know where I'm going and I know the truth, and I don't have to be what you want me to be. I'm free to be what I want' (p. 149).

Ali provides Mojitola with a 'coming out' model through which she is able to locate her own sense of belonging in the world. The Mojitola/Ali relationship represents, in microcosm, a relationship based upon solidarity and identification within the deterritorialised space of the African diaspora. This sense of the African diaspora as the glue that binds their relationship is introduced at the beginning through the griot, and is later extrapolated in a presentation that Mojitola gives at school entitled 'The History of the Shuffle' (p. 111). The title of her speech is inspired by Ali's trademark moves in the boxing ring, which he christened the 'Ali shuffle' and introduced in his fight against Cleveland Williams in 1966:

Mojitola: Shuffle has always been a feature of dances on the African continent:/Africans shuffled for celebration,/and shuffled in grief./To
maintain traditions,/and shuffled in chains./Shuffled shackled in
pain./On the slave ships./On the auction blocks [. . .] And from
the shuffle/came tap/and from tap/came Jazz/and Jazz equals/
everything we are/and all we can be./All our Black possibilities./
Our roots/and our routes/to being free./So shuffle is a move-
ment/is a memory/is a state of mind./And when Muhammad Ali
did *his* shuffle in the ring/he was doing so much more than boxing
or dancing,/he was saying/Me, We.

(pp. 112–113)

Mojitola's history of the shuffle highlights that Ali's dextrous footwork in the boxing ring resonates beyond physical movement. Through Ali's per-formance of the shuffle, the movement articulates an embodied African diasporic cultural and political tradition. The 'shuffle' communicates central ideas in the play of African cultural continuity and community based upon shared experiences in the diaspora. Through Ali, Mojitola forges a connec-tion between the self and the African diaspora and therefore finds a sense of belonging encapsulated in Ali's poem 'Me. We'.[5]

This diasporic history and cultural tradition based upon 'routes' allows Mojitola to create a sense of identity and belonging by accessing histories, stories, traditions and cultures beyond the geographic, cultural and temporal confines which define the national identity from which she experiences exclu-sion. This mode of belonging is contrasted with a traditional sense of Britishness that draws upon a vocabulary of historical rootedness through which to articu-late a national identity. This idea is expressed in the play when the Ali versus

Cleveland Williams fight, after which he christened the term 'Ali shuffle', is projected onto the stage during a scene when Mojitola is singing 'When a Knight Won His Spurs'(p. 106) at school assembly. The scene contrasts the ways in which history and tradition are appropriated. In England, through the singing of the song and its reference to Arthurian legend, culture and history rooted in England's white past is transferred. In contrast, through the history of the shuffle Adebayo highlights an alternative history and moral code, which does not stem from a sense of nationalism but rather transnationalism.

In *Race, Sport and Politics: The Sporting Black Diaspora*, Ben Carrington develops a Gilroy-inspired conceptual space he calls the 'sporting black Atlantic'. Black athletes, he argues, have, through their successes, acquired a political weight which operates on a transnational level and resonates throughout the black diaspora (2010, p. 201). Ali's outspokenness on issues of American race relations and refusal to fight in the Vietnam War made him a national and global hero and a symbol in the struggle for racial equality. As Eldridge Cleaver argues, despite Ali's political and religious allegiances, his sense of self-pride, self-belief, and refusal to bow to white mainstream America's demands, were the values that consolidated his broad appeal and iconic status in the minds of many African Americans (2003, p. 303). *Muhammad Ali and Me* dramatises the impact that Ali's international career had upon Mojitola's parochial London suburban experience. It draws attention to Mojitola's friendship with Ali as a survival strategy that allows her to shape her own reality, unhampered by the constraints of place. Thus, *Muhammad Ali and Me* gives theatrical form to Carrington's notion when Africa and the USA coalesce within Mojitola's London bedroom. It is in this borderless space that Mojitola is able to imagine and, in turn, to concretely forge her identity.

Adebayo's work engages with the black American literary tradition by drawing upon slave narratives, African American icons, myths and history to inform her narratives. Through her re-working of the trope of the Talking Book, Adebayo not only appropriates but also re-imagines these traditions to articulate her journey to consciousness and sense of self as black British. *Desert Boy* [2010, Albany Theatre], Adebayo's third full-length play, is dedicated to the memory of Stephen Lawrence and explores the criminalisation of contemporary black British youth through the historical context of slavery. (In contrast to her previous works, Adebayo wrote the play – with music and direction by Felix Cross – but did not perform in it or weave in autobiographical elements). *Desert Boy* is an epic story that begins in Deptford, South-East London with a young black man, Soldier Boy, who has a knife in his stomach. Desert Man, appears on the beach and transports the wounded Soldier Boy back in time. Soldier Boy becomes a witness to Desert Man's life as the play chronicles how he was sold into slavery, transported to the USA, fought as a Loyalist on the side of the British in the

American War of Independence, was granted passage to Britain, and how in Britain he was arrested for theft and sentenced to prison in Australia. By engaging with themes of black male youth delinquency and contextualising them in the historical experience of slavery, the play echoes Kwei-Armah's *Elmina's Kitchen*. Although Kwei-Armah's and Adebayo's approach and style are very different; nevertheless, for both writers, their representation and articulation of contemporary black British issues often rely upon and are told through African American experiences as recorded in literary traditions (prose, poetry, and drama) and/or expressed in popular culutre and polemics.

Notes

1 Other works by Adebayo include *Matt Henson, North Star* [2009, rehearsed reading Lyric Hammersmith], about African American Mathew Henson who was a member of the first expedition to the North Pole in 1909. Her piece, *I Stand Corrected* premiered in South Africa before being staged in the UK at the Oval House Theatre in 2012. The piece, co-created with South African Mamela Nyamza, explores the issue of corrective rape in South Africa through physical theatre/dance.
2 For another solo performed piece that explores the writer/performer's personal experiences of being raised in foster care, see Lemn Sissay's *Something Dark* [2004, Contact Theatre].
3 For information about Denise Wong and Black Mime Theatre Company, see Goodman (1993, 1996). Adebayo was an ensemble member of Black Mime Theatre's devised piece *Dirty Reality II* [1995, Nottingham Playhouse], directed by Wong, which explored the theme of intra-racial relationships and mixed-race children through physical theatre and dance.
4 In 2008 *Moj of the Antarctic*, funded by the British Council, toured to Botswana, Malawi, Mauritius and South Africa.
5 Ali first recited his poem, referred to as the shortest poem in the English language, at a lecture he gave at Harvard University.

Works cited

Adebayo, M. 2008. Moj of the Antarctic: An African odyssey. In: Osborne, D. ed., *Hidden gems*. London: Oberon Books, pp. 149–190.
———. 2011. Muhammad Ali and me. *Mojisola Adebayo: Plays one*. London: Oberon Books, pp. 65–150.
Anderson, B. 1991. *Imagined communities: Reflections on the origin and spread of nationalism*. Revised edition. London: Verso.
Ashcroft, B., Griffiths, G., and Tiffin, H. 1989. *The Empire writes back: Theory and practice in post-colonial literatures*. London: Routledge.
Carrington, B. 2010. *Race, sport and politics: The sporting black diaspora*. London: Sage.
Cleaver, E. 2003. The Muhammad Ali – Patterson fight. In: Wiggins, D. K., and Miller, P. B. eds., *The unlevel playing field: A documentary history of the African American experience in sport*. Urbana: University of Illinois Press, pp. 303–305.

Cook, W., and Tatum, J. 2010. *African American writers and classical tradition.* Chicago: The University of Chicago Press.

Craft, W., and Craft, E. 1969. *Running a thousand miles for freedom; or, the escape of William and Ellen Craft from slavery.* New York: Arno Press.

Dawson, G. 1994. *Soldier heroes: British adventure, empire, and the imagining of masculinities.* London: Routledge.

Douglass, F. 1999. *Narrative of the life of Frederick Douglass, an American slave, written by himself.* Oxford: Oxford University Press.

Gates Jr., H. L. 1988. *The signifying monkey: A theory of African-American literary criticism.* New York: Oxford University Press.

Gilbert, H., and Tompkins, J. 1996. *Post-colonial drama: Theory, practice, politics.* London: Routledge.

Gilroy, P. 1993. *The black Atlantic: Modernity and double consciousness.* London: Verso.

Goddard, L. 2008. Mojisola Adebayo in conversation with Lynette Goddard. In: Osborne, D. ed., *Hidden gems.* London: Oberon Books, pp. 142–148.

Goodman, L. 1993. *Contemporary feminist theatres: To each her own.* London: Routledge.

———. 1996. *Feminist stages: Interviews with women in contemporary British theatre.* New York: Taylor and Francis.

Gubar, S. 1997. *Racechanges: White skin, black face in American culture.* New York: Oxford University Press.

Holloway, J. E. 2005. *Africanisms in American culture.* 2nd edition. Bloomington: Indiana University Press.

Jacobs, H. 2001. *Incidents in the life of a slave girl.* Mineola, NY: Dover.

King, K. 1988. Audre Lorde's lacquered layerings: The lesbian bar as a site of literary production. *Cultural Studies.* 2(3), pp. 321–342.

Krasner, D. 2002. *A beautiful pageant: African American theatre, drama and performance in the Harlem Renaissance, 1910–1927.* New York: Palgrave Macmillan.

Lorde, A. 1982. *Zami: A new spelling of my name.* London: Sheba.

Morrison, T. 1987. *Beloved.* New York: Alfred Knopf.

Osborne, D. 2009. 'No straight answers': Writing in the margins, finding lost heroes: Mojisola Adebayo and Valerie Mason-John in conversation with Deirdre Osborne. *New Theatre Quarterly.* 25(1), pp. 6–21.

———. 2013. Skin Deep, a self-revealing act: Monologue, monodrama, and mixedness in the work of SuAndi and Mojisola Adebayo. *Journal of Contemporary Drama in English.* 1(1), pp. 54–69.

Taumann, B. 1999. *Strange orphans: Contemporary African American women playwrights.* Wurzburg, Germany: Konigshausen & Neumann.

Tizard, B., and Phoenix, A. 2002. *Black, white or mixed race?: Race and racism in the lives of young people of mixed parentage.* Revised edition. London: Routledge.

Walker, A. 1982. *The color purple.* New York: Harcourt Brace Jovanovich.

Wilson, A. 1987. *Mixed race children: A study of identity.* London: Allen & Unwin.

Wilson, H. E. 1983. *Our Nig; or, sketches from the life of a free black, in a two-story white house, north: Showing that slavery's shadows fall even there.* New York: Vintage Books.

SECTION II
The Caribbean

4

CREOLISATION AND THE CREOLE CONTINUUM IN CARIBBEAN BRITISH DRAMA

Trinidadian-born Mustapha Matura began his career writing about the experiences of Caribbean immigrants and their children in 1970s Britain. Increasingly, however, the Caribbean became the setting for his work. In an interview he stated: 'it's more important where we're coming from. I think we've got to get that clear as a basis, and then we can go anywhere! There's no mental or creative challenge for us here [. . .] The challenge lies in the Caribbean' (qtd in Peacock, 2006a, p. 189). Given that Matura was born in Trinidad and moved to the UK as an adult this sentiment may seem unsurprising. Looking back to the Caribbean for inspiration might seem less relevant to second-generation Caribbean British playwrights. This chapter argues, however, that the Caribbean remains a space with which contemporary black British drama continues to engage. The Caribbean also provides an important and overlooked theoretical model for discussing black British drama in the form of creolisation. The emergence of new cultural identities in post-war Britain and their representation in contemporary black British plays has been discussed in relation to multiculturalism, multiracialism and hybridity (see Derbyshire, 2007; Peacock, 2006b; Sierz, 2011, pp. 228–231). Creolisation, however, is helpful as a model for thinking through processes of cultural mixing specifically linked to the Caribbean and embedded in the region's history of slavery and colonisation. It also shifts the discussion away from black/white binaries that characterise identity and cultural politics in the USA (and how this has impacted on black British drama) towards a more fluid understanding of racial and ethnic categories. Creolisation and the notion of the creole enables new ways of thinking about the dramatic representation of the social and cultural transformations that have occurred in Britain as a result of post-war Caribbean migration. Similarly, thinking about culture as process has implications for understanding the representation and negotiation of blackness, Britishness *and* black Britishness as articulated in dramas since the 1970s.

Creolisation's emphasis on process and mixture enables a longitudinal perspective attuned to cultural (dis)continuity, bringing into view the complex historical and contemporary relations between black Britons and the Caribbean as a geographic, cultural and theoretical space. At its broadest, creolisation refers to a process of cultural inter-mixture which produces new (creole) cultural forms. The Spanish word *criollo*, from which the word 'creole' derives, is thought to have its roots in the Latin *creara* (to create) (Cashmore qtd in Cohen, R., 2007, p. 371). The term *criollo* was initially used in the sixteenth century to distinguish a person born in the 'New World' from their 'Old World' European parents and from the so-called 'native' population.[1] By the early eighteenth century the word's association with white Europeans had been extended and was being used to describe slaves who had not been born in Africa (Cohen, R., 2007, p. 371). From the late seventeenth century, the term creole also began to be used to describe the mixed languages spoken by New World inhabitants.

The '(post) creole continuum' (DeCamp, 1971) encompasses the spectrum of the language from the standard form (acrolect) on one extreme, with a more mixed version (mesolect) in the middle and, at the other end, full/deep/pure creole or patois (basilect). In the Anglophone Caribbean, the acrolect is standard Caribbean English. The basilect reflects a range of linguistic influences, including West African words brought over during slavery, and varies in its structural difference from English depending on the area. The creole continuum highlights how language use is inflected by socio-economic discourse and contexts. The acrolect, with its historical proximity to the language of the (former) colonial master and its contemporary status as an official language, affords it a higher prestige than the basilect, which is associated with the lower/slave classes.

According to Melanie Otto, 'the notion of what it means to be "creole" goes far beyond issues of language. It affects every aspect of Caribbean life' (2007, p. 97). Today, creole describes Caribbean languages, cultural (including culinary) practices and connotes a Caribbean ethnicity. Creole peoples, languages and cultures are not confined to the Caribbean; however, the colonial occupation of the various islands by Spain, the Netherlands, France and the United Kingdom and their use of African slaves and later Chinese and South Asian indentured labourers has resulted in complex social, cultural and racial fusions, making this region, in many ways, the creolisation prototype.[2]

As a theoretical term, creolisation describes processes of cultural mixture. Creole societies in the Caribbean developed out of extreme hardship and struggle. In *The Development of Creole Society in Jamaica, 1770–1820* (1971), poet and historian Edward/Kamau Brathwaite argues that society in Jamaica (and the wider Caribbean) emerged as a result of encounters between European settlers and African slaves, a meeting which produced 'a cultural action – material, psychological and spiritual – based upon the stimulus/ response of individuals within the society to their environment and – as white/black, culturally discreet groups – to each other' (1971, p. 296). Brathwaite's model of a creole society, later developed in *Contradictory Omens: Cultural diversity and Integration in the Caribbean* (1974b), does not imply the erosion of ethnic distinctions. For Brathwaite, creolisation occurs in the Caribbean as the result of the dual and symbiotic actions of *acculturation* and *interculturation* (1974b, p. 11). The former process refers to the way in which African slaves and their descendants adopted the dominant European culture (essentially a process of coercion) which gave rise to 'Afro-creole' culture, and the latter to how the African culture of the slaves was integrated by the European culture (a more subtle process of 'osmosis') rendering a 'Euro-creole' (Richards, 2007, p. 225). Hybridity and syncretism convey similar meanings to creolisation; however, hybridity has its roots in biological sciences, describing the reproductive results of two different animal or plant breeds/ varieties. Syncretism has tended to refer to the mixture of religious beliefs and practices. Like the employment of the term hybridity in postcolonial theory, theoretical uses of creolisation are attentive to tracing subaltern strategies of cultural resistance. However, where postcolonialism finds combative approaches to cultural colonisation in common across formerly colonised peoples (hence the application of the non specific term 'hybridity' to describe cultural encounters and intermixture), creolisation draws attention to the Caribbean's specific history of slavery and multiple colonial masters. Mimi Sheller argues that we should resist emptying creolisation of its specificity as a term not only associated with the New World, but with the experience of slavery (2003, pp. 192–196). Creolisation enables us to think of the Caribbean-origin population in Britain not as a simple diaspora marked by the single event of arrival in Britain, but as a double diaspora whose ancestral homeland is in Africa.

Scholars from the Francophone Caribbean have been instrumental in developing the concept of creolisation and what it means to be creole. Martinican Édouard Glissant's notion of *antillanité* (1989, 1997) describes 'Caribbeanness' in terms of the region's geography. In this conceptualisation, displacement, movement and mixture define Caribbean identity and culture whereby *essence* becomes meaningless and must be replaced by the continually evolving notion of *relation* (Munro and Shilliam, 2011, p. 173). In Glissant's model, ethnic distinctions and roots are de-emphasised: 'To assert peoples are creolized, that creolisation has value, is to deconstruct in this way the category of "creolized" that is considered as halfway between two "pure" extremes' (Glissant, 1989, p. 140). By avoiding the pursuit of an origin, hierarchies of centre and periphery are undermined. This understanding of Caribbean culture and identity challenged the Afrocentric model of Négritude which had emerged during the 1930s, developed in particular by Martinican Aimé Césaire, Senegalese Léopold Senghor and Guyanese Léon Damas. In its opposition to denigrating colonial discourse, the Négritude movement celebrated apparently identifiable African and/or Black cultural traits. Glissant's model, influenced by Gilles Deleuze and Félix Guattari's concept of the 'rhizome' which describes social and cultural formations as non-linear, heterogeneous and 'anti-genealogical' (2004, pp. 3–28), rejected these ideas as homogeneous and essentialist. The turn towards poststructuralism and the emphasis on cultural heterogeneity and culture as process has also influenced the thinking of cultural theorists of Caribbean origin in the UK. Stuart Hall's and Paul Gilroy's work consistently draws attention to how nationalist and imperialist discourses constructed Britishness as racially homogenous. Their deconstruction of such assumptions has highlighted Britain as a nation that has long been creolised.

Creolisation theory has also influenced arts practices. The process of alteration and difference from the parent or source culture/language that the term describes has meant that historically the word creole has carried with it pejorative connotations associated with notions of impurity and corruption. For this reason, an awareness of the socio-political implications of occupying points along an ethno-cultural and linguistic continuum has been integral to decolonising political and artistic discourses. With the independence of many of the Anglophone islands in the Caribbean in the 1960s, new national and regional cultural identities needed to be imagined and defined. The word creole and its association with inferiority began to be re-appropriated to signify instead a positive national identity that celebrated newly independent nations and the region's unique ethnic and cultural makeup. The languages from the Caribbean in particular began to be employed by Caribbean playwrights not only to reflect the way in which people in a region, from a particular class and in a particular situation, may speak, but also to draw attention to and critique the historical and social forces which have shaped *how* they speak. As Gilbert and Tompkins state, within postcolonial national contexts 'the use of variant Englishes offers one effective means of refusing to uphold the privilege of the imperial language as it has dominated both the theatre and the wider social realm' (1996, p. 177).

As a poet and a theorist, Brathwaite also had a significant impact on black arts practices in the Caribbean and in the UK. Brathwaite argued for the need to re-assert the suppressed 'Afro-creole' folk culture into a poetic approach that utilised creole/patois, or what he termed 'nation language'. The approach emphasises the African contribution to Caribbean English (its rhythms, pronunciation, syntax) and folk traditions (storytelling, music as social comment such as Calypso based on African satire). Although the term nation language was only coined later in *History of the Voice* (1984), Brathwaite's ideas and their application emerge earlier during his involvement in the British-based Caribbean Arts Movement (CAM) in the late 1960s and early 1970s. The recuperation of Caribbean indigenous practices rooted in African traditions became a key artistic strategy for black artistic expression in Britain. According to Walmsley, the CAM

> set the stage for trends now dominant in Caribbean arts, especially in poetry with its stress on orality and performance, its use of 'nation language' and the rhythms of everyday speech. It foreshadowed many of the directions of the so-called 'black arts' in Britain.
>
> *(1992, p. xviii)*

Brathwaite's project to elucidate African survivals in Caribbean folk culture and harness them in his writing drew on previous artistic movements with similar Pan-African and Afrocentric aims, such as the African American Harlem Renaissance in the 1920s and the Francophone Négritude movement of the 1930s. It also echoed similar conversations occurring at the time in the USA.[3] Creolisation discourse provided a compass with which the CAM's members could orient their artistic expression in both content and form. The influence of the CAM and creolization discourse can also be traced in black British plays which explore being Caribbean and British.

The shift from Caribbean to black British is prominently articulated in plays by the second-generation writing since the 1980s; however, the process of transformation and difference that creolisation, or becoming creole, implies is also expressed by first-generation dramatists. In other words, black

British culture did not begin with those born in Britain. Its seeds were sown as soon as the first-generation arrived, as soon as Britain became their home – unwelcoming or otherwise. Previously, plays by writers living in Britain in the inter-war period were set in the Caribbean, such as Jamaican Una Marson's *At What A Price* [1932] in 1933 at the YWCA in London and Trinidadian C.L.R James' *Toussaint L'Ouverture* in 1936 at the Westminster Theatre in London. Similarly, plays produced in the immediate post-war period, such as Trinidadian Errol John's *Moon on a Rainbow Shawl* [1958, Royal Court][4] and Jamaican Barry Reckord's *Flesh to a Tiger* [1958, Royal Court][5] tended to be set in their respective home lands. In the 1970s plays by first-generation immigrants such as Michael Abbensetts, Alfred Fagon and Mustapha Matura emerged which were populated by immigrants and examined the implications of being *of* but not *in* the Caribbean. It was noted by one reviewer at the time that these works represented the emergence of a 'West-Indians-in-Britain culture', distinct from 'a new Anglo-Caribbean culture' (Page, 1980, p. 99). Second-generation or 'black British' writers who emerged in the 1980s continued to register the development and formation of new Caribbean British cultures. Plays by writers such as Caryl Phillips and Winsome Pinnock explored what it meant to be born and raised in a different country to one's parents. (Phillips was born in St. Kitts but grew up in Leeds from the age of four months). From their vantage point that straddled their parents' homeland and the country of their birth, the struggle to belong in either location emerged as a major theme in their work. In these cases the Caribbean, personified through the parental generation or represented as a place to which a character travels in search of their roots, is ambivalently portrayed as a location that both hinders and helps identity formation and a sense of belonging. The portrayal of characters suffering from identity angst has abated in works by second-generation Caribbean British playwrights who emerged in the 1990s and first decade of the 2000s such as Roy Williams, Kwame Kwei-Armah and debbie tucker green. Nevertheless, all three writers continue to engage with the Caribbean: their plays that are set in the UK are populated by different generations of characters of mainly Caribbean origin and, in some cases, works are partly or entirely set in the Caribbean, such as Kwei-Armah's *Big Nose*, tucker green's *trade* [2004, The Other Place] and Williams' *Kingston 14* [2014, Theatre Royal Stratford East]. For second-generation playwrights writing since the 1980s, the Caribbean remains an important cultural and ideological space and their representations reveal the ways in which Caribbean culture is appropriated, reformulated, transformed or resisted in the British context. The occupancy of multiple identities and sustenance of transnational social and cultural ties is not just a first-generation experience but persists among subsequent generations. As Hall states of those born in Britain, 'they come from the Caribbean, know that they are Black, know that they are British. They want to speak from all three identities. They are not prepared to give up any one of them' (1991, p. 59). The tensions that arise from centripetal indigenous versus centrifugal transnational identifications find articulation in the concept of creolisation or more specifically the model of the creole continuum.

The post-war mass migration from the Anglophone Caribbean to Britain reverses the pre-modern Old to New World journey and reconfigures it, rendering it a voyage from the familiar Old World Caribbean to an unfamiliar New World Britain (see Osborne, 2011, p. 489). The world to which these immigrants were coming to was, of course, neither new nor unknown. Caribbean immigrants came to Britain with an array of assumptions about the motherland gleaned through their colonial education and upbringing. The anticipated journey to Britain and experience of rejection on arrival is a common theme in first-generation dramatic and literary narratives. The underlying motivation that drew Old World Europeans to the New World is paralleled in the Caribbean immigrants' dreams and hopes of building a better life in Britain. This reversal of the American dream (possibly the most famous articulation of New World hopes) recurs in plays by first- and second-generation playwrights (see, for example, John's *Moon on a Rainbow Shawl*, Pinnock's *A Hero's Welcome* and Kwei-Armah's *Big Nose*). People arriving from the Caribbean may have felt they knew something about Britain and Britishness; however, the experience of living in an unfamiliar environment was a revelation. Like the pioneers of the New World, the first generation's initial exposure to Britain is told through and evaluated against the topography. The British environment not only reflects the social and political temperature of life in the UK, it is seen as a force that shapes experience. Characters find themselves trapped in a cold hostile new world, living in cramped conditions and working in menial jobs. A breakdown in marriage between a husband who can adapt to life in England and a wife who cannot is portrayed in Michael Abbensetts' *Sweet Talk* [1973, Royal Court Theatre]. The play charts the challenges faced by Tony and Rita, attempting to make a life for themselves in London. The small bedsit in which the play is set draws attention to the challenges faced by Caribbean immigrants susceptible to landlord racism and exploitation which forced many to live in cramped, squalid conditions. Although they both struggle in England, Tony remains optimistic. He is determined to become British despite the obstacles: 'How many years you reckon we got to live in this country before they stop callin' us immigrants?' (2001, p. 71). Rita, however, who begins the play 'very tired' (p. 15), becomes more and more weak as the piece progresses. When she miscarries she decides to leave London and return to Trinidad to recuperate. The unborn child, conceived in the cold, cramped room, and her subsequent miscarriage which threatens her life, symbolises the stillbirth of the British dream. By the end of the play, Tony and Rita's marriage has broken down and Rita returns to Trinidad leaving Tony in England. Matura's *As Time Goes By* [1971, Traverse Theatre] presents another wife unable to cope with a new life in England. Batee advises the recently arrived Thelma: 'an' don't stay a minute longer dan yer have ter stay, is a evil kinda ting dat does rub off on yer if yer stay too long' (Matura, 1992a. 62). Batee's words attribute the land with a transformative power where, just by being in Britain, its malevolence 'does rub off on yer'. Refusing to integrate, each night she retreats into her dreams of return: 'a pray dat when a open me eyes in de morning a go see de sun shining, home' (p. 63). Survival in this 'brave new world' depends on the ability to adapt.

The New World environment was believed to have a corrupting effect on the body and mind (Bauer, R. and Mazzotti, 2009, p. 1). There is research that demonstrates the psychological effect of migration in the contemporary. In the UK there is a higher risk of psychotic disorders among immigrants, especially among African-Caribbean and black African groups (Bhugra and Gupta, 2011, pp. 66–67). Contributing factors include 'social exclusion, urban upbringing and discrimination' (Singh and Kunar, 2010, p. 67). This idea finds expression in Abbensetts' *Sweet Talk* when Tony highlights the psychological impact of un-belonging through his description of a woman he sees on his way to work at the tube station:

Tony: Only she always screams and screeches at everybody . . . English people pretend they can't see her . . . her distress. *(Pause)*. Lord only knows how long she's been in this country. *(Pause. Tapping his forehead)*. In here. She's gone in here . . . People talk about how we can't get proper jobs in this country, decent accommodation. But what nobody as yet really knows about is the price we're payin' up here.

(2001, p. 40)

Plays that link black people in Britain suffering from mental illness to the experience of migration and/or racism include Bonnie Greer's *Munda Negra*; Oladipo Agboluaje's *The Hounding of David Oluwale* [2009, West Yorkshire Playhouse] and Linda Brogan and Polly Teale's *Speechless* [2010, Traverse Theatre].

Initially the term creole did not convey an inter-racial dimension; however, it was not long before it signified people of mixed-race parentage. Hall recalls how in the immediate post-war period inter-racial relationships were the ultimate taboo in Britain and the dominant fear that underwrote racism (2000, p. 92). In *As Time Goes By,* Batee's aversion to white English women and insistence that she 'want no white girls coming into my house' (p. 42) is an example of numerous plays by black male writers in the 1970s and 1980s representing the negative aspects of black/white relationships which echo the fear New World colonists had of the 'natives' sexually compromising and corrupting their men and women. Similar anxieties emerge in Abbensett's *Sweet Talk,* Fagon's *Death of a Black Man,* Matura's *Party/Black Pieces,* and Phillips' *Strange Fruit* and *The Shelter* [1983, Lyric Hammersmith]. Plays by black women, such as Pinnock's *Talking in Tongues,* reverse the male-centric insecurity of black women dating white men by representing black male characters who cheat on black women with white women. In *Leonora's Dance* [1993, Cockpit Theatre], Zindika explores the push and pull of opposing national and racial identity camps on her protagonist whose crisis of identity as second generation and mixed race manifests itself in mental disorder (see Goddard, 2007a). According to Bauer (2010), studies from the 1950s and 1960s tended to conclude that mixed-race children suffered from identity problems as a result of not being accepted by the black or white community. Since the 1970s, however, she has argued research reveals that mixed-race children often experience a positive identification with both parents. For instance, Barbara Tizard and Ann Phoenix's study of mixed-race youth conducted in the early 1990s (and revised in the early 2000s) revealed that, increasingly, mixed-race people in the UK were claiming a 'dual identity' (2002, p. 4). Since the 1980s, plays featuring mixed-race characters often conform to the earlier held view, equating being mixed race with identity angst. Representations of mixedness reveal characters with an acute sense of un-belonging, alienated by black and white people. Plays about mixed families often portray them as dysfunctional, with issues of race lying at the heart of the turbulence. Examples of such plays include Ikoli's *Scrape off the Black* [1980, Riverside Studios], Linda Brogan's *What's in the Cat* [2005, Contact, Manchester] and Arinze Kene's *God's Property* [2013, Albany].

The disjuncture that arises between parents born in one country and their children in another, a process which according to Caryl Phillips bears 'strange fruit', recalls the original meaning of the word creole. In the sixteenth century, the earliest theories of the creolisation process focused on the dispositional difference that occurred among children of Old World parents born in the New World. For Spanish scholars in early modern times this change was perceived 'as profoundly disturbing, as evidence of a cultural "'degeneration'" (Bauer, R. and Mazzotti, 2009, p. 1). Those born in the hot climates of the New World were seen as morally inferior, lazy and less sophisticated than their parents who, by dint of their birth, could claim the cultural pedigree of the Old World. Tellingly, one of the definitions of the verb form 'to creolize' in *The Oxford English Dictionary* defines the verb 'to spend the day in a delectable state of apathy' (qtd in Bauer, R. and Mazzotti, 2009, p. 5). Thus, as Antonello Gerb states, 'the distinction was not ethnic, economic, or social, but geographical. It was based on a negative *jus soli*, which took precedence over the *jus sanguinis*' (qtd in Stewart, 2007, p. 1). In Matura's *As Time Goes By* the character Albert, a Trinidadian who works for London Underground, has a son, Skin Head, who has fully acculturated into the British way of life. As his name suggests, Skin Head is a caricature who has assimilated late 1960s British skinhead youth culture (not to be confused with the right-wing subculture that developed in the late 1970s and 1980s with the same name). Constantly berated by his father for having lost the values, culture and language of Trinidad (and compounded for his having not chosen a respectable model of British culture to identify with), Skin Head is represented as an inferior character, a version of a modern-day creole.

Those born in Britain, like the Old World creoles, are marked by their difference by being *of* but not *in* the Caribbean and thus not able to fully claim it as home. The relationship between a Caribbean-born mother and her two British-born sons, Alvin and Errol, provides the central conflict in Phillips' *Strange Fruit*. The theme of disconnection between parent and children dominates the play and the weather is a key way through which this difference is explored. Alvin, the eldest, visits the Caribbean in the hope that he will gain insight into his heritage and identity. However, his visit to his mother's homeland leads to his bitter disillusionment. For Alvin, the first-generation's nostalgic remembering of the Caribbean is undermined by the harsh political and economic reality of the region he witnesses during his visit:

Alvin: Well, what is it, man, that West Indians here always mention when they talk about home? . . . The weather. The weather, Errol, and picking fucking mangos off a tree. They've been here too long. You know what it's really like, man, and the same will be true in Africa. It's full of all the diseases of decolonisation, which they don't realise has eaten away at their islands in the sun. Inflation, unemployment, political violence – remember them? Fucking weather!

(1981, p. 69)

Alvin's mother's selective memory of her homeland has created a simplistic binary of good Caribbean/bad Britain that she has passed on to her children. As a result, both sons, like their mother, have become trapped in the past. Alvin's experience in the Caribbean shatters his imaginary sense of a homeland and highlights not, as he thought it would, his belonging, but his un-belonging.

Plays which stage black Britons visiting the Caribbean draw attention to the way in which they have evolved in different directions from their (grand) parents and throw into relief questions of home and belonging. In Winsome Pinnock's *Talking in Tongues* [1991, Royal Court], Leela and Claudette escape to Jamaica for a holiday after Leela discovers her boyfriend is having an affair with a white woman. For Claudette, who believes in black separatism, going to Jamaica is a return home. She differentiates between herself and the white Americans who she refers to as 'tourists' (1995, p. 204). However, her mission to 'rest, eat, drink, soak up as much sun as I can stand and fuck everything that moves' (p. 204) aligns her behaviour with the white American visitors. Her ideals of black sisterhood are undermined by her affair with local married man Mikie. She rationalises her conquest of him as a victory over the tourists by making them jealous; however, as Sugar, Mikie's partner, sums up, her behaviour highlights her disconnection from Jamaica:

Sugar: I don't understand you people at all. Mikie right. He say you all sick, say unno come out here because you broken people . . . You come here looking for . . . You tell me what you looking for. Unno tourist think you belong here. But you come out and you don't know where to put yourself: one minute you talking sisterhood, the next minute you treating us like dirt. You just the same as all the other tourists them.

(p. 223)

Through Claudette, Pinnock raises the thorny issue of the gulf that separates the working class living in the Caribbean from the Caribbean diaspora who benefit from the economic advantages of life in Britain. Leela, in contrast, is searching for a sense of wholeness. When she and Claudette cut off a white woman's hair while she is sleeping, it symbolises an act of revenge against historical white oppression. However, the act does not bring Leela closer to her sense of self, but rather reveals how damaged she has become. Furthermore, Sugar is blamed for the hair-cutting incident and loses her job. Leela's actions are rendered self-centred and expose the damaging repercussions of her attempt to find redemption in Jamaica. Ultimately, the play undermines simplistic notions of racial solidarity and critiques the idea of returning to an ancestral and imagined home as a panacea for addressing internalised oppression.

The exploitation of language to indicate broader socio-political issues has been carried over to Britain by Caribbean dramatists writing about the immigrant experience. In first-generation plays set in Britain, characters from various Caribbean nations are featured giving voice to the regional diversity of the Caribbean immigrant population. Language usage as a signifier of class and the ability of some to manipulate their speech depending on the situation is also a feature of these works. For instance, in Matura's *As Time Goes By,* the Indo-Trinidadian protagonist Ram, a self-appointed spiritual guru and immigrant life coach, changes his language from a thick Creole when speaking to his wife Batee to near Standard English when giving advice to his Afro-Trinidadian visitors in order to assert his 'professional' status. This moment in the play draws attention to the creole continuum and highlights the ways in which users can understand and employ a range of positions along the continuum ('code-switch') depending on the situation in which they find themselves (Wardhaugh, 2010, pp. 53–83). In *Sweet Talk,* Abbensetts indicates that Tony and Rita's accents should be slightly different as Tony 'has been over in England longer than his wife has, so he has less of a West Indian accent than she has' (2001, p. 15). The subtle difference in accent reinforces the play's theme of immigrant survival: the fractures in their relationship are located in the tension between cultural adaptation and retention and Rita's accent is a marker of her refusal to become Anglicised.

The language in these plays persistently draws attention to the cultural shifts occurring in the transition from Caribbean to black British and the ideological positions at stake in this process.[6] In *As Time Goes By,* although Ram perceives his ability to adapt as positive, through his mimicry of his white English clients' simple vocabulary and repetitive rhythms, Matura reveals his adaptation as a survival strategy but one that is ultimately undermined by the hollowness of the language he imitates. Matura's satirical portrait implies that to lose one's language or accent is to compromise the integrity of one's cultural identity. Matura returns to his exploration of the second-generation's sense of un-belonging and their attempts to assert an authentic 'black' identity by speaking 'black' in *Welcome Home Jacko* [1979, The Factory]. In *As Time Goes By,* Matura uses language to critique adaptation to British life by adopting its language. In *Welcome Home Jacko,* he reverses his stance and critiques those who are born in Britain and yet root their sense of self in an imagined Caribbean/Africa. *Welcome Home Jacko* depicts a group of young offenders in a community centre who are trapped within a dead-end system. Their entrapment, Matura implies, is exacerbated by their identification with a Rasta belief system. For these youth, Britain is a place of oppression defined as 'Babylon' (enemy territory). In defiance, they identify with the Caribbean and Africa as their 'true' and spiritual homeland. However, Matura exposes their belief-system as rooted in fantasy and based on ignorance. In an exchange between one of the youths (Zippy) and a black middle-class volunteer (Gail), Matura undermines the youths' allegiances:

Gail: Where are you from?

Zippy: Me from Jamaica.

Gail: You were born in Jamaica?

Zippy: No, we born in London, but me people from Jamaica.

Gail: But you speak with a Jamaican . . .

Zippy: Cha, me could talk London if me wanted to but me is a Rastafarian so me talk Ja.

Gail: I see

Zippy: Yer all genuine Rasta man him a talk Jamaican or else him not genuine.

(1992b, pp. 261–262)

The sense of betraying one's blackness by not adopting a Rasta/Caribbean identity is strongly conveyed in this exchange between Gail and Zippy, both black Britons. Gail, however, is middle-class and speaks with an English accent. As a result, one of the other youths, Marcus, tells her 'you a not one a we' (p. 280) and that 'she a Ras clart hypocrite black woman' (p. 289). In *Strange Fruit* the multiple influences that inflect Errol and Alvin's speech (patois, Standard English, African American slang) highlights their attempts to anchor their identity to a notion of 'Black' culture in order to assert a perceived authentic identity and to differentiate themselves from white Britishness. However, when Alvin returns from his pilgrimage to his mother's homeland in the Caribbean, Errol is surprised that he has not returned with a stronger accent with which to bolster his black identity:

Errol: You might have picked up a bit of the ling. You know, add a bit of authenticity to the banter.

Alvin: Oh that lingo. The English language.

(Phillips, 1981, p. 62)

Alvin's sarcastic retort is indicative of his personal journey within the play as he slowly comes to untangle himself from imposed markers of authentic blackness.

'Nation language' can be seen to operate at the dramatic structuring and aesthetic as well as linguistic level. Historical experiences of racial mixing in the Caribbean meant that Black nationalism 'pivoted less on notions of racial authenticity than on the tense relations between the metropolitan-identified neo-colonial elite and the non-European culture of the subaltern masses' (Dawson, 2007, p. 54). The implication for radical arts practices was to focus on popular cultural forms (p. 54). In 1971, the Trinidadian actor, playwright and academic, Errol Hill, who spent time in Britain during the late 1940s and early 1950s, presented a blueprint for a total Caribbean theatre praxis.[7] For Hill, theatre had the potential to facilitate social change in the region but first it 'must consciously slough off the accretions of an imported culture which remain alien to the large majority of West Indian peoples' (1972, p. 37). Hill promoted a creolised aesthetic drawn from indigenous folk culture 'developed by the largest sections of our society who, torn from their roots, had no place but the West Indies to turn for a cultural heritage and who therefore built their culture out of the memory of their past and the experience of present physical and economic slavery' (p. 37).[8]

Out of this anti-colonial sentiment, which saw playwrights turn to grass-roots experiences and popular traditions for inspiration, developed the 'yard play'. Judy Stone identifies the yard play as a type of Caribbean naturalistic drama set in 'a barrack-yard, where several households, having little more in common than their poverty, struggle in forced intimacy for their day-to-day existence' (Stone, 1994, p. 32). The barrack-yard, where life is 'a perpetual public drama' (Rohlehr, 1996, p. 199), has provided numerous writers with a way in which to structure their dramas and represent the state of the nation. *Moon on a Rainbow Shawl* is often cited as the prime example of this genre. Plays by British-born playwrights adopting this tradition for their works set in the Caribbean include Winsome Pinnock's *A Hero's Welcome* (see Goddard, 2007b, pp. 47–48) and Roy Williams' *Starstruck*. Echoes of the yard format also emerge in plays set in Britain. The close proximity of accommodation in urban working class communities provides a means to structure meetings between neighbours and, through the disintegration of private and public boundaries, facilitate broader social and cultural conversations. For instance, the adjacent gardens of terraced houses in Roy Williams' *The No Boys Cricket Club* and the communal park of a council estate in Kofi Agyemang and Patricia Elcock's *Urban Afro-Saxons* [2003, Theatre Royal Stratford East] provide the outside spaces for characters to meet and where (un)neighbourly and neighbourhood negotiations occur. In *Urban Afro-Saxons*, with its tagline 'what makes you British?', it is in the shared park that cultural and national identities and allegiances are performed, claimed or rejected.

Black British theatre companies have allowed practitioners and audiences to maintain close cultural contact with the Caribbean. As Britain's longest running black-led theatre company, Talawa, founded in 1985, has played an important role in bringing a Caribbean theatrical presence to the British stage. In its early years and under the artistic direction of founder Yvonne Brewster, Talawa staged a number of canonical British dramas, notably an all-black production of Oscar Wilde's *The Importance of Being Earnest* [1989, Tyne Theatre and Opera House] and a multiracial production of Shakespeare's *King Lear* [1994, Nia Centre] with Ben Thomas in the title role. This approach continues under the current artistic director, Michael Buffong who has programmed black-led productions of Arthur Miller's *All My Sons* [2013, Royal Exchange] and a new production of *King Lear* [2016, Royal Exchange]. Jatinder Verma, who founded the British Asian theatre company Tara Arts in 1977, coined the term 'Binglish' (1996) to describe creolised theatre practices emerging from work by black and Asian British practitioners. 'Binglish', like nation language, refers to 'a form of spoken English as much as a *process*' (p. 194). Similarly, Binglish is a praxis which 'challenge[s] or provoke[s] the dominant conventions of the English stage' (p. 194). These productions can be viewed as instances of counter-discursive praxis that creolise the classics (cf King-Dorset, 2014).

Sensitivity towards linguistic and cultural mixture and their shifting meanings are a hallmark of Caribbean drama, and one that has equally carried over to black British plays. So too are attempts to challenge dominant cultural forms and foreground marginalised cultural practices and linguistic expressions. The name 'Talawa' was taken from a Jamaican patois word 'tallawah' which translates as 'strong/tough' and which features in an expression 'she likkle but she tallawah' which means 'watch out, the little woman could be dangerous' (Brewster, 2006, p. 88). Victor Ukaegbu points out this name articulates an attitude of defiance in the face of mainstream marginalisation as well as expressing the company's artistic approach as rooted in the Caribbean and other black cultural practices (2006, pp. 125–126). Alongside black-led productions of Euro-American canonical plays, the company has produced many important Caribbean plays.[9] Creolisation discourse is entwined with a self-conscious desire to forge a positive identity through knowledge of and re-connection with the past. The reclamation of history is of underlying concern: 'A grounding in history is seen as an essential precondition for the realization of both individual and collective freedom' (Gilroy, 1987, p. 207). This emerges particularly in plays that treat slavery. The history of slavery has been a vital way in which to interrogate Caribbeanness, particularly its damaging affect on the psyche, exemplified in Dennis Scott's *An Echo in the Bone* [1974], which was staged in the UK by Talawa in 1986 at the Drill Hall. Black British playwrights have also explored slavery's traumatic legacy, as seen in the discussion of Kwei-Armah's work in Chapter 3. In these cases, historical recuperation is balanced with the desire to make sense of the present through the past. As a result, slavery's devastating social and cultural consequences are frequently mapped onto contemporary issues facing black people in Britain, locating black British experiences within an historical continuum of oppression stretching back to slavery.

The Caribbean's slavery past has also provided a potent model to articulate ways in which to overcome injustice. The Haitian Revolution (1791–1804), which led to the creation of the independent black-led republic of Haiti, has become iconic in the struggle for black self-determination. According to Hill, the Haitian Revolution is an event that has 'engendered more plays by black authors than any other single event in the history of the race' (1986, p. 414). One of the earliest dramatisations of the Haitian Revolution was also one of the earliest plays by a black writer to be staged in Britain. In 1936, C. L. R. James' *Toussaint L'Ouverture* received its world premiere at the Westminster Theatre in London. *Toussaint L'Ouverture* was written from research James had been compiling for his book on the same subject *The Black Jacobins: Toussaint L'Ouverture and the San Domingo Revolution* (1938). James' drama possibly marks the first time that the Caribbean history of slavery was used in a play by a black writer living in Britain, using allegory to confront contemporary British politics. In this instance, the play resonated an anticolonial message and the author's Pan-Africanist political beliefs. In 1986, James' play, now re-written and re-named *The Black Jacobins* (1976), was revived by Talawa at the Riverside Studios, London. Directed by Yvonne Brewster, the play was the company's inaugural production and was funded by the GLC as part of its Race Equality Unit's 'Black Experience Arts Programme'. The racial tensions in Britain at the time, with the race riots of 1981 and 1985 a recent memory, motivated Brewster to stage the story of an inspirational historical role model. The 1986 production provides a bridge to 1936 and draws attention to the time in-between the two points, highlighting the global and local changes that have occurred for black people – not least the achievement of independence for many African and Caribbean countries. A play by a theatre company established by black women, directed by a black woman, starring many black actors who were born in Britain or who came from abroad and trained at British drama schools, the existence of a black press that reviewed the show, and the play's high black attendance figures demonstrate the remarkable gains for black theatre since the 1930s. A comparison of the reviews, which in 1936 display a racist tone, were all but gone in the critical reception in 1986. In 1936, *The Daily Mail* deemed the play 'propaganda' (Disher, 1936) and in the *Sunday Times*, instead of revolutionary heroes, the slaves were described as a 'grotesque army of negro warriors' (G.W.B, 1936). The acting ability of the black cast members was, at best, patronising. The *Observer* (Brown, 1936) described the performance as having 'its own natural humour and charm', and the *Daily Mail* noted, aside from Robeson's sometimes 'thrilling' performance, 'how the many less gifted players of colour in the cast were enjoying themselves' (Disher, 1936). Despite receiving positive reviews, Robeson's acting is nevertheless attributed to his blackness. *The Times* stated: 'his method is unusual and its merit hard to define. By the rules that apply to others it is clumsy, but his appearance and voice entitle him to rules of his own, justifying the directness of his attack upon his audience' (Anon, 1936). By 1986 the language of the reviews had completely changed: 'this is the sort of show . . . that lends dignity and credibility to the British black theatre movement' (Coveney, 1986). Despite these considerable achievements, institutional and popular racism was still pervasive. Talawa's funding of over £80 000 from the GLC as part of their attempt to nurture black culture may have been unimaginable in Britain in 1936; but it is also a reminder of the racial hostility that had developed since.

The Haitian Revolution inspired a more direct comparison with black experiences in Britain in Amani Naphtali's *Ragamuffin* [1988, Oval House Theatre] which responded to the 1985 Broadwater Farm race riot. Black Theatre Cooperative brought to the London stage the story of Toussaint L'Ouverture's South American counterpart in Shango Baku and Aninha Franco's *Zumbi – Flame of Resistance* [1995, Theatre Royal Stratford East], a musical historical drama about an uprising led by slave Francisco Zumbi in Brazil in the seventeenth century. The play made direct comparison with the plight of black people in Britain by splicing the seventeenth century narrative with examples of police racism in contemporary England. The production elicited strong reactions among the public and in the press. David Lister, writing in *The Independent*, described it as 'highly emotive' and that it 'urges blacks to use violence against whites, especially the police' (1995, p. 9). In a statement,

Black Theatre Co-operative responded saying that 'the stories it portrays are based on real-life experiences from the black community' and that 'it is an affirmation of black culture' (qtd in Lister, 1995, p. 9). In these instances, the Caribbean is seen as a revolutionary space which can be mapped onto the UK to provide and imagine resistance to oppression.[10]

Although creolisation brings with it an awareness of mixedness and process, it is sometimes paradoxically employed to articulate fixity in order to inform national political or separatist discourses. Elements of Caribbean culture which legitimate hyper masculinity, violence and racism cannot idealistically be seen as a counter culture that challenges the master hegemony. The seeming dominance of dramatic representations of black youth gang culture, estate life and language of the 'ghetto' in the 2000s has prompted some scholars to criticise playwrights who claim that they are simply portraying reality for perpetuating stereotypes (see Beswick, 2014; Osborne, 2006, pp. 89–90). The ways in which Caribbean culture is harnessed to challenge or legitimate personal and group identity is explored in the following chapters in this section.

Black British cultural theorists have helped to shape the overriding scholarly conclusion that black theatre in Britain has contributed to the re-articulation of Britishness and British theatre. Despite this, the term creolisation is rarely seen in analyses of black British drama. However, creolisation provides a productive analytic model. Black British drama can be seen to hold a position along a continuum between British dramatic traditions and approaches more rooted in the Caribbean and Africa. For some, experiences of racism, marginalisation and un-belonging have fostered cultural retentionist approaches. In such cases, African-origin cultures of the Caribbean are emphasised as a means of asserting and maintaining a distinct cultural heritage and identity. Yet, their articulation within the British context means that, even while these practices are harnessed, they are changed to suit new needs and specific contexts. In other words, they are extended to Britain but, in the process, become adapted, and (re)creolized to produce new and distinct forms.

Notes

1 The places that European explorers claimed to have 'discovered' were, of course, not new to the people living there. Nevertheless, I use these problematic terms because they are key to this discussion which locates the processes and products of creolisation within the historical context of Caribbean colonisation, slavery and migration.

2 For works that analyse the process of creolisation and formation of Creole societies, see Brathwaite (1971), Mintz and Price (1992) and Nettleford

(1978). For overviews of the history of the term creole and analyses of the application of creolisation theory, see Buisseret and Reinhardt (eds.) (2000) and Shepherd and Richards (eds.) (2002). For a theoretical precursor to creolisation, see Fernando Ortiz's concept of 'transculturation'(1940/1947). For a discussion of creolisation in relation to global processes of cultural intermixture, see Hannerz (1987, 1992).

3 Brathwaite's essays 'Jazz and the West Indian Novel' (1967) and 'The African Presence in Caribbean Literature' (1974a) draw attention to this debt. He also cites the influence of Aimé Césaire and Léopold Senghor.

4 *Moon on a Rainbow Shawl* has been revived in the UK four times: in 1986 at the Theatre Royal Stratford East, directed by Errol John; in 1988 at the Almeida, directed by Maya Angelou; in 2003 as the inaugural production for Eclipse Theatre, directed by Paulette Randall; and in 2012 at the National Theatre directed by Michael Buffong, who became artistic director of Talawa that year.

5 *Flesh to a Tiger* was originally produced under the title *Della* in 1953 in Jamaica and then as *Adella* in 1954 at the Theatre Centre, London. Reckord's other plays staged in the UK include *You in Your Small Corner, Skyvers, Don't Gas the Blacks* [1969, the Open Space], revised as *A Liberated Woman* [1971, Greenwich Theatre], *Give the Gaffers Time to Love You* [1973, Royal Court Theatre], *X* [1974, Royal Court Theatre] and *Streetwise* [1982, Albany Empire], a musical adaptation of *Skyvers*.

6 For linguistic discussions about the evolution of 'British Black English' or 'British Creole' and its Caribbean influences, see, for example, Patrick (2004) and Sutcliffe (1984).

7 For a view similar to Hill's on the value of carnival for Caribbean theatre, see writer/director and active CAM member Marina Maxwell's, 'Toward a Revolution in the Arts' (1970).

8 In particular, Hill saw Trinidad's Carnival as a model for developing a theatre that employed forms such as stick fighting, calypso, steelpan and masquerade in order to capture what he identified as 'a pervasive and predominant rhythm in the life of our people – in the drums, in music, in dance and movement, in vocal sounds including speech' (1972, p. 38). Plays about and which draw on Carnival for their themes and aesthetics staged in the UK include Errol Hill's musical *Man Better Man* [1960] which represented Trinidad and Tobago in the Commonwealth Arts Festival held in Britain in 1965; Matura's *Play Mas* and *Rum an' Coca-Cola* [1976, Royal Court Theatre]; Irish-born Helen Camps' Trinidad Tent Theatre's production of *J'Ouvert*, which toured the UK in 1982; Earl Lovelace's dramatisation of his novel *The Dragon Can't Dance* [1986], staged by Talawa in 1990 at the Theatre Royal Stratford East, directed by Yvonne Brewster; *Carnival Messiah* based on Handel's oratorio at the West Yorkshire Playhouse in 1999, directed by Geraldine Connor; and Christopher Rodriguez's *High Heel Parrotfish* [1996], which explores the intersection of Carnival and drag and was staged by Talawa in 2005 at Theatre Royal Stratford East, directed by Paulette Randall. Trinidad's Carnival underwent another transformation when it was transplanted to the British context in the form of the Notting Hill Carnival. The festival developed as an expression of a more generalised Caribbean culture as other traditions, especially Jamaican-inspired reggae and Rastafarianism were incorporated (see Cohen, A., 1980, p. 79). Dramas about Carnival in Britain that

explore themes of protest include Winsome Pinnock's *A Rock in Water* and Edgar White's *Man and Soul* [1982, Riverside Studios].

9 Talawa has also championed the Jamaican pantomime, particularly stories featuring the folkloric spider-man trickster Anansi. Similar tales are found in West Africa. Their survival across the Middle Passage and Anansi's innate trickery encapsulate the ability to overcome oppression and are well suited to the satirical family-friendly pantomime genre. The first Jamaican-style pantomime to be staged in Britain was *Anansi and Brer Englishman* written by Manley Young and directed by Yvonne Brewster for The Dark and Light theatre company's Christmas show in 1972. It was set in Brixton and told the story of a love affair between Anansi's daughter and a Conservative council official's son. Since 1972, pantomimes staged featuring Anansi include: Manley Young's *Anansi and the Strawberry Queen* staged by Dark and Light in 1974 and directed by Norman Beaton; Jimi Rand's *Anansi's Royal Quest* in 1983 at the Arts Theatre; and LTM's *Anansi Come Back* [1993] which toured to London in 1995 where it played at the Hackney Empire. Talawa's pantomime productions include: *Itsy Bitsy Spider: Anansi Steals the Wind* by Jean 'Binta' Breeze, Jackie Kay and Christopher Rodriguez in 2002 at the Southbank Centre and in 2003 at the Bloomsbury Theatre; Trish Cooke's *Anansi Trades Places* in 2007 at the Shaw Theatre; and Geoff Aymer's *Anansi and the Magic Mirror* in 2009 at the Hackney Empire.

10 For a timeline and details of theatre productions about slavery in Britain since 1807, see the website *Trading Faces: Recollecting Slavery* (Terracciano, 2008).

Works cited

Abbensetts, M. 2001. Sweet talk. In: Abbensetts, M.: *Four plays*. London: Oberon, pp. 11–72.

Anon. 1936. Stage Society: 'Toussaint L'Ouverture' by C.L.R. James. *The Times* [The Times Digital Archive]. 17 March. [Accessed 29 January 2017].

Bauer, E. 2010. *The creolisation of London kinship: Mixed African-Caribbean and white British extended families, 1950–2003*. Amsterdam: Amsterdam University Press.

Bauer, R., and Mazzotti, J. A. 2009. Introduction. In: Bauer, R., and Mazzotti, J. A. eds., *Creole subjects in the colonial Americas: Empires, texts, identities*. Chapel Hill: University of North Carolina Press, pp. 1–60.

Beswick, K. 2014. Bola Agbaje's *Off the Endz*: Authentic voices, representing the council estate: Authorship and the ethics of representation. *Journal of Contemporary Drama in English*. 2(1), pp. 97–122.

Bhugra, D., and Gupta, S. 2011. *Migration and mental health*. Cambridge: Cambridge University Press.

Brathwaite, E. K. 1967. Jazz and the West Indian novel, part 1. *BIM*. XI(44), pp. 275–284.

———. 1971. *The development of Creole society in Jamaica, 1770–1820*. Oxford: Clarendon Press.

———. 1974a. The African presence in Caribbean literature. *Daedalus*. 103(2), pp. 73–109.

————. 1974b. *Contradictory omens: Cultural diversity and integration in the Caribbean.* Mona, Jamaica: Savacou Publications.

————. 1984. *History of the voice: The development of nation language in Anglophone Caribbean poetry.* London: New Beacon Books.

Brewster, Y. 2006. Talawa theatre company, 1985–2002. In: Davis, G. V., and Fuchs, A. eds., *Staging new Britain: Aspects of black and South Asian British theatre practice.* Brussels: P.I.E.- Peter Lang, pp. 87–106.

Brown, I. 1936. The week's theatres. *The Observer.* [ProQuest Historical Newspapers]. 22 March. [Accessed 29 January 2017].

Buisseret, D., and Reinhardt, S. 2000. *Creolization in the Americas.* Arlington: Texas A & M University Press.

Cohen, A. 1980. Drama and politics in the development of a London carnival. *Man.* 15(1), pp. 65–87. Available from: http://www.jstor.org/stable/2802003

Cohen, R. 2007. Creolization and cultural globalization: The soft sounds of fugitive power. *Globalizations.* 4(3), pp. 369–384. [Accessed 2 March 2016]. Available from: http://dx.doi.org/10.1080/14747730701532492

Coveney, M. 1986. The Black Jacobins/Riverside Studios. *Financial Times.* [The Financial Times Historical Archive]. 27 February. [Accessed 30 January 2017].

Dawson, A. 2007. *Mongrel nation: Diasporic culture and the making of postcolonial Britain.* Ann Arbor: University of Michigan Press.

DeCamp, D. 1971. Towards a generative analysis of a post-creole speech continuum. In: Hymes, D. ed., *Pidginisation and creolisation of languages.* Cambridge: Cambridge University Press, pp. 349–370.

Deleuze, G., and Guattari, F. 2004. *A thousand plateaus: Capitalism and schizophrenia.* London: Continuum.

Derbyshire, H. 2007. Roy Williams: Representing multicultural Britain in *Fallout. Modern Drama.* 50(3), pp. 414–434.

Disher, M. W. 1936. Mr. Paul Robeson's Thrilling Part. *Daily Mail.* [Daily Mail Historical Archive]. 17 March. [Accessed 30 January 2017].

Gilbert, H., and Tompkins, J. 1996. *Post-colonial drama: Theory, practice, politics.* London: Routledge.

Gilroy, P. 1987. *'There ain't no black in the Union Jack': The cultural politics of race and nation.* London: Hutchinson.

Glissant, E. 1989. *Caribbean discourse: Selected essays.* Charlottesville: University Press of Virginia.

————. 1997. *Poetics of relation.* Ann Arbor: University of Michigan Press.

Goddard, L. 2007a. Middle class aspirations and black women's mental illness in Zindika's *Leonora's Dance,* and Bonnie Greer's *Munda Negra* and *Dancing on Blackwater.* In: D'Monté, R., and Saunders, G. eds., *Cool Britannia.* Basingstoke, UK: Palgrave, pp. 96–113.

————. 2007b. *Staging black feminisms: Identity, politics, performance.* Basingstoke, UK: Palgrave Macmillan.

G.W.B. 1936. Toussaint L'Ouverture: A Play by C.L.R. James. *The Sunday Times.* [newspaper clipping]. 22 March. London: Victoria and Albert Museum Theatre Collection.

Hall, S. 1991. Old and new identities, old and new ethnicities. In: King, A. ed., *Culture, globalization and the world-system: Contemporary conditions for the representation of identity*. London: Macmillan, pp. 41–68.

———. 2000. Reconstruction work: Images of postwar black settlement. In: Proctor, J. ed., *Writing black Britain, 1948–1998: An interdisciplinary anthology*. Manchester: Manchester Universtiy Press, pp. 82–94.

Hannerz, U. 1987. The world in creolisation. *Africa*. 57(4), pp. 546–559.

———. 1992. *Cultural complexity: Studies in the social organization of meaning*. New York: Columbia University Press.

Hill, E. 1972. The emergence of a national drama in the West Indies. *Caribbean Quarterly*. 18(4), pp. 9–40.

———. 1986. The revolutionary tradition in black drama. *Theatre Journal*. 38(4), pp. 408–426.

James, C. L. R. 1938. *The Black Jacobins: Toussaint L'Ouverture and the San Domingo revolution*. London: Secker & Warburg.

———. 1976. The black Jacobins. In: Hill, E. ed., *A time . . . and a season: 8 Caribbean plays*. Trinidad: University of the West Indies, pp. 355–420.

King-Dorset, R. 2014. *Black British theatre pioneers: Yvonne Brewster and the first generation of actors, playwrights and other practitioners*. Jefferson, NC: McFarland & Company.

Lister, D. 1995. Play 'intimidates white audiences'; Drama urging violent black protest stirs inner-city tensions. *The Independent*. 7 July. p. 9.

Matura, M. 1992a. As time goes by. *Matura: Six Plays*. London: Methuen, pp. 1–66.

———. 1992b. Welcome home Jacko. *Matura: Six Plays*. London: Methuen, pp. 237–294.

Maxwell, M. 1970. Toward a revolution in the arts. *Savacou*. September (2), pp. 19–32.

Mintz, S., and Price, R. 1992. *The birth of African-American culture: An anthropological perspective*. Boston, MA: Beacon Press.

Munro, M., and Shilliam, R. 2011. Alternative sources of cosmopolitanism: Nationalism, universalism and créolité in Francophone Caribbean thought. In: Shilliam, R. ed., *International relations and non-Western thought: Imperialism, colonialism and investigations of global modernity*. Abingdon, UK: Routledge, pp. 159–177.

Nettleford, R. M. 1978. *Caribbean cultural identity: The case of Jamaica: An essay in cultural dynamics*. Kingston: Institute of Jamaica.

Ortiz, F. 1947. *Cuban counterpoint: Tobacco and sugar*. de Onis, H., Trans. New York: Knopf. (Original work published 1940).

Osborne, D. 2006. The state of the nation: Contemporary black British theatre and the staging of the UK. In: Godiwala, D. ed., *Alternatives within the mainstream: British black and Asian theatres*. Newcastle upon Tyne, UK: Cambridge Scholars Press, pp. 82–100.

———. 2011. Roy Williams. In: Middeke, M., Schnierer, P., and Sierz, A. eds., *The Methuen drama guide to contemporary British playwrights*. London: Methuen, pp. 487–509.

Otto, M. 2007. The Caribbean. In: McLeod, J. ed., *The Routledge companion to postcolonial studies*. Abingdon, UK: Routledge, pp. 95–107.

Page, M. 1980. West Indian playwrights in Britain. *Canadian Drama*. 6(1), pp. 90–101.

Patrick, P. 2004. British creole: Phonology. In: Kortmann, B., and Schneider, E. W. eds., *A handbook of varieties of English, I: Phonology*. Berlin: Mouton DeGruyter, pp. 231–243.

Peacock, D., Keith. 2006a. Home thoughts from abroad: Mustapha Matura. In: Luck-hurst, M. ed., *A companion to modern British and Irish drama: 1880–2005*. Oxford: Blackwell, pp. 188–197.

———. 2006b. The question of multiculturalism: The plays of Roy Williams. In: Luckhurst, M. ed., *A companion to modern British and Irish drama: 1880–2005*. Oxford: Blackwell, pp. 530–540.

Phillips, C. 1981. *Strange fruit*. Ambergate, UK: Amber Lane.

Pinnock, W. 1995. Talking in tongues. In: Brewster, Y. ed., *Black plays: 3*. London: Methuen, pp. 171–225.

Richards, G. 2007. Kamau Brathwaite and the creolization of history in the Anglo-phone Caribbean. In: Paul, A. ed., *Caribbean culture: Soundings on Kamau Brathwaite*. Kingston, Jamaica: University of the West Indies Press, pp. 218–234.

Rohlehr, G. 1996. Images of men and woman in the 1930s calypsos. In: Donnell, A., and Lawson Welsh, S. eds., *The Routledge reader in Caribbean literature*. London: Routledge, pp. 198–205.

Sheller, M. 2003. *Consuming the Caribbean: From Arawaks to zombies*. London: Routledge.

Shepherd, V., and Richards, G. 2002. *Questioning creole: Creolisation discourses in Carib-bean culture*. Oxford: James Currey.

Sierz, A. 2011. *Rewriting the nation: British theatre today*. London: Methuen Drama.

Singh, S. P., and Kunar, S. S. 2010. Cultural diversity in early psychosis. In: French, P., Smith, J., Shiers, D., Reed, M., and Rayne, M. eds., *Promoting recovery in early psycho-sis: A practice manual*. Oxford: Wiley-Blackwell, pp. 66–72.

Stewart, C. 2007. Creolization: History, ethnography, theory. In: Stewart, C. ed., *Cre-olization: History, ethnography, theory*. Walnut Creek, CA: Left Coast Press, pp. 1–25.

Stone, J. 1994. *Studies in West Indian literature: Theatre*. London: Macmillan.

Sutcliffe, D. M. E. 1984. British Black English. In: Trudgill, P. ed., *Language in the Brit-ish Isles*. Cambridge: Cambridge University Press, pp. 219–238.

Terracciano, A. 2008. *Trading faces: Recollecting slavery*. [Online]. [Accessed 21 October 2016]. Available from: http://www.tradingfacesonline.com/index.asp

Tizard, B., and Phoenix, A. 2002. *Black, white or mixed race?: Race and racism in the lives of young people of mixed parentage*. Revised edition. London: Routledge.

Ukaegbu, V. 2006. Talawa theatre company: The 'likkle' matter of black creativity and representation on the British stage. In: Godiwala, D. ed., *Alternatives within the mainstream: British black and Asian theatres*. Newcastle upon Tyne, UK: Cambridge Scholars Press, pp. 123–152.

Verma, J. 1996. The challenge of Binglish: Analysing multi-cultural productions. In: Campbell, P. ed., *Analysing performance: A critical reader*. Manchester: Manchester University Press, pp. 193–202.

Walmsley, A. 1992. *The caribbean artists movement, 1966–1972: A literary and cultural history*. London: New Beacon Books.

Wardhaugh, R. 2010. *An introduction to sociolinguistics*. 6th edition. Oxford: Wiley-Blackwell.

5

COMING TO VOICE

Roy Williams' *The No Boys Cricket Club, Lift Off, Fallout* and *Sing Yer Heart Out for the Lads*[1]

Since Williams' début with *The No Boys Cricket Club* [1996, Theatre Royal Stratford East] he has maintained a prolific presence in British theatre. Williams cites plays such as Nigel Williams' *Class Enemy* [1978, Royal Court Theatre] and Barrie Keeffe's trilogy *Barbarians* [1977, Greenwich Theatre], which he was introduced to at school, as important influences. These plays' social-realist depictions of British working-class youth set in urban environments, written in a youth vernacular and their exploration of masculinity would profoundly shape Williams' approach.[2] Initially Williams' plays explored themes of identity politics and stereotyping within a domestic setting. However, while retaining a focus on the domestic, Williams' later and most successful plays (in terms of their critical reception and staging in mainstream venues) have been set against the backdrop of larger socio-political events: the Macpherson Report and the murder of Damilola Taylor in *Fallout* [2003, Royal Court Theatre]; The Iraq war in *Days of Significance* [2007, Swan Theatre]; the race riots of the 1980s in *Sucker Punch* [2010, Royal Court Theatre] and the 2011 London riots in *The Loneliness of the Long Distance Runner* [2012, York Theatre Royal].[3] Williams' plays draw attention to the shifts that have resulted in Britain's increasingly multicultural and multiracial demographic. Peacock, defining multiculturalism as an ideal which 'refers to immigrants and the indigenous population preserving their cultures and interacting peacefully within one nation' (2006b, p. 531), concludes in his analysis of Williams' plays that they contribute towards this ideal by highlighting 'the cultural, social and political forces' that underlie 'inter- and intra-racial relations' (2006b, p. 540). Derbyshire, on the other hand, interprets multiculturalism as a socio-political policy rather than an ideal. He argues that Williams' plays provide a critique of such policy 'that may disguise rather than address structurally perpetuated inequalities among racial groups' (2007, p. 417). However, the way in which many of Williams' characters speak, dress, act, and imitate each other suggests that Williams' definition of multiculturalism is somewhat different. For Williams, multiculturalism is less to do with discrete cultures struggling to co-exist and refers rather to what Gilroy identifies as 'the complex pluralism of Britain's inner-urban streets' which result in 'kaleidoscopic formations of "trans-racial" cultural syncretism' (2000, p. 310). This understanding of multiculturalism, or rather its effects, is synonymous with creolisation. It describes the same process of cultural intermixture and creation of new forms. This chapter explores the ways in which Williams' plays engage with this process through an analysis of their use of language. It draws attention to how Williams examines the tensions and possibilities that occur when cultural boundaries are blurred through how his characters speak and what they say. Of equal importance are his uses of symbolic and spatial language to draw attention to the ways in which social identities and belonging are oriented, defined and transgressed. Williams' theatrical worlds can be seen to model the social and cultural shifts that are re-defining Britain and Britishness.

Caribbean voices

Williams has described his early plays, *The No Boys Cricket Club*, *Starstruck* [1998, Tricycle Theatre], and *The Gift* [2000, Birmingham Repertory Theatre] as belonging to a Jamaican trilogy (2004, p. xi). *The No Boys Cricket Club* is set in both London and Kingston and *Starstruck* and *The Gift* are set entirely in Jamaica. The plays' central exploration of the theme of migration echoes the works of first-generation playwrights as well as plays by second-generation writers such as Winsome Pinnock, who Williams credits as an inspiration.[4] *The No Boys Cricket Club* (2002) is set between London in 1996 and Kingston Town in 1958. The play focuses on Jamaican immigrant Abi, whose existence in London is characterised by struggle: she lives in a council house, her husband passed away, and her two wayward children, Michael, twenty-six, and Danni, nineteen, still live at home and expect her to support them. The representation of the family and inter-generational conflict between parents born in the Caribbean and their British-born children is reminiscent of Caryl Phillips' *Strange Fruit*. In the stage directions Phillips stipulates:

> The language in *Strange Fruit* has to be a careful mixture of West Indian English (patois), Standard English, and English working-class regional dialect. In the language one should be able to detect the socio-cultural confusion which undermines any immediate hopes of harmony within the body politic of the family.
>
> *(1981, p. 5)*

Similarly, Williams indicates the cultural chasm that exists between parents and children through language. In *The No Boys Cricket Club* Abi's discordant life in London is represented by noise. The play's peaceful opening, which sees Abi daydreaming about her childhood in Jamaica while she hangs out the washing, is interrupted by a cacophony of swearing neighbours and her arguing children. Abi's relationship with her children is characterised by constant fighting and arguing. Communication in the household has broken down because Abi and her children don't speak the same language. This is both literal – Abi's Jamaican dialect and expressions contrast with her children's London English – and figurative – they do not share Abi's Jamaican values: they talk back to her, disobey her and ridicule her Jamaican traits and the way she speaks.

The representation of the children who do not share their mother's values suggests that their British birthplace and upbringing is the source of their undisciplined behaviour (this idea also emerges in Agbaje's *Gone Too Far!*, discussed in the next chapter). The representation of good Caribbean/bad Britain seems to subscribe to and reverse the same Old World stereotypes that identified those born in the New World (or 'creoles') as morally inferior. However, through his plot and dramaturgy Williams is careful not to suggest such a reductive dialectic. Williams employs a magical device that allows Abi to time-travel back to Jamaica and revisit key moments of her childhood. Yet, the experience does not result in Abi becoming trapped in the past. She does not nostalgically yearn to return to the country of her birth. Neither is her return characterised by disillusionment and a rejection of both the Caribbean and Britain, leaving her with an ultimate sense of un-belonging. Instead, Abi's interface with her past becomes a revitalising experience, equipping her with the wherewithal to face up to the challenges in her present. Abi's 'return' to London is accompanied by the reclamation of her voice. Her language becomes more assertive and she takes the first steps towards regaining control of her life. The play, which began with shouting, ends with Abi laughing as the lights fade.

The play's staging, which fluidly moves between scenes set in present-day London and Kingston in 1958, provides a representation of the Caribbean within Britain. By collapsing time and space in such a way, the play gives form to the workings of memory. It reveals the homeland as a site of potential power, a memoried archive from which to draw on in a bid to reinvigorate the self in the host-land. The two locations can become one if they are imaginatively allowed to co-exist and not irrevocably separated in a then/now, there/here binary. Any attempt to change the past is naïve. Rather, Williams suggests, living with the past and making it usable in the present is the way forward.

Williams' engagement with Jamaica suggests a coming to terms with his own present and his own voice. Williams' employment of a more magical realist style in his Jamaican trilogy, in contrast to the gritty realism of his later plays set in the UK, suggests the Caribbean as a locale that exists first and foremost in his imagination. The Caribbean is used as a space through which to process where, as a member of the second generation, he is 'at', and less about where his parents were 'coming from':

> I didn't quite know what kind of a writer I wanted to be so I chose to write about my mum's past rather than about my own life. I don't think I was ready to write about me, or my generation, black British living in today's society. I thought, you've got to look back before you can go forwards. And I felt I wanted to understand my mother's generation, how it was for her.
>
> *(qtd in Sierz, 2006, p. 115)*

As seen in the previous chapter, Williams' perspective contrasts with Matura's belief that 'it's more important where we're coming from' (qtd in Peacock, 2006a, p. 189). The idea of Abi finding her voice in the Caribbean is replicated in Williams' experiences as a writer and the reception of his work. So too are the play's portrayal of inter-generational divisions and first-generation anxieties about the loss of the homeland's culture and values in their British-raised children. Williams recalls two responses from the public for his use of swearing in *The No Boys Cricket Club* and *The Gift*:

> It was almost identical: 'You're a good writer, it's very important what you're doing because you're black, but do we need that kind of

language?' It's like getting a dressing down from my mum. So I just say,
Yes Ma'm, no Ma'm.

(qtd in Sierz, 2009)

This 'burden of representation' (Hall, 1988; Mercer, 1994, pp. 233–258), or
the pressure to be the 'voice' of the community and thereby represent black
people or issues in a certain way, recurs as something black playwrights have
constantly had to navigate. The expectation to conform to certain values
associated with a notion of British theatre 'proper' also emerges. One British
theatre critic, arguably representing a 'standard' middle-class white British viewing culture, took offence at the acting style of *The No Boys Cricket
Club* stating that 'a more experienced director' would have 'prevented the
type of declamatory acting (the flashing eyes and overplayed patois) that so
often bedevils black productions' (Bartholomew, 1996). Attending the same
production at Theatre Royal Stratford East Aleks Sierz recalls the audience
reacting to a moment when Abi is accidentally hit by her son by shouting
out in anger at his actions (2009). Such an engaged and vocal audience suggests that the larger-than-life acting style was appropriate to the performance
conditions. However, the criticism of the acting style highlights the pressures
facing playwrights (and directors and actors) to conform to certain perceived
British standards. Arguably, these expectations have an impact on what a
playwright chooses to represent or is commissioned to represent. In turn, this
has an effect on subsequent playwrights who might ascribe to, or who are
expected to ascribe to, successful precedents. (This is discussed further in the
following chapter in relation to Bola Agbaje's work).

Williams' Jamaican trilogy should not be relegated to an immature
back-catalogue and only invoked to narrate his coming of age as a black
British writer. In *Kingston 14* Williams demonstrates his investment in the
country of his parents birth by writing what was described in the press as a
'state of the nation' look at Jamaica (Williams, H., 2014). The fact that the
play needed surtitles to translate the fast-paced dialogue written in patois
demonstrated Williams' deft command of Jamaican culture and his handle
on this aspect of his heritage.

Colonial discourse

A hallmark of Williams' plays is the use of explicit and shocking language.
The language (including body language) in Williams' works provocatively
engages with racial stereotypes. Williams could be seen to be perpetuating

such stereotypes by not drawing attention to their origination in colonial discourse. This becomes increasingly problematic if a venue is attended by a mainly white middle-class audience. Arguably, however, Williams' plays do problematise the essentialist perspectives that underwrite colonial ideology by presenting and then undermining stereotypes.

In *Lift Off* [1999, Royal Court Theatre] Williams explores the friendship between Tone, who is white, and Mal and Rich who are both black. *Lift Off* was written between *Starstruck* and *The Gift* and is Williams' first play to focus exclusively on contemporary Britain. In line with Williams' plays of this period, there is a strong element of magical realism. The protagonist Mal, for example, is haunted by the ghost/memory of his dead school friend Rich. The play also moves between the characters' school-days and the present. However, the play is set entirely in the UK and does not deal with the theme of migration in any way. *Lift Off* stylistically and thematically provides a bridge between Williams' Jamaican trilogy and his later work.

In this representation of multicultural, urban England, proximity to whiteness is no longer prized. Instead accoutrements of blackness are valued on this creole continuum. Ethnic allegiance is first and foremost signified through linguistic and physical codes. In *Lift Off* Tone attempts to emulate the 'ideal' of black masculinity which Mal embodies. Tone, formerly Tony, sees blackness and its accompanying signifiers of strength and sexual prowess as a means by which to gain respect. He apes Mal by also speaking in patois and copying the way he dresses. When he beats Mal in an arm-wrestle he declares: 'I'm blacker than yu Mal!' (Williams, 2002, p. 171). Tone's performance of blackness undermines and challenges essentialist notions of race and ethnicity by representing how culture can be imitated and adopted. Tone's behaviour recalls Bhabha's concept of mimicry, whereby the colonised subject assimilates the culture of the coloniser. Creating an imperfect replica, Bhabha argues, provides the possibility of subversion, whereby 'mimicry is at once resemblance and menace' (1994, p. 86). However, in Williams' play Bhabha's concept is ironically reversed. Williams challenges homogenous notions of blackness. Williams is not presenting Tone's imitation of Mal as a coup for blackness. Instead, Williams raises concerns about the idea of authentic blackness; what this notion looks like and how and to whom it is being ascribed. The destruction wrought by those trading in it, whether through material objects or cultural codes, is a trope in Williams' plays. His critique of contemporary British urban youth culture exposes and undermines notions of blackness as something that can be defined. For in defining or essentialising blackness, it is rendered tangible and attainable. The result is its exploitation as cultural capital. The play begins in a playground on a council estate where we first meet Mal, Rich and Tone as boys. The setting reiterates how racial identities and stereotypes of blackness are circulated, traded, reproduced and acquire meaning through social practices from a very young age.

The violent and promiscuous Mal is drawn as the black male stereotype. Mal aspires to an idea of hyper masculinity and capitalises on white women's fascination with the stereotype of black male sexual prowess. Mal's internalisation of black stereotypes is brought into question when he learns he is dying of cancer. The treatment requires blood from a black person but there are not enough donors. Mal's situation leads to a complex state whereby he at once assumes and rejects stereotypes: he has sex with Tone's sister, makes her pregnant, and wants no part in being the father. When Tone, furious, calls him a 'nigger' (Williams, 2002p. 232), he retorts:

Mal: Yes! Thas wat I am, and niggers don't care Tone, it's not in us. I mean we'd rather stuff our faces wid fried chicken, go out and teif, fuck whoever we like, than give blood to one of our own who badly needs it – who could die if he don't get it . . . We do wat everyone thinks, wat everyone expects, so give 'em wat they want, go for the pussy.

(p. 232)

By performing to expectation, Williams indicates Mal is a victim of a destructive cyclical pattern of black male behaviour shaped by and perpetuated through stereotypical representations. Williams reiterates this through Rich who does not subscribe to the ideal of blackness held by Mal and Tone. He does not speak 'black' and he is sensitive and shy. As a result, he is perceived as weak, likened to a homosexual, and seen as worse than a white person. When Rich refuses to join a gang and engage in school fights, Mal deems him unworthy of being black and verbally assaults him: 'He ain't black. Fuck knows wat he is' (p. 235). Rich's refusal to prove that he's 'hard' (p. 192) stems from his fear of becoming abusive like his father. The bullying Rich experiences for not being black *enough* results in his death. Williams harrowingly draws attention to the circulation, internalisation and embodiment of stereotypes and their physical and psychic destructiveness.[5]

In *Joe Guy* [2007, New Wolsey Theatre] Williams explores the pressures to conform to a type of blackness from an intra-racial angle. The protagonist Joe, a professional football player of Ghanaian heritage, is taunted by his Caribbean British peers because of his Ghanaian accent and how he looks – his darker skin colour and the shape of his nose and lips focus the taunts. In response, he changes his image to conform to a stereotype of Caribbean British masculinity. When we first meet Joe he is an awkward, shy character. His transformation from African British to Caribbean British occurs with him alone on stage repeatedly rehearsing a new accent and aggressive attitude. In this moment Williams once again draws attention to how identity is constructed and performed as the audience witnesses Joe subscribe to what he perceives as a more powerful and authoritative black identity. (This issue of intra-racial relationships between black Britons of African and Caribbean descent is discussed in the following chapter).

'Ghetto' voices

In *Fallout*, Williams presents us with racism's alienating effects on British society. The play explores the intersecting worlds of gang-culture on a British council estate and the police using two actual events as a starting point: first, the murder and subsequent botched investigation of Damilola Taylor in 2000;[6] second, Williams examines the police as an institution in the wake of the 1999 Macpherson Report, published after Stephen Lawrence's murder, which concluded that the police were 'institutionally racist'.[7] In particular, the media frenzy surrounding the murder of Damilola rekindled a public fear of violent youth crime. Because of the murder in which a black Nigerian boy was killed by other black youths, 'black-on-black' violence became the new 'buzz' word and an 'underclass' of dangerous black youths was identified by the media as the new malaise afflicting urban Britain.[8]

Through his representation of the gang of youths Williams introduces us to a subculture that has severed itself from mainstream British society. The gang dresses in African American-inspired hip-hop hoodies and trainers; speaks a combination of London Estuary, Jamaican patois and African American slang. Their cultural references are also derived from black America. For example, they refer to police as '5–0s' after the television show *Hawaii 5–0* and frequently use the word 'nigger'. Referring to a moment when the gang discusses whether Mike Tyson or Lennox Lewis was the better boxer Derbyshire argues:

> Through their banter the group reaffirms its subcultural identity, reifying blackness and maleness to the point of prejudice and misogyny. Their refusal to adopt the codes and mores of white England is

underscored by their subject (Mike Tyson) and their means of expression, which draws on American street slang and Jamaican patois.

(2007, p. 425)

The disaffected gang's identification with America, not Britain, as the epitome of 'cool', highlights anti-nationalism as part of their anti-Establishment identities. In Jewelle Gibbs' discussion of African Caribbean gang culture in London she draws attention to existing research that has highlighted how belonging to a gang for some youth 'may function as a bridge between the West Indian culture of their parents, from which they are alienated, and the British culture of their host country, from which they are excluded' (2013, p. 93). The gang's language highlights how subcultural identification has shifted away from Jamaican Rastafarianism of the 1970s and 1980s towards Jamaican 'yardie'/'gansta'-inspired patois and African American 'ghetto' slang. In these representations, we see acculturation occurring transnationally, as black British youth are influenced by, and identify with, dominant representations of black hyper-masculinity in black American and Caribbean hip-hop culture. In her study of diasporic identities of second and third-generation Caribbean British youth, Tracey Reynolds finds that identification with cultures from the Caribbean and the USA such as hip-hop and dancehall is a result of the experience of marginalisation in the UK and feeling of belonging that is achieved through 'participation in transnational rituals and networks' (2006, p. 1099).

Williams' representation of the gang raises questions around the assumption of the apparently inherent oppositional nature of creolisation. For Mercer, the transference of Caribbean languages to Britain and its 'creolisation' which has led to a black British vernacular fulfils a postcolonial oppositional agenda within the metropolitan centre:

Across a whole range of cultural forms there is a 'syncretic' dynamic which critically appropriates elements from the master-codes of the dominant culture and 'creolises' them, disarticulating given signs and re-articulating their symbolic meaning. The subversive force of this hybridizing tendency is most apparent at the level of language itself where creoles, patois, and black English decentre, destabilise and carnivalise the linguistic domination of 'English' – the nation-language of the master-discourse – through strategic inflections, re-accentuations and other performative moves in semantic, syntactic, and lexical codes.

(1988, p. 57)

However, the view that creolisation is inherently oppositional is thrown into question especially when the focus becomes more about retention than intermixture. In his representation of the gang Williams challenges dominant assumptions regarding black gang culture. As Derbyshire argues, the play draws our attention to structural inequalities, which have resulted in the youths' alienation from mainstream society (2007, p. 424). However, Derbyshire also suggests, based on his reading of Stuart Hall and Tony Jefferson's (eds.) *Resistance through Rituals: Youth Subcultures in Post-War Britain* (1993), that the gang's violent subculture is predicated on resistance to deeply ingrained social racism. Despite contextualising their delinquency, Williams' primary aim is not absolution by finger pointing at society's innate racism – although these are clearly factors that have shaped the youth's behaviour. Rather, through the black-on-black murder and the reaction of the gang in its aftermath, he highlights the youth's agency. In doing so Williams provocatively challenges notions of black youth as victims.

The murder of Kwame confounds the notion that black gang culture can be entirely explained as a product of cultural resistance to white oppression. In his critique of subculture theory as developed in the 1970s and 1980s by the Birmingham Centre for Contemporary Cultural Studies, Rupa Huq argues that because subculture was examined only in terms of its existence as a response to oppression, theorists tended to overlook the negative aspects of their case studies (2006, p. 16). Furthermore, Huq notes, if subculture arises solely from resistance then it presupposes the inevitability of violence, 'rendering it excused as much as explained' (2006, p. 16). In *Fallout,* Williams' portrayal of the youths and, for most of them, their apparently unfazed attitude towards the murder they have committed presents a challenge to a liberal audience well versed in the social causes that lie at the foundations of dysfunction. Had Williams' aim been merely to reveal the gang as a product of society's failings he may have followed David Wilson's argument in *Inventing Black-on-Black Violence* that if we are to 'supplant the meaning system of "black-on-black violence"' then the portrayal of violence needs to be not one of 'agency-infused kids rambunctiously roaming inner cities' but instead a depiction of 'hurt, hopeless, and searching youth in societally created settings' (2005, p. 159). Instead, Williams balances the youth's victimisation by demonstrating them equally as perpetrators, as agents in their own undoing and, crucially, in their tentative steps towards reformation at the end.

This sense of agency is carried through in the play's performance. Without an interval and with scenes that transition seamlessly into one other, the pace is relentless as the audience witnesses acts of un-premeditated violence and anger spontaneously erupts, allowing little time for reflection before the scene changes. Reviews comment on Ian Rickson's direction as achieving a 'bruising, confrontational production' (Spencer, 2003) with a 'visceral impact' (Billington, 2003). Countering this tone of seething aggression is the humour that Williams brings to the dialogue – even the last line of the play is said in jest as Shanice tells Dwayne that they can date but: 'Yu ain't grindin me' (2008, p. 117). This humour and the experience of high-octane acting over-shadows the more subtle message of social causality, complicating whether responsibility lies either with society or the individual.

The characters of Shanice and Dwayne also make important decisions that lead them to transformation at the end. Shanice's remorse guides her to confess to Emile that Kwame never tried to 'sex' her (p. 102) and that it was in fact she who made a pass at him, which he rejected. Her confession, beyond revealing that the murder was in part the result of adolescent jealousy, is seen as a brave act in a world where a bruised ego is enough motivation to kill. And it is Dwayne's feelings for Shanice that prevent him from shoot-ing Emile. The play ends with Shanice and Dwayne having a re-match of a football game they played as children seven years before. This re-creation of their childhood symbolises a fresh start through a return to innocence. It is unlikely that their lot will change dramatically, nevertheless it underlines their desire to start anew and marks a moment of self-intervention. The social oppression experienced by the gang, the killing of Kwame and the emphasis on the characters' own decision-making all combine to present a gang of youths that are at once oppressors and products of their own oppression, disal-lowing any comfortable categorisation of good/bad and victim/perpetrator. Furthermore, in revealing the gang members as both victims and perpetrators, Williams highlights their agency. This unsettles the debate around racism which perpetuates the placement of 'the white "us" of British society' at its centre (Barry and Boles, 2006, p. 299).

Although *Fallout* was a critical success, there were murmurs in the press regarding the negative issues surrounding representation of black people in the theatre (see Koenig, 2003). This response to *Fallout* reflects a wider debate about black representation. While black theatre in the first decade of this millennium has enjoyed unprecedented prominence in the number of plays produced and the high profile venues in which they have been presented, this prominence has been accompanied by a proliferation of images of black hyper-masculinity, urban poor and themes of violence and male sexuality. Such representations, it could be argued, play into the hands of dominant dis-courses, which stereotype black youths as violent, predatory and dysfunctional and ignore the diversity of black people's experiences. Williams, however, refuses to yield to representational expectations claiming that 'positive role models, of whatever race, make dull characters, because they don't really exist' (2009), that he is not writing about 'all' but only 'some black people,' and that he 'can't be a spokesman for a whole culture' (Williams qtd in Sierz, 2009). Echoing Hall's declaration of 'the end of the innocent notion of the essential black subject' (1988, p. 28), in *Fallout* Williams presents and simultaneously undermines stereotypes through complex characterisations, which fly in the face of representational expectation and complicate critical generalisations.[9]

Nation language

According to Benedict Anderson, 'the nation was conceived in language, not in blood, and that one could be "invited into" the imagined community' (1991, p. 145). In *Sing Yer Heart Out for the Lads* [2002, National Theatre] Williams explores whether the language of British nationalism has evolved and tests the extent to which racial differences still patrol the borders of national belonging.

The play is set in the King George pub in south-west London where the pub's football team assembles to watch the 2000 England versus Germany World Cup Qualifier. The lads are a stereotypical group of young, white, working-class football fans: they are big drinkers, violent, foul-mouthed, misogynist, patriotic, xenophobic, homophobic and racist. Complicating the stereotype of the English lad is Barry who, with St. George's flags painted on his face, acts and behaves exactly like his fellow white, racist teammates, but is the only black member of the football team. In contrast, his brother Mark has come to extricate Barry and take him home to visit their sick father. The screening of the live match in the pub and the reactions it evokes in the lads initiates a debate around national belonging and Britishness. Representing the far right is Alan, a member of a political group resembling the British National Party, and his protégé Lawrie. Lawrie wants to 'make a bomb or summin, go down Brixton and blow every one of them up' (Williams, 2004, p. 222), while Alan sources the arguments of Enoch Powell to demonstrate that 'the blacks, the non-whites, have absolutely nothing in common with the Anglo-Saxon Celtic culture' and that 'if they want to practice their black culture and heritage, then they should be allowed to do it in their own part of their world' (p. 188).

The dualist nature of competition, mirrored in the England versus Germany game, pervades the play's exploration of national belonging, which pits black against white in a tussle for the British title. These divisions reveal how a sense of 'Britishness' operates through binaries of inclusion/exclusion and proffers a scathing critique of multicultural rhetoric that maintains cultures can live in harmony without taking into account the oppressive nature of the dominant ideology. Williams' play seems to support Gilroy's argument expounded in *There Ain't No Black in the Union Jack,* in which Gilroy demonstrates how discourses of national belonging in the post-war era were re-defined in reaction to non-white immigrants. As a result, distinctions between race and ethnicity were collapsed. Culture became 'almost biologized by its proximity to "race"' (1987, p. 61) which effectively rendered Blackness and Britishness as 'mutually exclusive' (p. 55).

This division is spatially represented in the play. In the play's pub setting, Williams establishes a territorial microcosm, complete with borders and ethnic affiliations and provides a glimpse into the operations of the 'imagined community' at work. In the 2004 production at the National Theatre, the Cottesloe space was transformed into a replica traditional English pub with the audience positioned at tables placed around the central area of performance. Through their proximity, the audience becomes implicated not just as witnesses, but as punters/regulars themselves in this culturally familiar space. The space of the play is divided between the interior of the pub and the outside estate, creating a literal and symbolic border. The King George pub, decorated in St. George's flags, is the microcosmic representation of an historic England. The pub is both a home to three generations – Jimmy, Gina and Glen – and 'a home from home' (Williams, 2004, p. 160) for the lads. It is within the bosom of this (surrogate) family that a culture based on racial difference is nurtured and transmitted: 'Families are therefore not only the nation in microcosm, its key components, but act as the means to turn social processes into natural, instinctive ones' (Gilroy, 1987, p. 43). When Glen's mobile phone and jacket are taken by Bad T, Glen's grandfather Jimmy offers to teach Glen to fight so he 'can go back, sort 'em out' (p. 183) and Becks advises Glen to defend himself by creating an all-white gang in retaliation: 'get yerself some white boys, Glen, stick together, show sum pride' (p. 212). The cycle of racism, perpetuated through the institution of the family/pub finds its apex when Glen stabs Mark and Glen succumbs to and echoes the racism that has been ricocheting around the pub all day with his final words: 'He's a black bastard, they all are' (p. 234).

The space of the estate outside, inhabited by the black youths Duane and Bad T, represents the space of the alien/other and is seen as a threat to the core English values of the King George. Glen's association with Duane and Bad T is framed in terms of cultural corruption. As Gina notes, it is because 'he's been hanging round with them black kids from the estate' (p. 135) that he now listens to rap music and speaks using patois inspired slang:

Jimmy: I can't even understand half the things they're [the rap musicians] saying.
Glen: Ca you ain't wid it guy.
Gina: English, Glen, we speak English in here.

(p. 135)

Like Tone in *Lift Off*, Glen is desperate to become part of the black gang run by Bad T and his sidekick Duane. However, such 'mixing' is viewed by Glen's family as a bastardisation of his Englishness. It is Glen's 'mixing' with the wrong crowd that drives the action of the play. When Bad T takes Glen's mobile and jacket it not only precipitates the mob of angry protesters outside the pub, it also leads to Glen, thwarted in his plans to kill Bad T, murdering Mark. The crowd of black protestors that develops outside the pub is a stark illustration of the way in which the preservation of Britishness is defined along territorial and cultural lines. The 'army of black kids out there' (p. 226) is not only a threat to the site of the pub, but when they are referred to as 'a whole bleedin tribe' (p. 227) and 'those monkeys out there' (p. 230), the colonial imagery distils the 'battle' into a defence of white supremacy against the black 'savages'.

Through the characters of Mark and Barry, Williams explores the implications of such ethnic protectionism upon black Britons through the reactions of cultural retention and acculturation respectively. Mark's objective in the play is to extricate Barry from the pub and its white laddish culture and take him home to visit his sick father and 'his own people' (p. 209). The desire to re-unite Barry with his roots reveals Mark's own retreat into cultural separatism as a consequence of his direct experiences of marginalisation resulting in a profound sense of un-belonging:

Mark: They don't want us here, Barry.
Barry: We were born here.
Mark: They don't care.

(p. 210)

Despite the word 'nation' coming from the Latin 'nasci' meaning 'to be born', Mark's experiences reveal that birthright far from guarantees entry into cultural citizenship. Mark's experience of racial abuse in the army where his CO 'was a racist wanker' (p. 214) has pushed him into a position of reactionary racism. On the other hand, Barry, desperate to be accepted by the dominant culture, is singing his heart out in support of England and ignores the casual racism of his friends.

In the same way that Glen is judged by his family, Barry's crossing of the imaginary border that separates white and black is seen as a betrayal of his roots by Mark. Where Britishness is defined by whiteness, the body becomes the site on which national belonging is first and foremost signified. Barry's allegiance is inscribed onto his skin in the form of a British Bulldog tattoo. The painted St. George's flags on his cheeks are seen by Mark as a mask of his 'true'/black identity. He tells him to 'wipe that shit off your face' (p. 167). Yet despite Barry's attempts to fit in, he is also ultimately rejected by his white football friends who, because of his blackness, perceive his cultural allegiance as being outside the pub and by extension the nation. Phil questions why Barry is not outside helping his brother Mark who is trying to placate the growing unrest:

Phil:	Barry, shouldn't you be out there?
Barry:	ENGLAND!
Phil:	Baz!
Barry:	Wat?
Phil:	He's your brother, you should be backing him up.
Barry:	I'm watchin the game,
Becks:	You ain't gonna miss anything.
Barry:	So why are you still here then?
Jason:	Cos we follow England.
Barry:	Wat you tryin to say, Jase?
Jason:	Nuttin.
Barry:	I'm not white enuff for England?

(p. 194)

In the play's climax the borders between the localised spaces, pub/estate/Wembley, collapse. When England loses, the lads' support is displaced onto the growing tension between black and white people in the pub. Lawrie laments 'this whole country's lost its spine', 'we ruled the world' (p. 229). Determined to salvage England's dignity, he challenges Barry to fight saying, 'Well, come on then, black boy, show us how English you are' (p. 230). Football's fundamental dualism resonates with the black versus white debate as the borders blur between the England versus Germany match and the pub versus the estate riot. The inside/outside space is traversed when two bricks are thrown through the pub window and open war is declared. For Lawrie, like a football match, there can only be one winner: 'Lass one standing at the final whistle, wins England' (p. 231). The chaos results in Mark's murder and Barry disowning England symbolised by wiping the painted flags from his cheeks. It appears that Alan's Powellist prophecy of 'rivers of blood' (p. 235) has come to pass.

Sing Yer Heart Out for the Lads is Williams' most pessimistic play. Despite commonality in class, environment and experiences, the play stresses that local identity is subservient to the larger question of national belonging. Although Lee, Gina, Glen (initially) and eventually Barry and Mark attempt to navigate the complexity of fitting between rigid cultural and racial essentialist models, their actions and voices are all but drowned out by the din of Alan and Lawrie's 'England for whites' (p. 186) polemic, the riot outside and the stark imagery and spatial delineations which underscore Britishness as defined by cultural/racial separatism. Barry's reaction to his brother's death: 'I'll kill all of yer. Come on, come on! Who wants me, come on! Yer fuckin white cunts, all of yer!' (p. 235) renders Lee's advice to Barry and final words of the play: 'Don't lose yerself' (p. 235) an inaudible bleat. Drawing similar conclusions to Gilroy, the play demonstrates that as long as Britishness is defined along constructs that conflate race and ethnicity, there never will be any black in the Union Jack.

Williams' is a complex theatre that blurs binaries of victim/perpetrator, society/individual and ethnicity/race. Beneath the turbulence of his dramas Williams hints at a social ideal defined by creolisation/inter-mixture rather than pluralism. He persistently draws our attention to the ruptures that result from the perversion of life's fundamental complexities to fit distinct and homogenous categorisations. In navigating these social fractures, Williams inevitably exposes himself to criticism. As Osborne states of *Fallout*, Williams treads 'a fine line between perpetuating negative typing of black people and staging aspects of black British working class experience to spark debate' (2006, p. 93). The sense of discomfort that arises from this precarious positioning is characteristic of Williams' style that deliberately uses stereotypes to create a tension between mainstream assumptions and a radical re-positioning of the black (and white) subject. The urge to incite debate is fostered by a belief that only through open dialogue can society arbitrate deep-seated prejudices and inequalities: 'Many pieces of drama (stage or screen) that address racial issues lose their bottle and drown themselves with wishy-washy liberal platitudes' (Williams, R., 2004, p. x). By not resorting to easy solutions and by highlighting possible causes and areas of redress for the issues he explores, Williams' work is at once reflective of a dysfunctional society as it is hopeful of the possibility of its redemption.

Notes

1 Some sections of this chapter were included in a chapter published as 'Roy Williams' in Rebellato, D. ed., 2013. *Modern British playwriting 2000–2009: Voices, documents, new interpretations*. London: Bloomsbury, pp. 145–168 and are reprinted with kind permission from Bloomsbury.

2 Williams' work does not slot easily into a particular generation of British playwrights. Suzanne Scafe (2007) criticises Aleks Sierz's omission of Williams' work in his book *In-Yer-Face Theatre: British Drama Today* (2001). She argues that Williams' style aligns 'almost perfectly' with Sierz's template (Scafe, 2007, p. 72). However, although explicit language and challenging subject matter are features of Williams' plays, on the whole they avoid graphic representations of sex and violence. As Kritzer shows, writers such as Williams, of a minority race or culture, not only replied to the 1990s 'in-yer-face' generation of writers but by bringing their race, ethnicity, and class to bear, 'revis[ed] its terms' (2008, p. 78).

3 Other plays by Williams that explore topical issues include gang culture and gun crime in *Little Sweet Thing* [2005, New Wolsey Theatre], the 1958 Notting Hill race riots in *Absolute Beginners* [2007, Lyric Hammersmith], immigration in *Angel House* [2008, New Wolsey Theatre] and the penitentiary system in *Category B* [2009, Tricycle Theatre]. His adaptation of *Antigone* [2014, Derby Theatre] was transplanted to the inner city and used the play's themes to explore contemporary gang culture.

4 *The No Boys Cricket Club* and its themes of inter-generational culture clash, the nostalgic sense of in-between-ness that characterises the immigrant condition and the dialogic relationship between past and present are reminiscent of Caryl Phillips' *Where There is Darkness* [1982, Lyric Hammersmith]. Similarly, the (broken) dreams of a better life in England in *Starstruck* echo Errol John's *Moon on a Rainbow Shawl* and Pinnock's *A Hero's Welcome* in theme and yard theatre format. *The Gift* explores the relationship between two sisters, one of whom was taken with her parents to England while the other remained in Jamaica, bringing to mind Trish Cooke's earlier treatment of the theme of the impact of Caribbean-British migration upon families in *Running Dream*.

5 See *Clubland* [2001, Royal Court Theatre] which also addresses themes of inter and intra-racial masculine identity and stereotypes.

6 For an analysis of the problematic investigation and trial of the case, see *The Damilola Taylor Murder Investigation: The Report of the Oversight Panel* (Metropolitan Police Service, 2002). Since *Fallout* was written, the Taylor trial was re-opened and two brothers, Danny and Ricky Preddie, were convicted of manslaughter in 2006.

7 Ten years after the Macpherson Report was published, a new report found that although improvements had been made within the Metropolitan Police, 'black communities [. . .] are disproportionately represented in stop and search statistics and on the National DNA Database' a gap which has increased since 1999. The report goes on to highlight that 'being subject to higher levels of stop and search and inclusion on the DNA Database perpetuates black people's over-representation in

the criminal justice system', and 'that any gains made by the use of stop and search may be offset by its potentially negative impact on community relations' (House of Commons Home Affairs Committee, 2009, p. 7).

8 For a response to the murder in the media, see, for example, 'How Violent is Britain?' (BBC News, 2000).

9 For a list of productions by black British playwrights staged in major London venues in 2003 and 2004, see Osborne (2006, pp. 82–83).

Works cited

Anderson, B. 1991. *Imagined communities: Reflections on the origin and spread of nationalism.* Revised edition. London: Verso.

Barry, E., and Boles, W. 2006. Beyond victimhood: Agency and identity in the theatre of Roy Williams. In: Godiwala, D. ed., *Alternatives within the mainstream: British black and Asian theatres.* Newcastle upon Tyne, UK: Cambridge Scholars Press, pp. 297–313.

Bartholomew, R. 1996. Theatre/the 'No Boys' Cricket Club Theatre Royal, Stratford East, London. *Independent.* 4 June. [Accessed 7 March 2016]. Available from: http://www.independent.co.uk/arts-entertainment/theatre-the-no-boys-cricket-club-theatre-royal-stratford-east-london-1335527.html

BBC News. 2000. How violent is Britain? [Online]. 10 December. [Accessed 27 October 2016]. Available from: http://news.bbc.co.uk/1/hi/talking_point/1048339.stm

Bhabha, H. K. 1994. *The location of culture.* London: Routledge.

Billington, M. 2003. Fallout: When racism isn't black and white. *The Guardian.* 18 June. p. 24.

Derbyshire, H. 2007. Roy Williams: Representing multicultural Britain in *Fallout. Modern Drama.* 50(3), pp. 414–434.

Gibbs, J. T. 2013. Gangs as alternative transitional structures: Adaptations to racial and social marginality in Los Angeles and London. In: De Anda, D., and Becerra, R. M. eds., *Violence: Diverse populations and communities.* New York: Routledge, pp. 71–100.

Gilroy, P. 1987. *There ain't no black in the Union Jack': The cultural politics of race and nation.* London: Hutchinson.

———. 2000. Cruciality and the frog's perspective: An agenda of difficulties for the black arts movement in Britain. In: Procter, J. ed., *Writing black Britain, 1948–1998: An interdisciplinary anthology.* Manchester: Manchester University Press, pp. 307–320.

Hall, S. 1988. New ethnicities. In: Mercer, K. ed., *Black film, British cinema: ICA documents 7.* London: Institute of Contemporary Arts, pp. 27–31.

Hall, S., and Jefferson, T. 1993. *Resistance through rituals: Youth subcultures in post-war Britain.* London: Routledge.

House of Commons Home Affairs Committee. 2009. *Macpherson report – ten years on.* [Online]. London: The Stationery Office. [Accessed 27 October 2016]. Available from: http://www.publications.parliament.uk/pa/cm200809/cmselect/cmhaff/427/427.pdf

Huq, R. 2006. *Beyond subculture: Pop, youth and identity in a postcolonial world.* Abingdon, UK: Routledge.

Koenig, R. 2003. Fallout, Royal Court, London. *The Independent.* [Online]. 23 June. [Accessed 29 January 2017]. Available from: http://www.independent.co.uk/arts-entertainment/theatre-dance/reviews/fallout-royal-court-london-110027.html.

Kritzer, A. H. 2008. *Political theatre in post-Thatcher Britain: New writing, 1995–2005.* Basingstoke, UK: Palgrave Macmillan.

Mercer, K. 1988. Diaspora cultures and the dialogic imagination: The aesthetics of black independent film in Britain. In: Cham, M. B., and Andrade-Watkins, C. eds., *Blackframes: Critical perspectives on black independent cinema.* Cambridge, MA: MIT Press, pp. 50–61.

———. 1994. *Welcome to the jungle: New positions in black cultural studies.* London: Routledge.

Metropolitan Police Service. 2002. *The Damilola Taylor murder investigation review: The report of the oversight panel: Chaired by Right Reverend John Sentamu.* London: Metropolitan Police Authority. [Accessed 4 March 2016]. Available from: http://image.guardian.co.uk/sys-files/Guardian/documents/2002/12/09/damilola.pdf

Osborne, D. 2006. The state of the nation: Contemporary black British theatre and the staging of the UK. In: Godiwala, D. ed., *Alternatives within the mainstream: British black and Asian theatres.* Newcastle upon Tyne, UK: Cambridge Scholars Press, pp. 82–100.

Peacock, D., K. 2006a. Home thoughts from abroad: Mustapha Matura. In: Luckhurst, M. ed., *A companion to modern British and Irish drama: 1880–2005.* Oxford: Blackwell, pp. 188–197.

———. 2006b. The question of multiculturalism: The plays of Roy Williams. In: Luckhurst, M. ed., *A companion to modern British and Irish drama: 1880–2005.* Oxford: Blackwell, pp. 530–540.

Phillips, C. 1981. *Strange fruit.* Ambergate, UK: Amber Lane.

Reynolds, T. 2006. Caribbean families, social capital and young people's diasporic identities. *Ethnic and Racial Studies.* 29(6), pp. 1087–1103.

Scafe, S. 2007. Displacing the centre: Home and belonging in the drama of Roy Williams. In: Anim-Addo, J., and Scafe, S. eds., *I am black/white/yellow: An introduction to the black body in Europe.* London: Mango, pp. 71–87.

Sierz, A. 2001. *In-yer-face theatre: British drama today.* London: Faber and Faber.

———. 2006. What kind of England do we want? Roy Williams in conversation with Aleks Sierz. *New Theatre Quarterly.* 22(2), pp. 113–121.

———. 2009. The arts desk Q & A: Playwright Roy Williams. *theartsdesk.com.* [Online]. 24 October. [Accessed 26 October 2016]. Available from: http://www.theartsdesk.com/theatre/theartsdesk-qa-playwright-roy-williams

Spencer, C. 2003. Estate of the nation. *The Telegraph.* [Online]. 19 June. [Accessed 27 October 2016]. Available from: http://www.telegraph.co.uk/culture/theatre/drama/3596889/Estate-of-the-nation.html

Williams, H. 2014. Kingston 14, review: Goldie has a menacing presence in stage début. *Independent.* [Online]. 4 April. [Accessed 27 October 2016]. Available from: http://www.independent.co.uk/arts-entertainment/theatre-dance/reviews/kingston-14-review-goldie-has-a-menacing-presence-in-stage-début-9237932.html

Williams, R. 2002. *Roy Williams plays 1: The no boys cricket club; Starstruck; Lift off.* London: Methuen Drama.

———. 2004. *Roy Williams plays 2: Sing yer heart out for the lads; Clubland; The gift.* London: Methuen.

———. 2008. *Roy Williams plays 3: Fallout; Slow time; Days of significance; Absolute beginners.* London: Methuen Drama.

———. 2009. Black theatre's big breakout. *The Guardian.* [Online]. 27 September. [Accessed 26 October 2016]. Available from: https://www.theguardian.com/stage/2009/sep/27/black-theatre-roy-williams

Wilson, D. 2005. *Inventing black-on-black violence: Discourse, space, and representation.* Syracuse, NY: Syracuse University Press.

6

AFRICAN ACCENTS

Bola Agbaje's *Gone Too Far!*, *Detaining Justice* and *Off the Endz*

In 2010, journalist and cultural critic Lindsay Johns wrote a controversial article in *The Evening Standard* entitled 'Black Theatre is Blighted by its Ghetto Mentality' (Johns, 2010). The article was written in response to the title of British Nigerian Bola Agbaje's play, *Off the Endz* [2010, Royal Court Theatre]. Johns had not seen *Off the Endz* when he wrote his article but he anticipated 'yet another derivative black street play, probably set on a council estate, and probably with lots of patois and pimp-rolling protagonists to boot' (2010). Such dramas, he argued, have come to dominate representations of black British experiences. And, despite the increased number of black plays in the mainstream, this provides a veneer of 'multicultural bonhomie', but the reality is the persistent presentation of a monocultural and stereotypical experience:[1]

> For the ghetto is not black London's only reality. What about my reality? My milieu is comprised of barristers, doctors, media and arts types. We'd like our reality represented too. And I know for a fact that none of us spells 'ends' with a 'z'.
>
> *(2010)*

Johns was, in part, correct in his assumptions about *Off the Endz*. Despite being about upward mobility, the play is set on a council estate and features gun-toting, drug-dealing black youth. Agbaje's (b. 1981) experiences growing up on the North Peckham Estate in London have clearly influenced her thematic choices and writing style.[2] Her début *Gone Too Far!* [2007, Royal Court Theatre], like *Off the Endz* was also set on a council estate.[3] The estate setting and focus on youth crime align her plays with successful works by Caribbean British playwrights that treat similar themes, for instance Williams' *Fallout* which was also staged at the Royal Court (cf Goddard, 2015, pp. 155–172). As a British-born woman of Nigerian heritage Agbaje brings a different voice to the black British theatre landscape. Plays such as *Gone Too Far!*, *Detaining Justice* [2009, Tricycle Theatre], and *Belong* [2012, Royal Court Theatre] reflect the impact the growing black population of African origin is having on the British theatrical landscape. (This is discussed in detail in the following chapter). These plays don't tend to focus on black/white British relations. Instead, they explore intra-racial encounters between black people in Britain of Caribbean and/or of African origin.[4] What is of interest in this chapter, and read in relation to the previous chapter on Roy Williams, are the ways in which Agbaje's plays intersect with black British theatrical representations by Caribbean-origin playwrights with a similar profile. Agbaje's dramas, like Williams', focus on issues of cultures meeting and mixing. In Agbaje's plays we see the same actions of *acculturation* and *interculturation* at play identified by Brathwaite (Brathwaite, 1974, p. 11) in his conception of creolisation. But, whereas Williams has mainly charted the creolisation process occurring at the meeting of Caribbean and white British cultures in his plays, Agbaje's plays chart the cultural negotiations occurring as a result of meetings between African and Caribbean diasporas in Britain.

Gone Too Far!

Gone Too Far! is set on a south London estate and follows two brothers who are sent by their mother to buy milk. Essentially the play is a moral tale about the pressures facing teenagers to conform. Ikudayisi, the eldest brother, grew up in Nigeria and is proud to be a Nigerian, whereas Yemi, the younger sibling, was raised in the UK and spurns his heritage in favour of an adopted black Caribbean British identity. What begins as a benign errand turns into a journey of self-discovery as the brothers come into contact with a range of characters on the estate including a Bangladeshi shopkeeper, two white cockney policemen, an old white woman and the local gang. Through the brothers' interactions with the play's other characters and each other, Agbaje explores the various social forces which compel individuals to adopt various personas. As the play progresses, Yemi begins to re-evaluate his feelings towards his Nigerian heritage. But, it is the brothers' interaction with the local gang which drives the play to its climax. When Ikudayisi is accidentally stabbed in the arm trying to separate Yemi from a fight with gang-member Razer, the moment marks the turning point in Yemi's transition from an angry youth to a proud black Briton of Nigerian heritage.

In *Gone Too Far!*, Agbaje demonstrates a malleable identity and ability to code-switch as an important survival strategy employed by minorities to gain social acceptance. This tactic, the play suggests, is not restricted to youths facing peer pressure. For instance, Yemi and Ikudayisi's mother replaces her strong Nigerian accent with 'a very English voice' (2007, p. 4) when she is speaking on the telephone. The mother's adoption of an English persona when interacting with the outside world via the faceless medium of the telephone demonstrates her belief that she is more likely to be treated with respect if she masks her Nigerian origins. Likewise, the Bangladeshi shopkeeper makes every effort to proclaim his English nationalism by 'wearing an England shirt and a headscarf' (p. 7) and decorating his shop with England flags. When Yemi insinuates he may be a terrorist, the shopkeeper turns off his Islamic music and replaces it with the England World Cup anthem. Both examples, although comedic, reveal the increasing pressure some immigrants may feel in a post – 9/11 and 7/7 Britain to 'perform' their integration into English society.

The gang, on the other hand, has constructed identities in opposition to mainstream expectations. Their dress, language and value-system, which prizes violence and extreme masculinity, is redolent of the characters who populate Roy Williams' plays. In their study of inner-city black British young men, Louise Archer and Hiromi Yamashita observed that:

> dominant and attractive/popular ('hegemonic') discourses of masculinity were drawn from black Caribbean sources, mixed with US black 'rap' elements and grounded within a local London context. These identities were 'personified' in the myth of the 'rude boy' or 'bad boy'.
> *(2003, p. 122)*

Agbaje provides some insight into the gang's antisocial behaviour by highlighting some of the structural inequalities which face black British youth. The bleak estate setting is one indicator of the way class shapes identity and may foster a sense of disenfranchisement among the youth. Agbaje also hints at the perpetuation of institutional racism. In the scene in which Yemi and Ikudayisi come into contact with two white policemen Agbaje could be seen to be implying that black youth are often pushed into a position of social opposition

as a result of systemic discrimination. When the police find Yemi and Ikudayisi play-fighting, they assume that because of Yemi's black British accent
he is of Jamaican origin and that he is antagonising the Nigerian Ikudayisi.
While they are sympathetic to Ikudayisi, Yemi is automatically pigeonholed
as a cannabis-smoking criminal. However, Agbaje does not undermine the
notion that the police may be acting on institutionally racist assumptions or
'profiling' by specifically targeting Caribbean-origin youth. Instead, during
the confrontation with the police, Yemi is represented as culpable of perpetuating negative police and black British youth relations. A similar critique of
belligerent behaviour towards authority is also a feature of Williams' dramas.
Yemi's behaviour lives up to the police's stereotype. He accuses the police
of racism and calls one of them a 'BATTY MAN!' (Agbaje, 2007, p. 62). In
contrast to Ikudayisi's more measured approach, Yemi's response is deliberately
provocative and inflames the situation. Yemi's aggressive reaction may have its
reasons rooted in historical structural inequalities; however, through Yemi's
reactions Agbaje seems to suggest this has become a self-destructive cycle.
Ikudayisi councils Yemi 'to learn to choose your battle' (p. 74) and that 'once
you stop thinking dat the whole world has declared war on you, you will see
how great your life is' (p. 74). In the end Yemi follows this advice. Despite
providing a basic socio-economic contextualisation of the problems faced by
some black youth in Britain, Agbaje's overall message in the play places the
onus on the individual to ultimately make positive lifestyle choices.

The play narrowly avoids essentialist representations. The fact the police
are kind towards Ikudayisi because they correctly assume he is of African
origin but they are hostile towards Yemi because they incorrectly assume
he is of Caribbean heritage indicates that differences between African and
Caribbean people are cultural and, therefore, learned. Nevertheless, Agbaje
seems to be raising a fairly politically incorrect notion by representing the
police's racism as not targeted to all black people but to a specific sector
of black youth who have adopted a Jamaican identity. The play seems to
support the idea that, in contrast to Nigeria, Jamaica provides a negative
influence on youth culture. The obnoxious Armani, a female member of
the gang, is a case in point. Despite being raised by her single white mother,
Armani – who was introduced to aspects of Jamaican culture via her relationship with a friend – has modelled her identity after her black Jamaican
father. Armani's wholesale embrace of a Jamaican identity includes an
adoption of the prejudiced system of 'colourism' (Walker, 1983) that has
historically structured social hierarchies in the Caribbean whereby near
whiteness and European phenotypes are valued over African ones. When

she learns that Yemi is of Nigerian (she had assumed Caribbean) heritage, she compliments him by saying that he does not 'look' African as he 'don't have big lips and big nose' (Agbaje, 2007, p. 18). And when Yemi insults her, she resorts to calling him racist names such as 'babatunde' (p. 21) and 'Kunta Kinte' (p. 32) and urges her boyfriend Razer to beat Yemi up 'because these Africans are forgetting their place' (p. 67). Armani justifies her racism against (and homogenisation of) Africans with the comment that 'back in da days they sold us off as slaves' (p. 36). The slave trade is alluded to as the explanation for hostile relations between African and Caribbean groups in Britain in other plays that examine the relationship, including Kwei-Armah's *Statement of Regret* and Roy Williams' *Joe Guy*. In response to a similar explanation in a Channel 4 television programme about relations between African and Caribbean communities in Britain, Archer and Yamashita state that 'these interpretations draw attention to how diasporic identities have social and geographic 'histories' that continue to influence modern manifestations and constructions beyond the immediate time/space boundaries' (2003, p. 122). Although the rest of the gang doesn't share her hostility, Armani's anti-African stance is revealed as an integral aspect of her constructed, and therefore lends authenticity to, her Jamaican identity.

Yemi's desire to fit in with the gang has also manifested a dislike for his Nigerian heritage. His internalised negativity is expressed by his disdain of his brother and his view of Nigerian culture as backward. Instead, he has constructed a Caribbean/black British-styled identity. His assimilation is so successful that the gang only discovers he has Nigerian roots when they meet Ikudayisi. Archer and Yamashita note the pressure on young black Africans to conform to the dominant Caribbean British culture. Among the subjects interviewed in their study at a London school they observed that:

> Distinctions were drawn between 'authentic'/'cool' Caribbean masculinities and Other/ridiculed African masculinities. Boys of African heritage were more likely to identify their ethnicity as 'black' (as opposed to 'Caribbean' boys) and used popular Caribbean styles of talk and dress. However, they were often ridiculed by Caribbean boys.
>
> *(2003, p. 122)*

Agbaje draws attention to her own experience growing up in London where she had to navigate her blackness in relation to the dominant

Caribbean-origin community. On her website she describes her first day in secondary school:

> I went around the classroom asking everyone where they were from and when I was asked I told my class mates I was half Jamaican and half African. Thinking back I don't know why I did it, I mean I know why at the time, I was ashamed of being African [sic] most African [sic] where I grew up were ashamed. It was cooler to be West Indian.
>
> *(2010a)*

Agbaje seems to indicate that Yemi's dilemma is the result of a confused identity and lack of self-pride which have lead to him making bad life choices. Yemi is on the brink of losing himself to the wrong crowd by assimilating Caribbean British culture. The remedy, Agbaje indicates, is for Yemi to reconnect himself to his Nigerian roots:

Ikudayisi: One minute you feel you don't fit in here because people are racist but then you don't want to be a Nigerian. You want to be left alone, but you complain you have no friends. Do you know who you are, Yemi?

Yemi: Yes, I'm a free person.
  [. . .]

Ikudayisi: How can you be free when you deny your own heritage? You don't like your name, you are ashamed of your language. If you are *so* free you won't care what people think about Nigeria and you will just be what you are.

(Agbaje, 2007, p. 46)

Through the character Blazer, Agbaje narrowly veers the play away from promoting a 'good African'/'bad Caribbean' dialectic. Blazer is also of Nigerian heritage but, unlike Yemi, he advocates a sense of pride in his African origins: he speaks Yoruba and believes 'us Nigerians need to stick together' (p. 55). However, his belief in the fundamental difference between people from Africa and the Caribbean belies his own racism:

Blazer: That's what makes us different.
Yemi: What does?
Blazer: Respect.

Yemi: From who?
Blazer: Da West Indians.

(p. 50)

Blazer has given up his Nigerian name; yet, he considers what he is doing as a strategic way to take control of the estate by infiltration: 'Gone are da days when mans take the piss out of this African! Cos I run this estate now . . . the roles have reversed now' (p. 53). Blazer's position as gang leader may point to a reversal of power; yet, it is a pyrrhic victory: his appropriation of an outward Caribbean British identity and essentialist beliefs hints at the problematic issue of reverse racism which perpetuates a cycle of violence and hate. Although Blazer claims the maxim 'Money, power, respect is what you need in life' (p. 51) to be an African 'truth' learned from his Nigerian mother, Blazer's notion of respect is more ideologically in-line with the 'gangsta' interpretation of the word which has nothing in common with its meaning within a traditional Nigerian context.

Agbaje reveals the warped values of the black British gang through Ikudayisi who is good-natured, polite, respectful of his elders, speaks English and Yoruba and has a firm understanding of when to pick one's battles based on growing up in Nigeria. Agbaje presents and contrasts a traditional Nigerian value system of respect, exemplified by Ikudayisi, with the way in which 'respect' has become hijacked and twisted to mean something taken (by violence and intimidation) not given. The play hints that the reason for this is a hostile reaction to authority as a result of individual and institutional racism. But Agbaje moves beyond this traditional perspective to highlight the cyclical self-defeating nature of such an aggressive defence mechanism. This is highlighted by the fact that it is merely a pair of trainers that is the catalyst for the knife fight between Yemi and Razer.[5] In reaction, Yemi, embracing what he believes to be his true identity, distils the fight between himself and Razer into an African versus Caribbean conflict declaring, 'I'm doing this for me. I'm gonna make people know who I am' (p. 74) and that 'These jams think they are better dan us Africans. Dat we ain't shit. That's why they robbed you [. . .] They treat Africans like they are beneath them. I AIN'T BENEATH NO ONE' (pp. 78–79). The case of mistaken identity – Yemi believes Razer took Ikudayisi's trainers, but actually it was a different gang member – underlines the pettiness of the African versus Caribbean conflict. Agbaje gets to the moral heart of the play during the knife-fight between Yemi and Razer when Ikudayisi pleads:

Ikudayisi: We are all BLACK! WE ARE ALL BLACK AND YOU ARE
ACTING LIKE WE ARE ALL DIVIDED! [. . .] Why are we
always fighting each other? Why can't we just get along? [. . .]
Yemi, you tell me you are free, be free to make the right choice.
Don't go down the wrong road. It's your choice, make the right
choice. GIVE ME THE KNIFE.

(p. 79)

Despite this call for solidarity and to let go of deep-seated intra-racial prejudices, the play ultimately presents a conservative view. It implies that black
Britain's youth problems stem from a sense of identity disconnect. The solu-
tion provided to Yemi is to acknowledge and embrace his Nigerian heritage.
However, as Yemi's bad attitude stems from his adoption of Caribbean traits, the
play problematically indicates that it is Caribbean culture which is responsible
for the negative aspects of some black British youth's behaviour. It also raises
questions around authenticity. Agbaje insinuates that one's moral path becomes
compromised if one is not true to their roots. By the end of the play, Yemi's
transformation has begun and he has started learning Yoruba. In the final scene,
Yemi is getting ready for a party. He 'picks up a basketball cap but then decides
on the traditional [Nigerian] hat. As he starts to put on his shoes he changes his
mind and goes for his trainers' (p. 82). The play ends with him singing: 'Green,
white, green on my chest, I'm proud to be a Nigerian!' (p. 82). His traditional
hat combined with trainers reveals him as a 'creole' or hybrid but, importantly,
one that has been redeemed only through the reclamation of his roots.

Detaining justice

During the televised election debate in 2010, in order to support his argument for greater immigration control, David Cameron used an anecdote
about a man he had met named Neal Forde:

I was in Plymouth recently and a 40-year-old black man actually made
the point to me. He said, 'I came here when I was six, I served in the Royal
Navy for 30 years, I'm incredibly proud of my country, but I'm so ashamed
that we have had this out of control system with people abusing it so badly'.

(qtd in Burkeman, 2010)[6]

Cameron carefully used a black man as an example in order to couch his
anti-immigration stance as non-racist and to make the point that if even

the immigrants are unhappy with immigration then there must be a serious problem. At the same time Cameron's words made an implicit distinction between those immigrants prepared to move to the UK and contribute to society and those that come to take advantage of it. Agbaje's *Detaining Justice* anticipates the complex issues of immigration and belonging in multicultural Britain that Cameron's anecdote raises.[7] In the play, Agbaje examines the themes of immigration and asylum from a predominantly black perspective. In doing so she holds up for scrutiny notions of multiculturalism and black solidarity in twenty-first century Britain. The plot centres around a Zimbabwean brother and sister, Grace and Justice, who have sought asylum in Britain. Grace has been granted leave to remain; however, her brother Justice's application has been refused and he is being held in a detention centre. Justice's case is being defended by Cole, a black British lawyer, and Chi Chi, his black British assistant, who both work for the not-for-profit Immigration Advisory Centre. Representing the Home Office seeking to repatriate Justice are Alfred, a black British case-worker, and Ben, a white British enforcement officer. Agbaje explores the broader immigrant experience through three cameo characters who are all illegal immigrants working as cleaners at a train station: Pra, a Ghanaian man who is also the pastor of a church; Abeni, a Nigerian woman and Jovan, a white Eastern European man.

Detaining Justice raises questions regarding the reception of immigrants and asylum seekers in multicultural Britain. As seen in the previous chapter on Roy Williams, there are debates as to what multiculturalism means. Whereas some perceive it as a policy that encourages intermixture, others argue multiculturalism preserves and promotes separatism. Since 9/11, the 2001 race riots in Bradford and the 7/7 bombings in London in 2005, however, critics of multiculturalism have become more vociferous.[8] The emphasis placed on foreigners to accept the homeland's values and way of life have become increasingly strong in discourses around immigration and national unity. To some extent, these views are held by the pragmatic Cole. His assistant Chi Chi, on the other hand, criticises the fact that while politicians may speak of the need for immigrants to integrate, the reality is that they receive such a hostile reception that, even if they wanted to, they cannot. Chi Chi argues that immigrants who have been granted leave to remain face such discrimination finding a job or in the work place that she does not 'know of *any* asylum seekers or immigrants who feels they can call this place their home' (Agbaje, 2009, p. 210). In her opinion, the problem faced by immigrants is not, as

Cole suggests, their difficulty to adapt, but the failure of the host society to accept them:

Chi Chi: *But it's not about adapting!* It's about acceptance and as much as this country goes on that they are accepting and how welcoming it is . . . it is not. If you ask me, the dodgy politicians chat absolute bollocks about Britishness and multi-whatever-you-want-to-call-it. It really gets to me sometimes. People here have this hatred towards asylum seekers, immigrants, and for what? Honestly, I'm telling them to go home to their countries cos I care. This country is bloody racist.

(p. 211)

However, despite Chi Chi's good intentions, she is revealed to be somewhat naïve and blinded by her Afrocentric politics. Despite not knowing how to pronounce the word 'colonisation', she makes nonsensical statements such as: 'Africa was a beautiful nation before the invader went there to mess it up' (p. 215). Her politics are revealed as separatist and rooted in reactionary racism when she is called a 'black cow' and retaliates by calling the person a 'white cunt' (p. 211). When Cole comes to work for the Immigration Advisory Centre, she assumes that because he is black he will be more committed to helping other black people. Cole, however, refuses the positive representation Chi Chi forces upon him. He does not want to be a black activist and hero. Instead his much more pragmatic approach centres around trying to be the best he can be. His decision to leave the Immigration Advisory Centre raises a question mark over Chi Chi's assumed notions of black solidarity.

Alfred, the black Home Office case worker, is the foil to Chi Chi. As opposed to trying to secure immigrants' leave to remain in the UK, Alfred's *raison d'etre* is to keep them out. Alfred has internalised the rhetoric that there are too many immigrants and that they are a burden on the state:

Alfred: Watch when your daughter grows up and she needs to look for a job. She is not going to stand a chance because all these damn immigrants would have come here and taken over. If it was up to you, these bloody lawyers and left-wing do-gooders, I bet you'd grant every asylum seeker not just leave to enter but free medical care and housing. Then when your daughter has no job, no house and has to queue for ten hours in the hospital you will only have yourself to blame with our soft approach and equal rights bullshit.

(p. 220)

Ironically, Alfred reacts to new black immigrants in the same manner as his grandparents might have been treated.[9] When Grace pleads with him to have pity on her brother, Alfred fails to sympathise, stating, 'I am not an immigrant' (p. 240). Grace's appeal to him on the level of black solidarity fails to resonate:

Grace: How can you condemn your own? You turn your back on people who need help. We are not animals. They use you to choose the fate of your own and you do not see the problem with that.

Alfred: I am British.

Grace: Are you not black? You see your own people suffering and you do nothing to help.

[. . .]

Grace: It is only the luck of the draw that you are here. Your family were once foreigners in this land.

Alfred: Unlike you and *your* people, my family did not smuggle themselves in a truck to get here. They walked proudly through the borders. They were British citizens from birth. They had the right to enter, work and settle here. They were invited to this country.

Grace: And what were they invited here to do? Was it not to work in jobs that the immigrants you hate so much do right now?! The invitation was not limited to *your* people. My father was invited to this country to work in 'your' hospitals. But instead of being a follower and going in search of a better world, he had hope our country will get better. He did not want to be a slave in another man's land. He was loyal to his own land.

(p. 242)

The exchange highlights the hegemonic nature of nationalism and national identity. Alfred seems oblivious to the history of how changes to immigration laws restricted non-white entry into Britain as well as contributed to racist discourses. The association of blackness with non-Britishness ran much deeper than birthright, as the racist views of Enoch Powell highlighted. Fear of non-white mass migration led to the 1962 and 1968 Commonwealth Immigration Acts which successively re-defined the rights to claim British citizenship. The 1971 Immigration Act introduced 'patriality' into the law which meant that only foreign-born people with a parent or grandparent born in the UK retained the right to citizenship. The change in law was effectively a 'colour ban' on immigration and, as Gilroy argues, meant that the words 'immigrant' and 'black' became interchangeable (Gilroy, 1987, p. 46).

Arguably, Alfred's words reveal that the white-only conception of British-ness has been re-defined in the post-war era. Yet Grace's responses highlight how contemporary anti-immigration discourse still depends on replicating notions of racial and cultural difference albeit in much more subtle terms. Alfred's words conjure a 'good black'/'bad black' immigrant scenario. His narrative of legitimacy depicts the Windrush generation with dignity, as people who were not only citizens but who were 'invited' to Britain. Afri-can refugees such as Grace (whose asylum claim has been accepted giving her right to remain) are portrayed as criminals and unwanted parasites. This imagery, in conjunction with the divisive '*your* people', contains unmistakable vestiges of imperial discourse which constructed the colonial 'other' as sav-ages and which Alfred has internalised. Agbaje's play insinuates that notions of Britishness have not fundamentally changed – the principles of exclusion based on racial and ethnic differences still exist.

Grace's revelation that her father once worked in Britain in a fairly high-status capacity in comparison to Alfred's more working-class ancestors subtly reveals class politics as a foundational reason behind African/Caribbean hostility. Secondly, Grace insinuates that black belonging in Britain is a mat-ter of historical chance. In the 1950s, both Grace's father and Alfred's parents would have been considered British citizens. Ultimately, the only difference between the two of them is that Grace's father decided to return to Zimbabwe and, between then and now, Britain changed its citizenship and immigration laws. Grace insinuates that not only is Alfred a traitor to his race by not help-ing her, but that his family members were sell-outs and self-serving by leaving the newly independent Caribbean in search of a more secure financial future in Britain. The implication is that her refugee status and politically-motivated departure from Zimbabwe were for more honourable reasons than economic security. Finally, Grace tells Alfred, 'You look down on me like I am so dif-ferent to you. We are all immigrants in this land! You should not be so blind to the truth' (Agbaje, 2007, p. 242). Her point raises the question of whether or not black people can be perceived as indigenous, and echoes a line from Michael Abbensetts' *Sweet Talk*, performed in 1973, when Tony says to his wife Rita, 'How many years you reckon we got to live in this country before they stop callin' us immigrants?' (2001, p. 71).

Racism remains as much a barrier to belonging for these new immigrants as it did in the post-war era. Agbaje indicates through the character of Ben, Alfred's white co-worker at the home office, that multiculturalism provides a politically correct veil which masks a persistent fetishisation of the 'other'. Initially, Ben appears to have adapted perfectly to life in multicultural Britain:

he speaks using black British slang, his favourite food is curried goat and rice and he is married to an Indian woman. However, for Ben multicultur- alism is a self-serving ideology that furnishes him with a new vocabulary, access to exotic foods and women and an excuse to support his adultery – he claims 'Monogamy in an English invention' (Agbaje, 2007, p. 217). Ben takes advantage of Grace by using his position of power to seduce her into think- ing that sleeping with him will help her brother's case. Ben's treatment of Grace serves as a metaphor for the powerlessness of asylum seekers and illegal immigrants. Whereas Caribbean immigrants came to the 'mother country' as citizens with rights, new arrivals from Africa come from the former colo- nies as non-citizens. Agbaje's play highlights the vulnerability of this sector: Justice's powerlessness at the hands of the guards at the detention centre is harrowingly portrayed when they force him to eat dog food; Pra and Abeni are too scared to stand up against ill-treatment by their employees and the public in case someone makes a complaint against them and they lose their jobs, recalling the tragedy that befell the exploited Chinese cockle pickers who died in Morecambe Bay in 2004.

The play provides an interesting point of comparison with plays by first-generation Caribbean writers produced in the 1970s. *Detaining Justice* portrays immigrants occupying low-paying and marginal positions in soci- ety. The train station where Pra, Abeni and Jovan work emphasises their transitory existence and echoes Matura's *As Time Goes By* in which the char- acters occupy similar jobs working for the London underground and buses. Similarly, the characters in *Detaining Justice* occupy an in-between position of ambivalent un-belonging: happy in neither home nor host-land. Like the Windrush generation, the immigrant characters in the play have come to Britain in search of a better life and, in the case of Grace and Justice, are flee- ing persecution. Agbaje's play suggests life in Britain as an immigrant in the twenty-first century is equally difficult to the post-war immigrant experi- ence. Menial jobs continue to be the only work available despite the characters occupying positions of status within their communities, such as Pra who is a pastor. The play also highlights how immigrants continue to be perceived in the host society to be taking jobs from local 'indigenous' people despite the fact they work in positions that many Britons might feel are below them. As Abeni states: 'They think they know what this country needs. But what they don't know is that they need us' (p. 205). Yet, in the twenty-first century, the terms have changed. The meeting between the settled/'indigenous' black community and new black African arrivals complicates notions of black Britishness and black solidarity. By bringing together histories of black migration, the play highlights the multiple reasons and routes behind black British belonging.

Off the Endz

In *Off the Endz* Agbaje represents a more generalised urban working-class black British experience. The play tackles the theme of upward mobility and inflated black masculinity. It depicts twenty-something businessman Kojo and nurse Sharon who are expecting a baby. They are preparing to move off the estate where they are living and into a better area with good schools for their unborn child. However, when their old friend David is released from prison he threatens to destroy their fragile future plans. To earn money quickly and easily, David begins to sell drugs. When Kojo loses his job because of the recession and is faced with spiralling debt he is easily co-opted into David's illegal enterprise. However, David's drug peddling encroaches on the local gang's territory run by gun-wielding ten-year-olds. In an attempt to kill David, Kojo is accidentally shot by one of the youths. The play ends with Kojo and Sharon ending their friendship with David and the couple preparing to re-build their lives.

Agbaje prefaces her play with a quote from Anne Frank: 'Parents can only give good advice or put them on the right paths, but the final forming of a person's character lies in their own hands' (2010b, n.p.). In essence, the play is a morality tale with a lesson that anti-Establishment behaviour rooted in blaming society is self-defeating. Self-improvement, Agbaje intones, is ultimately up to the individual and choices s/he makes. The sentiment, conveyed in Frank's quote, is echoed in the final scene when Kojo tells David: 'You're your own worst enemy. You are trapped in a mindset. In a way of thinking that is not helping you. You're the only one holding you back' (p. 75). The moral tone is consistent with *Gone Too Far!* and highlights Agbaje's personal connection with the issue of black male wasted potential. In fact, *Gone Too Far!* is dedicated to her brother who spent a year in prison for attempted robbery. Agbaje's description of her brother's actions and belief in his redemption resonates with both male characters in *Off the Endz*:

> He didn't work, he didn't go to college. He had that mentality of quick money, easy money is the way out, instead of working hard [. . .] He has made some really bad choices. But he's paid for his crime now, and he's got the opportunity to change his life.
>
> *(qtd in Costa, 2008, p. 26)*

David and Kojo are two sides of the same coin and represent the either/or scenario of a fundamental life-choice. When Kojo takes the bullet meant for David but survives, it symbolises his resurrection, and an opportunity to start life anew. Agbaje's plays often convey a strong moral lesson indicative of her strong Christian beliefs. She dedicates her plays to God and brings a moral conservativeness to her dramas which can be attributed to her traditional Nigerian upbringing.

Agbaje also brings a personal perspective to a subject in which, because of her brother, she has a vested interest. The note of hope at the end distinguishes *Off the Endz* from plays by some black male playwrights that deal with similar issues. Roy Williams and Kwame Kwei-Armah both examine the pressures facing young black men to conform to a world-view which emphasises hyper-masculinity, 'respect' and anti-Establishment sub-cultural belonging. However, their plays, in particular Williams' *Fallout* and Kwei-Armah's *Elmina's Kitchen*, end in tragedy and depict a cycle of damaged young men who grow up without fathers or whose fathers are bad role models. In *Off the Endz* however, Kojo survives and his son will grow up with a father.

Agbaje highlights the culture of machismo as the Achilles heel of urban black male experiences where kudos is gained by asserting oneself against the Establishment as well as against women. For example, David critiques Kojo's and Sharon's middle-class aspirations as evidence that they are 'slaves to the system' (p. 76) and accuses Kojo of pandering to and being emasculated by Sharon. The tone in *Off the Endz*, in contrast to Williams' and Kwei-Armah's plays, is not one of anger directed at the failures of the father-figure; rather, it expresses a hope that the men in the play will grow up and make the right decisions. As Billington points out, Agbaje 'resolves the dilemma by pinning her faith, somewhat unfashionably, in the solid virtues of work and family' (Billington, 2010, p. 40). As well as bringing a perspective to a theme typically dealt with by male writers, the play is also testament to the multiple identities Agbaje negotiates and is able to represent as a female black British and second-generation Nigerian British playwright.

Agbaje hints at Kojo's and David's West African heritages through their names and surnames respectively. However, beyond this she chooses not to draw attention to their ethnic backgrounds. Despite this assertion of their indigeneity – whether they are of African or Caribbean descent is of no relevance to the plot – her choice is revealing. By not highlighting their backgrounds, but by giving them Caribbean-influenced speech, Agbaje represents the way in which black Caribbean has become normalised as black British. The point the play seems to reinforce is that among black Britons, particularly working-class youth cultures, what eventually surfaces is a Caribbean-influenced identity as it has greater status than an African one.

Arguably, *Off the Endz* tries to straddle the working-class/middle-class divide by exploring characters attempting to escape the limited possibilities of the 'endz'. Her strong moral tone and hopeful ending provide an alternative to such plays as *Fallout* and *Elmina's Kitchen* which have been criticised for offering no 'way of changing this reality' and being 'more a cry of anger and despair than a call for change' (Sierz, 2004, p. 83). Ironically, however, it was the transparent morality of Agbaje's redemptive play which attracted the most criticism. Across the board critics tempered their praise of the play by suggesting it was somewhat 'schematic' (Spencer, 2010), 'sometimes overly direct' (Billington, 2010, p. 40) and, in the worst-case the reviewer for black cultural website 'Catch a Vibe' found the play 'had more in common with a TIE production on the dangers of drug dealing and mixing with the wrong crowd than an engaging piece of drama' (Williams, 2010).[10] The play's social-realist style, use of patois-inspired black British 'street' vernacular and exploration of black masculinity, crime and violent youth set on a council estate echo a glut of contemporary black British gritty urban dramas. In *Off the Endz*, Agbaje emulates a generic model, pioneered by Caribbean British playwrights and endorsed by mainstream theatres, in particular the Royal Court, that has proven highly successful in the last decade.

As the previous two chapters have shown, historically, Caribbean British experiences have powerfully shaped representations of black British culture and identity in the theatre. Creolisation provides a useful way in which to think about the ways in which Agbaje's plays, located at the interstice of African and Caribbean British experiences, explore and represent the evolution of black Britishness in the twenty-first century. Mainstream representations since the 2000s by second-generation Caribbean British playwrights such as Roy Williams have frequently portrayed urban youth cultures. Agbaje's plays intersect with this mainly male Caribbean British tradition. She writes to it by treating similar themes of youth crime and gang violence set on urban council estates and articulated by patois-inspired 'street' speech. Like in Williams' *Fallout* and *Joe Guy*, the good African/bad Caribbean dichotomy is also represented in her plays. As a second-generation Nigerian Briton and a woman, Agbaje's work also brings a different perspective to antecedent representations. Her plays feature African-origin protagonists and explore issues of particular import to the African, particularly Nigerian, diaspora in Britain. However, Agbaje also writes Caribbean/black British characters in order to explore these themes of African Britishness and belonging. Arguably, therefore, her exploration of identity is relational to a sense of Caribbean British identity and culture even while it gives rise to its own set of unique stylistic articulations and thematic interrogations.

In *Belong*, Agbaje explores the theme of return migration, principally through the protagonist who returns to Nigeria for a visit and then decides to stay and pursue his political career there. The characters in *Belong*, reflecting Agbaje's own family experiences, live between the UK and Nigeria. Agbaje dedicates the piece to her family in Nigeria and the play highlights Agbaje's diasporic positioning that has resulted in an interest in Nigeria as much as the UK. As a later work it contrasts with Roy Williams who began his career writing about the migratory experiences of his parents' generation before focusing on the UK. Arguably, this reflects the contemporary moment whereby migration is no longer as decisive as it was in the immediate post-war period. It points to the ability in the contemporary to imagine a more fluid transnational identity whereby Agbaje does not need to deal with the past and the 'there' in order to come to terms with the present and the 'here'.

Notes

1 Arinze Kene echoes this in a newspaper interview: 'He [Kene] points to his own family: they have lived in east London since his parents emigrated from Nigeria, yet none of his siblings has ever been involved in violent crime; two of them are graduates, and his brother is a photographer. "What about those stories?" he asks. "They're just as interesting." But he admits that he grew up surrounded by "bad influences", and came close to trouble himself' (Costa, 2013).

2 Agbaje lived for a brief period between the ages of six and eight in Nigeria but otherwise has spent the rest of her life in the UK.

3 *Gone Too Far!* premiered at the Royal Court as part of the Young Writers' Festival in 2007 and was revived in the main theatre in 2008. It won a Laurence Olivier Award for Outstanding Achievement and was also adapted by Agbaje into a film which was released in 2013.

4 Roy Williams treats the theme of African and Caribbean British relations most directly in his play *Joe Guy*, although similar issues emerge in *Clubland* and *Fallout*. Other plays which explore relationships between African and African Caribbean origin characters include Edgar White's *Man and Soul* [1982, Riverside Studios], Frank McField's *No Place to be Nice* [1984, Albany Theatre], Maria Oshodi's *The 'S' Bend* [1984, Royal Court Theatre]; Courttia Newland's *B is for Black* [2003, Oval House Theatre]; David Addai's *House of Agnes* [2008, Oval House Theatre] and *Oxford Street* [2008, Royal Court Theatre]; and Kwame Kwei-Armah's *Statement*

of Regret. Paul Boakye's *Boy with Beer* [1992, Man in the Moon Theatre] adds the theme of homosexuality to its exploration of intra-racial relationships.

5 Intra-racial violence over trainers also emerges in Roy Williams' *Fallout* when Kwame is murdered by the black British gang for his shoes. Violent crimes over shoes recall cases in the USA such as 15-year-old Michael Eugene Thomas who was murdered for his pair of Air Jordans in 1989.

6 The statement caused much derision in the press as it suggested that Neal Forde was ten years old when he served in the Royal Navy. Forde was in fact fifty-one and served in the royal Navy as a marine engineer for six years.

7 *Detaining Justice* opened at the Tricycle Theatre alongside Kwame Kwei-Armah's *Seize the Day* and Roy Williams' *Category B* for the theatre's 'Not Black & White Season'.

8 In September 2005, black Briton Trevor Phillips, as chair of the then CRE, sparked the debate over multiculturalism versus integration with his speech entitled: 'After 7/7: Sleepwalking into Segregation', in which he argued that in Britain 'we've focused far too much on the "multi" and not enough on common culture' (qtd in McGhee, 2008, p. 87). In 2006, Tony Blair reiterated this sentiment in his speech entitled: 'The Duty to Integrate: Shared British Values' (Julios, 2008, p. 153).

9 This theme is examined from a different angle in Kwame Kwei-Armah's *Let There Be Love,* about a Grenadian pensioner who is initially hostile to his Polish immigrant home helper.

10 Arinze Kene's *Estate Walls* received a similar critique in the press: 'although at points *Estate Walls* flies above the expected into the sublime it eventually lands, somewhat predictably, in the bosom of a conventional morality tale' (Bayes, 2010).

Works cited

Abbensetts, M. 2001. Sweet talk. In: Abbensetts, M. *Four plays*. London: Oberon, pp. 11–72.

Agbaje, B. 2007. *Gone too far!* London: Methuen.

———. 2009. Detaining justice. In: Agbaje, B., Kwei-Armah, K., and Williams, R. eds., *Not black and white*. London: Methuen, pp. 185–269.

———. 2010a. *Biography*. [Online]. Available from: http://bolaagbaje.com/bio.php

———. 2010b. *Off the endz*. London: Methuen.

Archer, L., and Yamashita, H. 2003. Theorising inner-city masculinities: 'Race', class, gender and education. *Gender & Education*. 15(2), pp. 115–132.

Bayes, H. 2010. Estate walls. *WhatsOnStage*. 6 October. [Accessed 8 March 2016]. Available from: http://www.whatsonstage.com/off-west-end-theatre/reviews/10-2010/estate-walls_11377.html

Billington, M. 2010. Beware old friends dealing drugs and dissatisfaction: Off the Endz. *The Guardian*. 20 February. p. 40.

Brathwaite, E. K. 1974. *Contradictory omens: Cultural diversity and integration in the Caribbean*. Mona, Jamaica: Savacou Publications.

Burkeman, O. 2010. Chapter and twitterverse: Cameron's debate anecdotes picked apart on web. *The Guardian*. 16 April. Available from: http://www.guardian.co.uk/politics/2010/apr/16/david-cameron-twitter-fact-checking

Costa, M. 2008. 'I suddenly thought, I know who I am'. Bola Agbaje turned a mis-spent youth on a south London estate into an award-winning play. *The Guardian.* 23 July. p. 26.

———. 2013. Arinze Kene: 'At home, I'm Nigerian. *I go out and I'm a British kid'.* [Accessed 4 March 2016]. Available from: http://www.theguardian.com/stage/2013/feb/25/arinze-kene-gods-property

Gilroy, P. 1987. *'There ain't no black in the Union Jack': The cultural politics of race and nation.* London: Hutchinson.

Goddard, L. 2015. *Contemporary black British playwrights: Margins to mainstream.* Basingstoke, UK: Palgrave Macmillan.

Johns, L. 2010. Black theatre is blighted by its ghetto mentality. *The Evening Standard.* [Online]. 9 February. [Accessed 29 January 2017]. Available from: http://www.standard.co.uk/news/black-theatre-is-blighted-by-its-ghetto-mentality-6709941.html.

Julios, C. 2008. *Contemporary British identity: English language, migrants, and public discourse.* Aldershot, UK: Ashgate.

McGhee, D. 2008. *The end of multiculturalism? Terrorism, integration and human rights.* Maidenhead, UK: Open University Press.

Sierz, A. 2004. 'Me and my mates': The state of English playwriting, 2003. *New Theatre Quarterly.* 20(1), pp. 79–83.

Spencer, C. 2010. Off the Endz at the Royal Court. *The Telegraph.* [Online]. 22 February. [Accessed 29 January 2017]. Available from: http://www.telegraph.co.uk/culture/theatre/theatre-reviews/7293100/Off-the-Endz-at-the-Royal-Court-review.html.

Walker, A. 1983. If the present looks like the past, what does the future look like? In: Walker, A. *In search of our mothers' gardens: Womanist Prose.* New York: Harcourt Brace Jovanovich, pp. 290–312.

Williams, K. 2010. Theatre review: *Off the Endz. Catch a Vibe.* 25 February. Available from: http://www.catchavibe.co.uk/theatre-review-off-the-endz/

SECTION III
Africa

7

HOME TO HOST-LAND AND THE HYPHEN IN-BETWEEN

African British diasporic dramas since the 1990s

Denton Chikura's play *The Epic Adventures of Nhamo the Manyika Warrior and his Sexy Wife Chipo* [2013, Tricycle Theatre] opens with the narrator imploring 'ye fathers of storytelling' to help him secure the perfect hero for his tale: 'I am speaking to you, Chinua Achebe! *You* Wole Soyinka and *you* Richard Pryor!' (Chikura, 2013, p. 3). While the first two names might be expected in a line-up of the holy trinity of African storytellers, the mention of African American comedian Richard Pryor secures the play's first laugh. The play, a satire of stereotypical representations of 'Africa' achieves its humour through bold references and a performance aesthetic that does not shy away from political incorrectness. For instance, the villain, semi-naked and clad in a zebra skin and grass costume, presents a folkloric stereotype which is both ridiculous and awkward to watch. Chikura was born in Zimbabwe and moved to the UK in 2002 as a young adult. From his vantage point as a naturalised Briton, his play comes across as an ode to his Zimbabwean homeland and Africa more generally. The play holds up ideas and assumptions of 'African' cultural authenticity for scrutiny and, from the start, explodes any expectations of a portrayal of 'traditional African' life. In the process, the piece communicates a strong sense of heart in its aim to challenge exotic and primitivist African stereotypes. Chikura's continued investment in his homeland reflects his diasporic consciousness and positioning in-between his home (Zimbabwe) and host-land (the UK). Using diaspora as a critical framework, this chapter discusses plays by African British playwrights staged in the UK since the

1990s, focusing on their negotiation of issues of migration and belonging. In order to provide a point of comparison with how black British playwrights of Caribbean heritage have been discussed, plays are grouped according to a writer's immigrant status, i.e. first-generation (moved to the UK as an adult) and second-generation (born in the UK to immigrant parents or came to the UK as an infant). The generational paradigm is further complicated by the introduction of the notion of the 1.5 generation to describe a cohort of African British playwrights whose experience of migration occurred when they were teenagers. The 1.5 generation have therefore spent formative years in at least two countries.

The Greek word 'diaspora' translates as 'the scattering of seeds' from *speiro* (to sow) and *dia* (over). As a result, horticultural metaphors are often used to describe diaspora processes (see Cohen, 1997). An image of a dandelion and its seeds being carried away by the wind to grow elsewhere is, as Cohen notes, commonly employed to represent diaspora (Cohen, 2015). The dandelion conveys the idea of transport, transplantation and transformation across spaces. As a result of growing up in a new environment, the new seedlings will resemble but not be identical to the parent plant. In the same way that theatre made by people of African origin contributes to an evolving sense of black and British theatre, such work still speaks to, and can be seen as an extension of, particular African theatre histories and cultures despite not being made in continental Africa.

While Caribbean migration to the UK began in earnest in the 1950s and peaked in the mid 1960s, migration from Africa gained momentum during the 1960s but increased exponentially since the 1990s (Owen, 2009). According to the 2001 Census the majority of the black population in Britain was of Caribbean origin. By 2011 the situation had dramatically changed with the number of people identifying as black African nearly double that of those identifying as black Caribbean (Office for National Statistics, 2012). Since the 1990s the African presence in British theatre has emerged more strongly in line with a community large enough to sustain it. Where a playwright has migrated from and why are important factors that shape the plays they produce. The African immigrant population is regionally, racially and ethnically diverse and includes economic migrants (both semi and skilled workers), refugees/asylum seekers and students (Bosveld and Connolly, 2006, p. 35). Given that the majority of the black African population in the UK who were born in Africa come from Nigeria (191,000 residents in the 2011 Census), it is perhaps unsurprising that the majority of African British playwrights are of Nigerian origin. Other countries with high numbers of black residents now living in the UK include Zimbabwe, Ghana and Somalia (Office for National Statistics, 2015, pp. 7–9).[1] The existence of an established literary/theatre tradition (by Western standards) and educational infrastructure in Nigeria and Zimbabwe may also account for the fact that theatre practitioners from these countries are relatively well represented. The majority of sub-Saharan African immigrants come from Commonwealth nations, reflecting how migration from Africa to Britain continues to be influenced by the legacy of colonialism (Barou, Aigner and Mbenga, 2012, p. 30). Despite this, since the 1990s a generation of people have come to Britain from developing African countries, without a lived experience of colonialism and who are more likely to have direct experiences not of racial but of class-based and ethnic oppression.

The notion of a homeland – material and symbolic – has traditionally been a defining characteristic for diasporic communities: their forced separation from it, desire to return and continued nationalism in the host country (Safran, 1991). Initially, diaspora described the dispersion of the Jews from Israel. As a result, typologies of diaspora have traditionally taken the Jewish experience of forced removal and exile as a starting point in defining its characteristics. More recently, diaspora has come to be applied to immigrant groups with a wider range of reasons for dispersal, including economic ones (Cohen, 1997). Diaspora can be used in a narrow sense to describe the bonds of affiliation that immigrants and their descendants have with their specific (parental) homelands, and the ways in which they negotiate their experience of the 'host-land'. Following this, the black African population in Britain can be subdivided into diaspora communities according to their respective countries of origin (e.g. Nigerian diaspora, Zimbabwean diaspora, etc.). This understanding of diasporic communities sits alongside the more encompassing notion of the African diaspora. According to Shepperson, frequently credited with coining the term, what unites black people outside of continental Africa is a shared ancestral homeland in Africa, forced removal or traumatic departure under slavery and later colonialism and experiences of marginalisation in current places of residence (1968, p. 152). Historically, the notion of Africa as an ancestral homeland has fostered bonds between continental Africans and black people in the diaspora, giving rise to complex relationships based on a sense of shared culture, history and politics (Butler, 2010). This has also had a powerful impact on creative practices. However, the main issues that emerge in conceptualising the African diaspora is that its 'members' do not all share a common ethnicity. Furthermore, their origins, time of dispersal, reasons for leaving and places of settlement vary enormously. The difference between a diaspora formed by slavery (the black Caribbean population), colonisation (immediate post-war African and Caribbean immigrants to the UK) and economic and political instability under majority black governments (African immigrants to the UK since the 1960s) and the meeting of these different diasporas who nevertheless find themselves housed under the same rubric raises interesting tensions.[2] These issues find representation in a number of African British plays as writers negotiate their place in Britain and in the theatre landscape in relation to both Britishness and black Britishness.

Pioneers

Before the 1990s there were, of course, African theatre practitioners working in British theatre in a number of roles. There is not the space to list their achievements here; however, some key practitioners are highlighted for contextual and mapping purposes. Playwrights based temporarily in Britain included Nigerian Wole Soyinka in the 1950s[3] and South Africans such as Alfred Hutchinson, Lewis Nkosi, Arthur (John) Maimane and John Matshikiza who lived in exile during apartheid (1948–1994).[4] A more permanent resident, Nigerian Yemi Ajibade, arrived in the UK in the 1960s and remained, working as an actor, director and playwright. Ajibade's plays set in England include *Parcel Post* [1976, Royal Court], about a bride who travels from Nigeria to London to meet her future husband for the first time and *A Long Way From Home* [1991, Tricycle], about a Nigerian 'Mafioso' who harbours illegal West African immigrants in his London nightclub during the late 1950s.[5] Temba Theatre Company, which means 'hope' in Zulu, was co-founded in 1972 by South African Alton Kumalo and Trinidadian Oscar James. (James then left the company to pursue an acting career).[6] The company was never exclusively African in its focus, although Kumalo did stage his own plays and programmed others by fellow South Africans.[7] When British-born Alby James (of Jamaican parentage) replaced Kumalo as artistic director in 1984, and until the company folded in 1992 after losing its Arts Council funding, the company presented two South African plays. These were a revival of Percy Mtwa, Mbongeni Ngema, and Barney Simon's *Woza Albert!* [1981] in 1986 and Mfundi Vundla's *A Visitor to the Veldt* in 1988. In fact, the 1980s witnessed a shift towards the consolidation of the Caribbean voice in black British theatre to which African theatre became more of an appendix than a vital part. This was reflected in the subject matter of the majority of black British plays produced at the time as well as in the programming choices of the main black theatre companies. During the 1980s and much of the 1990s, Black Theatre Co-operative/Nitro, Temba and Talawa, aimed to provide a repertoire which celebrated diverse black experiences; however, their programming choices reflected the heritage of the mainly Caribbean British management.[8]

Plays that engage with specific African countries and/or cultural practices by second-generation playwrights in the 1980s and 1990s are rare. For instance, Tunde Ikoli and Jackie Kay both had white British mothers and black Nigerian fathers. However, Ikoli was raised in foster care and Kay was adopted by a white Scottish couple. In *Chiaroscuro* [1986, Soho Poly], Kay explores the intersection of migration, gender and sexuality through four women, one of whom is of Nigerian origin. And, in *The Lower Depths: An East End Story* [1986, Tricycle], Ikoli adapts Maxim Gorky's play *The Lower Depths* [1902] by setting it in East London in a rooming house run by a Nigerian immigrant. However, reflecting their personal experiences, Nigeria is more remarkable for its absence than its presence in their work. In their own ways, both writers draw inspiration from black America in their examination of black/mixed-race Britishness; Kay (not unlike Mojisola Adebayo as seen in Chapter 3) through the influence of Audre Lorde and Ntozake Shange on her style and exploration of gender and sexuality, and Ikoli through his thematic exploration of black British urban experiences.

A number of key – mainly Nigerian – practitioners moved to the UK or came of age in the late 1980s and early 1990s. Their skillsets – which often crossed over into other areas – in education (e.g. Nigerian Rufus Orisayomi), writing (e.g. Nigerian Biyi Bandele), choreography (e.g. Ghanaian George Dzikunu and Nigerian Peter Badejo), music (e.g. British Nigerian Juwon Ogungbe), directing (e.g. British Nigerian Femi Elufowoju Jr.) and acting (e.g. Ghanaian/Sierra Leonean Patrice Naiambana), further helping African British theatre to gain a foothold. In particular, Femi Elufowoju Jr., who founded the theatre company Tiata Fahodzi has played a key role in the development of African British theatre, bridging its formative years in the 1990s to a position of greater visibility in the 2000s.[9]

Tiata Fahodzi was formed in 1997 by Elufowoju. The name is a mixture of Nigerian Yoruba and Ghanaian Twi and translates as 'theatre of the emancipated'. Alongside a few revivals, the company has championed new writing, fulfilling its aim to find a theatrical idiom through which to 'explore the workings of our African theatre tradition and find its compatibility with the British stage' (Elufowoju Jr. qtd in Cripps, 2005).[10] Their new writing platform, *Tiata Delights,* established in 2004, has also supported a range of African-origin writers whose plays have gone on to have full productions, including Ghanaian British Levi David Addai's *Oxford Street* [2008, Royal Court Theatre] and Nigerian British Lizzy Dijeh's *High Life* [2009, Hampstead Theatre]. If, as Brah argues, 'the concept of diaspora delineates a field of identification where "imagined communities" are forged within and out of a confluence of narratives from annals of collective memory and re-memory' (1996, p. 208), the performance of such plays forge and reinforce diasporic identity and culture by (re)connecting audiences with their (parental) homeland cultures. A case in point is Tiata Fahodzi's production of *The Gods Are Not To Blame* [1968] at the Arcola Theatre in 2005 which brought Yoruba rituals and cultural practices to the British stage also inspired Bola Agbaje to become a playwright: 'I was blown away by the performance and by the fact my culture was represented on stage and it wasn't watered down and there were no excuses, I just couldn't believe it' (Agbaje qtd in Fisher, 2012). The company subsequently produced Bola Agbaje's *Belong* [2012, Royal Court Theatre].[11] Tiata Fahodzi continues to play a key role in developing and bringing African British voices to the British stage.

First-generation

Dramas by first-generation playwrights produced since the 1990s need to be contextualised through the work that was produced by African playwrights in the pre-independence and immediate postcolonial period in Africa and the diaspora. For many of these writers a key objective was to find a way of working within an imposed European tradition of theatre and to make it their own. Although an autochthonous tradition was unachievable, numerous theatre practitioners have endeavoured to challenge, dismantle, and re-build Western notions of theatre in an 'African' image. Writers (a number of whom have been produced in the UK) such as Nigerians Wole Soyinka and Ola Rotimi, like their Caribbean and African American counterparts, drew on folk performance forms, language and mythology to shape and 'indigenise' their dramaturgy. In doing so, their work becomes an act of what Okagbue calls 'cultural affirmation', a way in which playwrights 'reclaim and recuperate the denigrated and emasculated cultural systems and practices of African and African-Caribbean peoples' (2009, p. 70). Postcolonial scholars have demonstrated how these techniques critique Eurocentric artistic assumptions, values and ideologies as acts of cultural resistance to (neo)colonialism (see, for example, Gilbert and Tompkins, 1996).

Despite the common denominator of being born in Africa, categorising first-generation African British playwrights in terms of their migratory histories is problematic. In addition to differences in approach to writing, their respective nationalities, ethnicities, ages and experiences shape their plays in different ways. Since the 1990s works by first-generation African playwrights staged in the UK continue to weave together African and Euro-American cultural strands; however, for some, particularly among younger playwrights, the motivation has shifted away from critiquing an imposed colonial culture. The difference in approach between Biyi Bandele-Thomas (often referred to as just Biyi Bandele) and Margaret Busby is a case in point. Bandele (b. 1967), a Nigerian-born poet, novelist and playwright, is the most high-profile first-generation African playwright to emerge in Britain in the 1990s. Plays by Bandele engage with his experience of growing up in post-independent Nigeria, marked by civil war, military dictatorship, corruption and the growing divide between the rich and poor as a legacy of the oil boom. His British début, *Rain; Marching for Fausa,* which is set in a fictional African country, explores and lampoons issues of government corruption, state brutality and censorship. As one reviewer noted, it elicited direct comparisons with Nigeria (Taylor, 1993). Subsequent plays set in Nigeria, including three adaptations, continue Bandele's satirical exposé of Nigerian society, centring around explorations of moral/spiritual and economic corruption.[12] Although Bandele engages with the political and social state of Nigeria, perhaps surprisingly, he does not contextualise this within the history of colonisation. Instead, he seems to place the blame on contemporary government greed, moral pollution and mismanagement. In contrast, Margaret Busby was born in Ghana (to a Ghanaian mother and Barbadian father) but educated in Britain. Although Busby has been living in England since long before the 1990s, it was in 1999 that she made her initial foray into writing for theatre. (She is most well known as Britain's first black woman publisher who co-founded the Allison and Busby publishing house in 1967 in London.) Despite Busby's works coming after Bandele's, they reflect an important distinction based on age and lived experience of an African country. Born in pre-independent Ghana and having spent a considerable time living in England, Busby's pieces are redolent of an anti-colonialist, Pan-Africanist approach. They aim to centre indigenous African performance traditions (e.g. *Sankofa* [1999, Connaught Theatre], a dance piece by Adzido Pan-African Dance Ensemble for which Busby provided and arranged the accompanying text), to recuperate events and people marginalised by Western historiography while drawing attention to African heroism (e.g. *Yaa Asantewaa – Warrior Queen* [2001, West Yorkshire Playhouse], also with Adzido), and to raise awareness of black peoples' historical experiences of suffering and trauma (e.g. *An African Cargo* [2007, Greenwich Theatre]).

The word *sankofa* translates from Twi (Ghana) as 'go back and fetch it' (Richards, 2007, p. 103). Sankofa is also the name given to an Asante mythic/ proverbial bird which flies forward while looking backwards. The notion of the Sankofa bird, often represented as looking backwards with an egg in its mouth, emphasises the value of past knowledge for posterity. It has become a diasporic symbol for communities attached to a literal or imagined homeland and metaphor which encapsulates an Afrocentric perspective that emphasises the importance of reclaiming one's historical and cultural roots (see Petty, 2008, pp. 16–51). It works, therefore, to describe first-generation writers who base most of their work in their homeland. This finds articulation in Busby's approach and identity. Despite living most of her life in England, Busby refuses the label English: 'I feel I am African – however long I have been here, I don't feel I am English' (Busby qtd in Roy, 2011). In contrast, Bandele's sense of self reveals a more fluid position. Having only moved to the UK in 1990, within a decade Bandele feels at home:

> I know London better than any other city in the world – including Lagos – and I know Brixton better than any other part of London. I really like it. It's a crazy place but I love the energy of it. There's a new coffee bar opening every fortnight, it's amazing. So that's home.
>
> *(qtd in Grimley, 1999)*

Although both Busby and Bandele write about the past, it is the way in which they approach it that is significant. Bandele's 1999 adaptation of Aphra Behn 1688 novella *Oroonoko: or, the Royal Slave* staged at The Other Place, Stratford-upon-Avon by the RSC, which deals with slavery, does not engage with issues of positive representation. As Wallace points out, Bandele 'situates his play neither in opposition to Behn's text nor as a corrective to her work' (2004, p. 266). In Behn's version, and later dramatic adaptations, such as Thomas Southerne's 1695 play of the same name, Oroonoko is portrayed as a 'noble savage', whose sale into slavery and eventual death is caused by white duplicity and greed. Bandele re-humanises Oroonoko, who, he feels, was written more as a symbol of anti-slavery than as a real person: 'I want to give the audience an idea of the complex society from which Oroonoko came, not some false nostalgia trip' (Bandele qtd in Cavendish, 1999). In Bandele's version, Oroonoko is not captured by white slavers but instead sold by the King of Coromantin's servant. Bandele describes Oroonoko not as a help-less and romanticised victim, but someone with his own flaws. For Bandele,

Oroonoko 'refuses to have an independent mind. That's what lands him into slavery' (qtd in Cavendish, 1999). Bandele's adaptation works against the notion of the noble savage by emphasising the weaknesses and mistakes of the Coromantins and of Oroonoko himself. As a result, Bandele's adaptation disrupts any automatic assumptions of postcolonial 'canonical counter-discourse' or 'writing back' (see Ashcroft, Griffiths and Tiffin, 1989) where one might expect to find them present.

The critical reception of plays set in Africa often reveals mainstream British assumptions of how certain African countries should be represented and the types of discourse writers 'should' be engaging with. For some British critics, the shift in focus away from the colonial past and consequent shift away from a British-centric perspective (regardless of whether Britain is negatively construed) seems difficult to accept. Billington's response to Bandele's *Marching for Fausa* praised the play's portrayal of 'the evils of dictatorship' but criticised its failure to address 'Western responsibility for African autocracy':

> Without doubting the play's documentary accuracy, I just wish it took a wider political perspective: it tells us nothing of the state's colonial history, current alliances or international standing. Bandele explores the symptoms of corruption and oppression without diagnosing their historical origins.
>
> *(Billington, 1993)*

But Billington misses Bandele's point, which is to stress agency. Speaking about his adaptation of *Oroonoko* and how he had chosen to focus on the culpability of the play's characters as opposed to seeking a polemic of blame, he states: 'I'm not interested in the philosophy of blaming someone else. I find that dishonest. It's important to say "I am the author of my destiny"' (qtd in Cavendish, 1999).

Younger first-generation African British dramatists are often less 'nativist' in their approach than the independence first-generation. This new wave tend not to draw attention to indigenous and Western practices in a dialectical way. Rather, they embrace the contradictions of specific contemporary African countries. They highlight their incongruities, frequently through comedy, without making an argument around indigenous/other. For Bandele, life in Nigeria is like living 'in a state of siege' where you have two choices: 'You either say it's crazy and retreat into a shell, or you just get into the thick of it and laugh' (qtd in Ehling, 2001, p. 94). For him, the absurd is 'a way of looking at life, at existence, that is itself full of pathos – and coming out grinning' (p. 94). Similar to Bandele's comedic approach, works by other first-generation practitioners such as Ghanaian/Sierra Leonean Patrice Naiambana's *The Man Who Committed Thought* [1999, Assembly Rooms, Edinburgh Fringe Festival], Zimbabwean/German/British Two Gents' *Vakomana Vaviri Ve Zimbabwe, or The Two Gentlemen of Verona* [2008, Oval House Theatre] and Zimbabwean/British Denton Chikura's *The Epic Adventure of Nhamo the Manyika Warrior and his Sexy Wife Chipo* prize irreverence. These works destabilise white and black Western assumptions of a monolithic Africa and challenge nostalgic Afrocentric imagery which predicates authenticity on traditional and indigenous – namely pre-colonial – cultural forms. The strong satiric, slapstick and absurd comedic vein and penchant for playing with the classics found in plays by a number of contemporary first-generation African writers is rarely found in plays by second-generation African British playwrights or non-African writers who write about Africa. These humorous plays contrast with the serious tone of white British representations of Africa and African touring productions, which often tend to present folkloric or negative images of Africa for Western consumption.[13] They also differ greatly in their representation from much of the heightened (non-specific) spirituality that finds representation in plays by a number of black British playwrights who invoke Africa in their work. These works disrupt stereotypical representations, intervening in the discourse and subscribing neither to the (at best) exotic and (at worst) primitivist visions of African countries and cultures that are frequently seen on the British stage.

1.5-generation

While older concepts of diaspora stress the desire to return to the homeland or play a part in its future, newer usages 'replace return with dense and continuous linkages across borders' (Faist, 2010, p. 12). In some cases, the terms 'first' and 'second' generation to group immigrants and their children respectively can be too rigid. Some black British playwrights, such as Arinze Kene who was born in Nigeria in 1987 but moved to the UK in 1991, might not have a strong memory of living in their natal land. For others, such as Inua Ellams who was born in Nigeria but moved to England aged 12 (and then to Ireland for three years and back to London), their lived experience in different countries has been highly formative. People who immigrated as children before their teens tend to be classified as first-generation immigrants; however, their experience of dual socialisation has led some sociologists to refer to them as the 1.5 generation.[14] The term 1.5 generation provides more flexibility to account for the different levels and patterns of acculturation and identification experienced by some immigrants (see Rumbaut and Rumbaut, 2005). Subtle differences between first, 1.5 and second-generation playwrights can be noted. Since the 1990s, the coming of age of a 1.5 generation whose engagement with themes of being from an African country and British and vice versa have brought refreshing perspectives to the Britishness debate.

There is a tradition of sending children back to African countries for a period of time to reconnect them with their parents' culture – see, for example, Ade Solanke's *Pandora's Box* [2012, Arcola Theatre]. There are also a small number of 1.5-generation African British theatre practitioners whose experience of migration moves in the opposite direction to the more typical example Ellams represents. (Ellams' plays are discussed in detail in the following chapter) Oladipo Agboluaje (b. 1968) and Femi Elufowoju Jr. (b. 1962) were born in the UK but moved to Nigeria with their parents when they were children and then re-located to Britain as young adults. Technically, they are second generation. Yet, in many ways the experiences of these playwrights aligns them more closely with first-generation writers. The lived experience of Nigeria is imprinted in their thematic and stylistic approach. Like first-generation playwrights, plays by these 1.5-generation writers incorporate a diversity of influences and owe a debt to Nigerian popular and high theatre. Soyinka's influence is visible particularly in Agboluaje's and Elufowoju Jr.'s adaptations of Western canonical texts. Following in the footsteps of African postcolonial dramatists, Agboluaje's adaptation of Brecht's *Mother Courage and her Children* [2004, Nottingham Playhouse], set in a fictional West African conflict zone, and Elufowoju Jr.'s *Macbeth*-inspired *Makinde* [2000, Oval House Theatre], re-situate the source texts within an African context. In doing so, these writers provoke a re-evaluation of these canonical texts from an African perspective. The use of comedy, especially slapstick, bawdy humour and satire, is a trait that is also shared by a number of first and 1.5 generation African British playwrights. Agboluaje acknowledges his debt to Nigerian popular theatre traditions stating: 'I grew up in the Nigerian tradition of satire, which is the main way in which writers attack the Establishment' (Luckie, 2007). Agboluaje's *The Estate* [2006, New Wolsey Theatre] and *Iyà-Ilé (The First Wife)* [2009, Soho Theatre][15], both produced by Tiata Fahodzi, are caustic portraits of the follies of all levels of Nigerian society. In-line with first-generation playwrights, these 1.5-generation writers exhibit a deep knowledge of Nigerian culture by incorporating a range of ethnically specific elements into their dramas. Different languages, cultural practices and beliefs are utilised to highlight character and situational nuances in a way that brings texture and depth to their representations. As British citizens, their relocation to the UK as adults is, in effect, a return 'home'. And, although citizenship and a sense of belonging are not necessarily coterminous, the holding of a passport does provide the individual with a sense of entitlement. This perhaps goes some way to explaining the confident and assertive African British idiom and acute diasporic consciousness that is a hallmark of their work. For instance, Agboluaje's *Early Morning* [2003, Oval House Theatre] is a satire about three Nigerian cleaners in a London office who plot to overthrow their white boss in a move to take over Britain and create a 'blackocracy'. Agboluaje fuses the African immigrant-in-Britain theme within a Nigerian comedic theatrical style that distinguishes the play from the treatment of similar themes by second-generation African British playwrights, such as Bola Agbaje's *Detaining Justice.*[16]

A number of these 1.5-generation African British playwrights could also be labelled 'Afropolitan'. The term describes the experiences of middle-class children of skilled migrants who left various African countries as part of a brain drain to the West following political disturbances and/or economic collapse. The term has gained in currency since Taiye Selasi's (2005) article in *The LIP Magazine* entitled 'Bye-Bye Babar'. Rejecting backward stereotypes of Africans peddled in US films such as *Coming to America* (to which the article's title refers), Selasi celebrates the coming of age of a new type of African immigrant who is successful, middle-class and cosmopolitan: 'Like so many African young people working and living in cities around the globe, they belong to no single geography, but feel at home in many' (2005). Unlike the first- and second-generation writers who tend to be more culturally aligned with their respective natal countries, these playwrights' works exhibit a high degree of cultural hybridity and are marked by their '*multi-locationality*' (Brah, 1996, p. 197).

Second-generation

Diaspora is a helpful concept for discussing how the cultural and geographic in-between-ness experienced by many immigrants and their children finds theatrical representation (see Griffin, 2003). However, although the concept of diaspora draws attention to the ways in which national boundaries are increasingly becoming eroded and is used as a trope to describe the subject's occupancy of multiple identities, diasporas are also paradoxically understood in terms of distinct communities. As Brubaker highlights, this notion of 'boundary-erosion' is at odds with diaspora as a concept which insists upon 'boundary maintenance' (2005, p. 6). Thus, 'diaspora can be seen as an *alternative* to the essentialization of belonging; but it can also represent a non-territorial *form* of essentialized belonging' (Brubaker, 2005, p. 12). A number of play-wrights works promote the values of holding on to one's culture. They also represent characters who resist acculturation and who persistently define peo-ple by perceived national traits and/or stereotypes. Maria Oshodi's *The S Bend* [1984, Royal Court Theatre], produced as part of the Young Writer' Festival, is significant as an example of a piece by a second-generation playwright of Nigerian heritage staged during the 1980s which explores cultural differences between people of African and Caribbean heritages in Britain. The Nigerian protagonist, Fola, is discouraged by her mother from associating with Carib-bean people who she sees as under-achievers and bad influences. Despite Fola's friendship with Claudette, who is of Caribbean origin, Fola perceives key cultural differences:

Fola: A high educational value in the African, and I guess a high material
        value in the West Indian, coupled with a lack of cultural identity.
                                                                (1986, p. 33)

Fola also holds the opinion that there is a power dynamic involved in friend-ships between people with African and Caribbean heritages. In her opinion, in order for such relationships to work, one culture must submit to the other:

Fola: one of the two has to make a sacrifice – sell out – and too often, in
        most cases, it's the African half [. . .] because African kids feel they are
        in the minority amongst blacks. Also there is a fear of being ridiculed
        by the majority of the black West Indian kids in this country.
                                                                     (p. 34)

In the end, determined to hold onto her cultural identity and values, Fola decides to return to Nigeria. The move, she hopes, will assist her to gain a stronger sense of self and to avoid 'the pressure of conflicting cultures' (p. 59) and 'a life torn by my submission to superficial cultural groups' (p. 60). Oshodi's play pre-empts themes that emerge in plays written in the 2000s of intra-racial conflict, the simplistic representation of good (studious) Africans and bad (materialistic) Caribbean people and the idea of the return to the homeland as an escape from negative Caribbean/black British influences.[17] In these plays, retaining one's culture is portrayed as a high priority amongst the Nigerian British community in particular. The practice of parents sending their children to Nigeria to be schooled is a way of minimising the cultural gap between Nigerian parents and British-born children. In *Gone Too Far!*, Agbaje hints at this practice. Unlike Yemi, the elder Ikudayisi has been schooled in Nigeria. As a result, he speaks Yoruba and is respectful of his elders. In contrast, the rebellious Yemi is told by his mother: 'You have no respect. It not your fault, it not your fault. It's my own, I have spoilt you too much. When I should have taken you to Nigeria, to boarding school, I let you stay here and now look at you' (2007, p. 6). The theme of sending children back to Africa for an education is explored in greater depth in Ade Solanke's début *Pandora's Box*. The play depicts a mother contemplating sending her son to school in Nigeria in order to dislocate him from the negative influence of his black British/African Caribbean peers. These plays suggest a growing concern among the British-Nigerian population in reaction to what is represented as an environment that is failing the upbringing and education of its youth, particularly young black men.

The tension between generations in families which have become increasingly fragmented by diasporisation highlights the strain on traditional lifestyles wrought by globalising processes. Janice Okoh's *Egusi Soup* [2012, Mumford Theatre], set in London, dramatises this conflict within a Nigerian British family. Mrs Anyia and her two daughters are preparing to return to Nigeria for the anniversary of their father's death. Conflict arises when Anne, the prodigal daughter, returns from living in New York and is unwilling to accept certain gender roles tradition demands. The theme of family fragmentation and loss of traditional values is underlined in the play's title, which refers to a Nigerian dish which has no fixed ingredients but is made up of whatever foods are available at the time. In this way, such African British plays written in the twenty-first century echo and extend African plays by the independence generation writing in the 1960s which examined the impact of colonisation and urbanisation on the traditional way of life by bringing a transnational experience to bear on the discussion of cultural and national identity.[18]

Second-generation African British plays since the 2000s also echo earlier works by Caribbean British writers who treated similar themes of migration and intergenerational culture clashes between immigrant parents and British-born children. For some writers, the source of generational conflict stems from the rigid views of the parent-generation versus the more cosmopolitan, liberal outlook of the British-born children. Levi David Addai's *House of Agnes* [2008, Oval House Theatre] typifies the culture clash between British-born children and their African-born parents. The play, with its titular tongue-in-cheek reference to Lorca's *The House of Bernarda Alba* [1945], is about a matriarch named Agnes who, after forty years in the UK, is moving back to her native Ghana. Before she leaves her house in her sons' care, she needs them to prove they are ready for the responsibility. However, when her eldest son Sol refuses to end his relationship with girlfriend Davina, who Agnes despises because she is of African Caribbean heritage, and she discovers that her younger son Caleb is having a secret relationship with a white woman and has lied about having a well-paid city job, Agnes decides not to return to Ghana.[19] The matriarchal Agnes is a symbol of tradition personified as conservative and immutable. The play's ending, with Agnes refusing to leave, ultimately points to an irreconcilable difference between the generations.

Improvements in transport and communication technologies have rendered migration since the 1990s less decisive than it was in the 1950s. African British dramas reveal less of an insistence upon British belonging than do plays by Caribbean-origin dramatists writing in the latter half of the twentieth century. Instead, the idiosyncrasies, pleasures and pains of occupying dual or multiple diasporic spaces are increasingly articulated. Contemporary second-generation African British playwrights include Bola Agbaje, Levi David Addai, Lizzy Dijeh, Arinze Kene, Ade Solanke, and Janice Okoh (all of whom except Addai (Ghana) are of Nigerian origin).[20] Plays by these writers reflect the complex cultural zone in which the second-generation are positioned. Kene encapsulates this experience of dual belonging: 'At home, I'm very Nigerian. You'll hear Nigerian music, my parents speak in Igbo, my mum's got her wrap on and cooks Nigerian food. Then I leave the house and I'm Arinze, the British kid' (qtd in Costa, 2013).

Addai's *Oxford Street* [2008, Royal Court Theatre] explores the intersecting themes of migration and multiculturalism. It presents a microcosm of contemporary London and its complex web of people of different cultures, creeds, and races. The play features characters from a range of nationalities and ethnicities (African, Caribbean, Brazilian, Polish, Bangladeshi, first- and second-generation immigrants) working together in a shop over the Christmas period. According to Dominic Cooke, then artistic director of the Royal Court, 'Levi's play [. . .] is the first I've read that nails down precisely the multicultural, multinational world of London right now: there's only one white British character in a cast of 10' (qtd in Billington, 2007). All of the characters, except the manager Steph from Essex, are working in the shop on a temporary basis with their eye on a better job. The play, a contemporary Dick Wittington-esque tale about dreams and their inevitable compromise, echoes Agbaje's *Detaining Justice* in its exploration of immigrants struggling to improve their lives. The promise of a better life emerges in works which explore social mobility or migration from the 'ghetto', such as Agbaje's *Off the Endz*, Arinze Kene's *Estate Walls* [2010, Oval House Theatre] and his *Little Baby Jesus* [2011, Oval House Theatre] which all depict African-origin characters struggling to escape the confines of inner-city London. In these urban dramas the theme of first- and second-generation culture clash is given a new twist as youth of African heritage come into contact with second- and third-generation peers who are of Caribbean origin.

Without the lived experience of two different nations, second-generation playwrights tend to set their plays in the UK; however, positioned between their parents' and British culture, their work is no less defined by (at least) two different cultural spaces. Virtually all of their plays privilege African and African-origin characters and the playwrights explore themes pertinent to their respective ethnic communities living in Britain. Kene attributes the structure of his plays, particularly leaving their endings unresolved, to Nigerian folklore and myths (qtd in Costa, 2013). Second-generation African British plays also primarily focus on the experience of being black in Britain and of African (usually Nigerian) heritage, or themes pertinent to the African immigrant community. However, in some cases these playwrights don't write African-origin characters. Their ability to write convincing characters of various ages and ethnicities reveals how the second-generation occupy a position between, and knowledge of, multiple cultures.

On the one hand, the second-generation experience of growing up as both African and British is a unique selling point. Their plays bring a fresh perspective to similar themes which have already been explored by Caribbean-origin playwrights, as well as providing documentation of new social trends shaping contemporary Britain. On the other hand, there is a dominance of urban representations in plays by this contemporary second-generation. This may, in part, be due to writers being shaped by white-run mainstream organisations and the kinds of 'black' theatre they perceive as relevant and saleable (see Goddard, 2015, pp. 11–13). Arinze Kene has observed:

> A lot of writers like myself – young, from London – write ourselves into a corner. We write what is expected of us, and often what's expected is knife-crime stories . . . I can speak from experience and say that it's easier to be listened to, to get your work on stage, if you depict the same old shit.
>
> *(qtd in Costa, 2013)*

Arguably, this is compounded by emerging African British writers reacting to the precedent of what 'sells', established by the success of writers such as Roy Williams and Kwame Kwei-Armah. Addai, Agbaje and Kene (all members of the Royal Court's Young Writers' Programme) emerged at a time when black plays being produced in the mainstream were dominated by themes about youth (particularly from the male experience), violence, crime, poverty, drugs, teenage pregnancy, and the 'underclass' written in a predominantly social-realist mode. Addai's *93.2 FM* [2006, Royal Court], about two South London community radio DJs, and his *Oxford Street*; Agbaje's *Gone Too Far!* and *Off the Endz*, all staged at the Royal Court, fit into this urban 'tradition'. Notably, their other plays which do not explore such gritty themes have been produced at different venues, such as Addai's *House of Agnes* (staged at the more community-orientated Oval House Theatre) and Agbaje's *Detaining Justice* (staged at the politically aware Tricycle Theatre). Second-generation African British playwrights, therefore, occupy a complex position located within an established mainstream and black British theatre tradition as well as within a second-generation African immigrant context which exerts its own specific set of influences on the content and style of their work.

As black playwrights in the UK, their work also interfaces with black British modes and discourses established by the dominant British-Caribbean second-generation who emerged in the 1980 and 1990s. Second-generation African British playwrights share similar traits with second-generation Caribbean British writers such as Winsome Pinnock, Kwame Kwei-Armah, and Roy Williams. Themes exploring the complexities of navigating a dual culture and identity are typical of second-generation plays regardless of specific ethnic heritages. Growing up in the 1980s and 1990s, Agbaje states:

> I didn't know if I was African or British. In England I was called African, in Nigeria a black girl with an English accent I was called British [*sic*] and when I returned to England with an African accent I was called African. I was so confused for a very long time.
>
> *(2010)*

Her words mirror Kwei-Armah's experience of growing up in London during the 1970s and 1980s. The shared sense of disequilibrium engendered by a state of un-belonging manifests itself in the work of both second-generation playwrights. However, the time at which they grew up has shaped their response to this identity crisis in different ways. Kwei-Armah's reaction is

typical of the second-generation of black Britons (predominantly of Caribbean origin) who were the first substantial group of black people who could
claim to be British through birthright and who came of age at a time in
Britain when racism was particularly virulent. For this cohort, their experience of racially motivated marginalisation from a national identity, coupled
with the difficulty they had in identifying with their parents' backgrounds,
combined to produce a profound sense of alienation. In reaction, this generation pursued a two-pronged yet interrelated approach: the exploration
and creation of an alternate cultural system which drew on the histories
and traditions from Africa and the black diaspora, and an assertion of their
Britishness achieved by dismantling and reconfiguring in their image what
being British signified.

New African arrivals since the 1990s, and their children who reached
adulthood in the early 2000s, confront the established black population in
Britain. This sector has its own history of race- and class-based oppression
that dates back to the 1950s and 1960s, and which has resulted in the formation of specific modes of social and cultural expression. Brah's notion of
'diaspora space' (1996, p. 205) emphasises the reciprocal relationship between
those who migrated to a place and those already there:

> In the diaspora space called 'England', for example, African Carib-
> bean, Irish, Asian, Jewish and other diasporas intersect among them-
> selves as well as with the entity constructed as 'Englishness', thoroughly
> re-inscribing it in the process.
>
> *(pp. 205–206)*

In this 'diaspora space' new black African arrivals also re-define notions
of black Britishness. The ways in which Englishness is constructed and
represented has evolved. The younger black playwrights in Britain have
reaped the benefits of previous generations' struggle for inclusion. Writing in the twenty-first century, African British playwrights' expressions
of identity are often refracted through multicultural discourses of difference as opposed to being underwritten by a sense of communal exclusion
based on racial grounds. Their plays are less concerned with challenging
the notion of a white and homogenous British identity. In many ways
they take their Britishness (or not) for granted and are more concerned
with highlighting issues specific to youth in contemporary multicultural
Britain.

Notes

1 The majority of African-born UK residents from South Africa identified as white/white British. Those from Kenya, Uganda and Tanzania identified as Asian/ Asian British and mainly arrived before 1981 (Office for National Statistics, 2015, pp. 7–9).

2 For a critique of how the conceptualisation of the African diaspora has been dominated by African American Atlantic discourses with specific reference to Gilroy's *The Black Atlantic*, see Zeleza (2005).

3 Soyinka came to England to study at Leeds university and then worked for a period as a play reader at the Royal Court in the late 1950s. During this time his play *The Swamp Dwellers* premiered as part of the University of London Drama Festival in 1958 and in 1959 *The Invention*, about apartheid in South Africa, was performed at the Royal Court'. Other productions of Soyinka's plays in the UK include the world premiere of *The Road* [1965, Theatre Royal Stratford East]; *The Trials of Brother Jero* [1960] in 1965/6 in Cambridge and Hampstead; *The Lion and the Jewel* [1959] in 1966 at the Royal Court; *The Strong Breed* [1964] in 1968 at the Mercury Theatre; the world premiere of *The Bacchae of Euripides* [1973, National Theatre]; *Before the Blackout* [1965] in 1981 in Leeds; the world premiere of *The Beatification of Area boy: A Lagosian Kaleidoscope* [1995, West Yorkshire Playhouse]; and *Death and the King's Horseman*, which received its UK premiere in Manchester in 1990 and was staged again at the National Theatre in 2009.

4 Plays by these South Africans staged in the UK arguably contributed to the transnational anti-Apartheid movement that campaigned for political change in South Africa. Lewis Nkosi's 1967 television play *Malcolm* was staged under the title *Virgin Malcolm Look Not So Pale: A Play* in 1970 at the ICA and *Rhythm of Violence* [1961] was produced by Temba in 1974. Arthur (John) Maimane's *The Prosecution* was staged in 1972 at the Bush Theatre (as a double bill with Nkosi's *Malcolm*). John Matshikiza's *Prophets in the Black Sky* was staged in 1985 at the Drill Hall and *In the Paddington Style* in 1988 at Soho Poly.

5 Plays by Ajibade not set in the UK include *Fingers Only* [1982, The Factory] – originally titled *Lagos, Yes Lagos* and first broadcast on radio in 1971 by the BBC African Service – and *Waiting for Hannibal* [1986, Drill Hall].

6 Kumalo came to the UK as a member of the cast of the township musical *King Kong* [1959] which played at London's Princess Theatre in the West End in 1961. He studied at Rose Bruford and then joined the Royal Shakespeare Company in 1968.

7 South African plays staged by Temba under Kumalo include his own piece *Temba* [1972, Young Vic], Lewis Nkosi's *Rhythm of Violence*, Athol Fugard's *No-Good Friday* and *Nongogo* [1958] in 1974 at the Sheffield Crucible, *Mister Biko* [1979, Roundhouse], by Andrew Carr, Alton Kumalo and Peter Rodda, and *Teresa* [1979, Cockpit Theatre] by Kumalo.

8 During the 1980s and 1990s Nitro (previously Black Theatre Co-operative) produced two plays about/set in Africa: Yemi Ajibade's *Fingers Only* in 1982 and *Waiting for Hannibal* in 1986. Talawa produced three: Ola Rotimi's *The God's are not to Blame* in 1989, Soyinka's *The Road* in 1992 and Biyi Bandele's *Resurrections in the Season of the Longest Drought* in 1994.

9 Collective Artistes, founded by African American Chuck Mike in Nigeria in 1988 and in the UK in 2002, has brought a number of plays exploring the Nigerian

experience to the British stage. While still based in Nigeria Collective Artistes co-produced Biyi Bandele's adaptation of Chinua Achebe's 1958 novel, *Things Fall Apart* [1997, West Yorkshire Playhouse and Royal Court] with the West Yorkshire Playhouse and the National Theatre Studio for the London International Festival of Theatre (LIFT). Since being based in the UK, productions of plays by African writers include Bandele's adaptation of Lorca's *Yerma* [2001, Edinburgh Fringe Festival]; *Sense of Belonging (The Tale of Ikpiko)* [2002, Arcola], about female genital mutilation in Nigeria and devised by Chuck Mike and the company; Femi Osofisan's adaptation of Euripides' *Trojan Women* called *Women of Owu* [2003] in 2004 at Chipping Norton Theatre and Oval House; Soyinka's *The Lion and the Jewel* [1959] at the Oxford Playhouse and Barbican Pit in 2005. The company's latest play *Zhe [noun]: Undefined* [2012, Soho Theatre], written by Mike and actors Antonia Kemi Coker and Tonderai Munyevu, blends the performers' life stories, exploring the malleability of gender identity and sexuality.

10 Tiata Fahodzi's first two productions were devised pieces that examined West African immigrants' experiences in Britain: *Tickets and Ties* [1997, Theatre Royal Stratford East] and *Booked!* [1998, Oval House]. Other plays by Tiata Fahodzi not mentioned in the body of this chapter include Adewale Ajadi's *Abyssinia* [2001, Southwark Playhouse], Roy Williams' *Joe Guy* [2007, New Wolsey Theatre] and a revival of Joe Penhall's award-winning *Blue/Orange* [2000] in 2010 at the Arcola Theatre.

11 When Elufowoju stepped down as Artistic Director of Tiata Fahodzi in 2010 he was succeeded by actor/playwright Lucian Msamati who ran the company until 2014. Msamati was born in the UK to Tanzanian parents but grew up in Zimbabwe. His programming clearly reflected his Southern African experience and marked the company's shift from favouring the West African/Nigerian British experience by programming *The epic adventure of Nhamo the Manyika warrior and his sexy wife Chipo* by Zimbabwean-born London-based writer Denton Chikura followed by *Boi Boi is Dead* [2015, West Yorkshire Playhouse] by Zimbabwean-born Leeds-based writer, Zodwa Nyoni.

12 Bandele's works set in Nigeria include *Resurrections in the Season of the Longest Drought* [1994, Cochrane], *Two Horsemen* [1994, The Gate], *Death Catches the Hunter* [1995, Battersea Arts Centre], *Me and the Boys* [1995, Finborough] and *Thieves Like Us* [1998, Southwark Playhouse]. Bandele has written adaptations of Achebe's *Things Fall Apart*; Aphra Behn's *Oroonoko* and Lorca's *Yerma*. Plays set in England include *Happy Birthday, Mister Deka D* [1999, Traverse, Edinburgh] for Told by an Idiot; and *Brixton Stories* [2001, Tricycle Theatre], a part adaptation of his 1999 novel *The Street*, which explores themes of death and exile set against the backdrop of multicultural Brixton.

13 Examples in the 2000s of representations of African countries defined by corruption, dictatorship, war, famine and disease, include Out of Joint's production of American J. T Rogers' *The Overwhelming* [2006, National Theatre], about the Rwandan genocide; Dominic Cook's staging of Shakespeare's *Pericles* for the RSC [2006, the Swan, Stratford-upon-Avon], set in an un-named war-torn African country; David Farr's staging of Brecht's *The Resistible Rise of Arturo Ui* [2008, Lyric Hammersmith], set in an un-named African state; Matt Charman's *The Observer* [2009, National Theatre], about Western observers in a fictional West African country during elections; Moira Buffini's *Welcome to Thebes* [2010, National Theatre], which explores a post-war African state's relationship with the West; and Out

of Joint's production of Stella Feehily's *Bang Bang Bang* [2011, Octagon Theatre], about NGO workers in the Democratic Republic of the Congo.

14 Generational cohorts can be complicated even further - for instance 1.25, 1.75 and 2.5 – depending on when during childhood immigration occurred or the number of immigrant parents a child has.

15 *Iyà-Ilé* won the Alfred Fagon Award for black British playwrights in 2009 and was nominated for a Laurence Olivier Award.

16 Plays by Agboluaje set in the UK, include *The Christ of Coldharbour Lane* [2007, Soho Theatre], which imagines the Second Coming occurring in Brixton with a Nigerian immigrant, Omo, as the son of God, and *The Hounding of David Oluwale* [2009, West Yorkshire Playhouse].

17 Oshodi is London-born and mixed-race (Nigerian father). Oshodi's plays include *From Choices to Chocolate* [1986, Riverside Studios], *Blood, Sweat and Fears* [1988, Battersea Arts Centre], *Here Comes a Candle* [1989, Oval House] and *Hound* [1992, Oval House Theatre].

18 See, for example, Obi Egbuna's 1966 play, *Wind versus Polygamy* (adapted from his novel of the same title), a comedy about a polygamous African chief which explores the theme of modern versus traditional African values.

19 The theme of love across the African and Caribbean 'divide' is also represented in Femi Oguns' début, *Torn* [2008, Arcola Theatre].

20 Arinze Kene was born in Nigeria in 1987 but moved to the UK in 1991 where he grew up in Hackney, London. Technically he is first-generation, but it is more helpful to see him as second-generation. (The same taxonomy may be applied to Caryl Phillips for example.)

Works cited

Agbaje, B. 2007. *Gone too far!* London: Methuen.

———. 2010. *Biography*. [Online]. Available from: http://bolaagbaje.com/bio.php

Ashcroft, B., Griffiths, G., and Tiffin, H. 1989. *The Empire writes back: Theory and practice in post-colonial literatures*. London: Routledge.

Barou, J., Aigner, P., and Mbenga, B. 2012. African migration in its national and global context. In: Attias-Donfut, C., Cook, J., Hoffman, J., and Waite, L. eds., *Citizenship, belonging and intergenerational relations in African migration*. Basingstoke, UK: Palgrave Macmillan, pp. 12–39.

Billington, M. 1993. Marching for Fausa. *The Guardian*. 15 January. p. 8.

———. 2007. 'You can sniff the best plays after half a page': If you want the freshest new writing, you have to look away from the mainstream, Dominic Cooke tells Michael Billington after a year as Royal Court director. *The Guardian*. 7 November. p. 28. [Accessed 9 December 2011]. Available from: https://www.theguardian.com/stage/2007/nov/07/theatre2.

Bosveld, K., and Connolly, H. 2006. Population. In: Dobbs, J., Green, H., and Zealey, L. eds., *Focus on: Ethnicity and religion*. Basingstoke, UK: Palgrave Macmillan, pp. 19–40. The ONS: http://www.ons.gov.uk/ons/rel/ethnicity/focus-on-ethnicity-and-religion/2006-edition/index.html

Brah, A. 1996. *Cartographies of diaspora: Contesting identities*. London: Routledge.

Brubaker, R. 2005. The 'diaspora' diaspora. *Ethnic and Racial Studies*. 28(1), pp. 1–19.

Butler, K. 2010. Clio and the griot: The African diaspora in the discipline of history. In: Olaniyan, T., and Sweet, J. H. eds., *The African diaspora and the disciplines.* Bloomington: Indiana University Press, pp. 21–52.

Cavendish, D. 1999. Oroonoko lives again. *The Independent.* 24 March. p. 11.

Chikura, D. 2013. *The epic adventure of Nhamo the Manyika warrior and his sexy wife Chipo.* London: Bloomsbury.

Cohen, R. 1997. *Global diasporas: An introduction.* London: UCL Press.

———. 2015. Seeds, roots, rhizomes and epiphytes: Botany and diaspora. In: Sigona, N., Gamlen, A., Liberatore, G., and Kringelback, H. N. eds., *Diasporas reimagined: Spaces, practices and belonging.* [Online]. Oxford: Oxford Diasporas Programme, pp. 2–7. [Accessed 23 October 2016]. Available from: http://www.migration. ox.ac.uk/odp/Diasporas Reimagined full book low res.pdf

Costa, M. 2013. Arinze Kene: 'At home, I'm Nigerian. *I go out and I'm a British kid'.* [Accessed 4 March 2016]. Available from: http://www.theguardian.com/ stage/2013/feb/25/arinze-kene-gods-property

Cripps, C. 2005. Authentic rhythms of Africa: The gods are not to blame. *The Independent.* 26 May. p. 49.

Ehling, H. 2001. Coming out grinning. In: Ehling, H., and Holste-von Mutius, C.-P. eds., *No condition is permanent: Nigerian writing and the struggle for democracy.* Amsterdam: Rodopi, pp. 91–97.

Faist, T. 2010. Diaspora and transnationalism: What kind of dance partners? In: Bauböck, R., and Faist, T. eds., *Diaspora and transnationalism: Concepts, theories and methods.* Amsterdam: Amsterdam University Press, pp. 9–34.

Fisher, G. 2012. Bola Agbaje, belong. *Afridiziak.* [Online]. 12 April. [Accessed 14 March 2013]. Available from: http://www.afridiziak.com/theatrenews/interviews/april2012/bola-agbaje-belong.html

Gilbert, H., and Tompkins, J. 1996. *Post-colonial drama: Theory, practice, politics.* London: Routledge.

Goddard, L. 2015. *Contemporary black British playwrights: Margins to mainstream.* Basingstoke, UK: Palgrave Macmillan.

Griffin, G. 2003. *Contemporary black and Asian women playwrights in Britain.* Cambridge: Cambridge University Press.

Grimley, T. 1999. Biyi is at home in many forms – and in Brixton. *Birmingham Post.* 27 April. p. 15.

Luckie, S. 2007. Playwright Oladipo Agboluaje on his new plays. *Theatre Voice.* [online radio]. Available from: http://www.theatrevoice.com/2175/black-voicesoladipo-agboluaje-the-playwright-talks-to-stev/

Office for National Statistics. 2012. Ethnicity and national identity in England and Wales 2011. [Online]. [Accessed 24 February 2016]. Available from: http://www.ons. gov.uk/ons/rel/census/2011-census/key-statistics-for-local-authorities-in-englandand-wales/rpt-ethnicity.html-tab-Changing-picture-of-ethnicity-over-time

———. 2015. 2011 census analysis: Ethnicity and religion of the non-UK born population in England and Wales. [Online]. [Accessed 24 February 2016]. Available from: https://www.ons.gov.uk/peoplepopulationandcommunity/culturalidentity/

ethnicity/articles/2011censusanalysisethnicityandreligionofthenonukbornpopulati
oninenglandandwales/2015-06-18

Okagbue, O. 2009. *Culture and identity in African and Caribbean theatre.* London: Adonis & Abbey.

Oshodi, M. 1986. The 'S' bend. In: Sulkin, D. ed., *Festival plays.* London: Longman, pp. 1–60.

Owen, D. 2009. African migration to the UK. [PowerPoint presentation]. African transnational and return migration conference, 29–30 June, Warwick. [Accessed 8 December 2011]. Available from: http://www2.warwick.ac.uk/fac/soc/crer/events/african/conference_paper/

Petty, S. 2008. *Contact zones: Memory, origin, and discourses in black diasporic cinema.* Detroit, MI: Wayne State University Press.

Richards,S. 2007. What is to be remembered? Tourism to Ghana's slave castle-dungeons. In: Reinelt, J. G., and Roach, J. R. eds., *Critical theory and performance.* Ann Arbor: University of Michigan Press, pp. 85–107.

Roy, A. 2011. Eye on England: Black & white. *The Telegraph, India.* 24 July. Available from: http://www.telegraphindia.com/1110724/jsp/7days/story_14280403.jsp

Rumbaut, R. D., and Rumbaut, R. G. 2005. Self and circumstance: Journeys and visions of exile. In: Rose, P. I. ed., *The dispossessed: An anatomy of exile.* Amherst: University of Massachusetts Press, pp. 331–343.

Safran, W. 1991. Diasporas in modern societies: Myths of homeland and return. *Diaspora.* 1(1), pp. 83–99.

Selasi, T. 2005. Bye-Bye Babar. *The LIP.* [Online]. 3 March. [Accessed 9 March 2016]. Available from: http://thelip.robertsharp.co.uk/?p=76

Shepperson, G. 1968. The African abroad or the African diaspora. In: Ranger, T. O. ed., *Emerging themes of African history: Proceedings of the International Congress of African Historians held at University College, Dar es Salaam, October 1965.* Nairobi: East African Publishing House, pp. 152–176.

Taylor, P. 1993. Cross-currents of darkness. *The Independent.* [Online]. 16 January. [Accessed 20 February 2011]. Available from: http://www.independent.co.uk/arts-entertainment/theatre-cross-currents-of-darkness-paul-taylor-on-marching-for-fausa-at-the-royal-court-and-heart-at-1478882.html

Wallace, E. K. 2004. Transnationalism and performance in Biyi Bandele's 'Oroonoko'. *PMLA.* 119(2), pp. 265–281.

Zeleza, P. T. 2005. Rewriting the African diaspora: Beyond the black Atlantic. *African Affairs.* 104(414), pp. 35–68. Available from: http://www.jstor.org/stable/3518632

8

MULTIPLE PERSONALITY DIASPORIC DISORDER

Inua Ellams' *The 14th Tale* and *Untitled*

Inua Ellams (b. 1984) is a poet, playwright, performer and graphic artist. He has lived in Nigeria, where he was born, and in Ireland and England. Because Ellams left Nigeria as an adolescent he can be described as being a '1.5 generation' Nigerian British immigrant (see previous chapter). The complex homeland/host-land relationship resulting from Ellams growing up in three different countries during his formative years have resulted in an acute sense of in-between-ness. The author's personal experience of migration and the diasporic condition focuses the thematic enquiry of his plays and are also evident at the level of writing and performance. His poetic writing is informed by a diverse range of influences, from hip-hop to the Romantic poets - he cites Mos Def and John Keats in particular as inspirations (Dent, 2008) – and his approach to performance draws on and combines Nigerian storytelling and performance poetry styles. This chapter highlights how *The 14th Tale* [2009, Arcola Theatre] and *Untitled* [2010, Bristol Old Vic], both written and performed by Ellams, intervene in existing black British dramatic representations through Ellams' exploration of the middle-class Afropolitan self. In turn, this raises questions regarding the ways in which contemporary African British playwrights position themselves in relation to established second-generation black British culture and dramatic traditions.

Ellams' first play, *The 14th Tale* (2009), recounts his early years spent in Nigeria and subsequent move with his family to the UK as a young boy.

It describes his journey and transformation across national spaces and over time, and performs the evolution of the self from boy to man, Nigerian to Nigerian British. After opening at the Arcola, *The 14th Tale* played at the Edinburgh Fringe Festival where it was awarded a Fringe First.[1] It later transferred to the National Theatre's Cottesloe theatre. For the National Theatre production, directed by Thierry Lawson, Ellams performed on an empty stage with a single chair set against a backdrop of jumbled black and white images drawn by Ellams in his clip art style: a mobile phone, an elephant, a British hospital sign, a calabash. Each picture on the strip of paper signifies a particular moment in the narrative, coming into focus when Ellams refers to it during the performance. Dressed in neutral clothes (t-shirt and trousers) against a virtually bare stage, Ellams creates images through voice and physicality.

The play begins in a British hospital where Ellams has just learnt that his father has had a stroke. The event provides the catalyst for his reminiscences of his life. The narrative flashes back to Ellams' birth and continues chronologically through five 'chapters' of his life, briefly returning to the hospital waiting room between sections. In the final section, we return to the present of the hospital waiting room. The narrative then moves forward in time as Ellams recounts the time spent with his father until his death. The five sections of the play (divided into chapters in the text) explore the following key moments:

1) Birth and early childhood in Nigeria.
2) Attending boarding school in Nigeria.
3) Moving to London when he is twelve and his school experiences.
4) Moving to Dublin when he is in his mid-teens; his school experiences there, his return to London and first experiences with girls.
5) At the hospital and the time spent with his father until his father's death

Although autobiographical, the piece is constructed as a dramatic story with flashbacks, a journey, obstacles, a crisis and a resolution. The events described in the play are 'true'; however, its dramatic construction blurs the boundaries between autobiography and story, rendering it more of, as its title suggests, a coming of age tale.

The 14th Tale describes Ellams' rite of passage from prankster to responsible adult. Ellams presents his impish nature as a hereditary trait passed through the male-line in his family. In doing so, he affirms his roots. Both his father and grandfather had reputations for being scoundrels and Ellams introduces himself as the next in 'a line of ash skinned Africans, born with clenched fists and a natural thirst for battle, only quenched by breast milk' (p. 7). Each time he gets into trouble his father reminds him that he will grow out of his naughtiness. His father's advice, 'there's a vague order to things, things happen when they are meant to, don't worry, your time will come' (p. 10) are repeated throughout the piece. When his father passes away, the play ends with a sense that his father's death is both an end and a beginning. It is this event which signals the end of Ellams' youth and the beginning of his adulthood. Similarly, as he takes on his new role, the space is left open for the next in line to inherit the family trickster role: 'I wonder when this story will reach my son and wonder more what he will do' (pp. 28–29).

By presenting his younger self as naughty, Ellams casts himself in the role of the trickster. Stories that feature trickster characters are found in societies throughout the world. Nigerian trickster stories present the trickster (often in animal but sometimes human or spirit form) as a rule-breaker whose mischief-making provides an entertaining yet moral lesson (see Pelton, 1980). Ellams' identification with the trickster underlines his 'Nigerianness'. The trickster stories also provide Ellams with a dramaturgical model. By establishing at the beginning of the play that he comes from a long line of tricksters, Ellams lends a mythic quality to his 'tale' redolent of the 'once-upon-a-time' beginning characteristic of Western folk tales. His journey, characterised by wayward exploits, ingeniously trickery, foolish methods of extricating himself from sticky situations, and crude humour imbue his 'self' character and narrative with the creative mischief and picaresque style which defines many trickster stories.

The 14th Tale charts Ellams' transformation into an adult but also into a diasporan. The moral function of trickster tales renders them conservative by nature. They are designed to strengthen community cohesion. The cyclical ending with Ellams growing up and out of his naughtiness and wondering how his son will assume the mantle suggests the fulfilment of his father's mantra regarding the natural order of things. Yet, by the end of the play, having witnessed the changes experienced by the protagonist, the desire for a neat ending that loops back to the start comes across more as an expression of hope than fact. The journey into his past as he waits in the hospital is typical of the homeward looking aspect of the diasporic condition. Through its use of flashbacks, the play reflects the workings of memory in its structure. In the play Ellams takes the audience back to his past and his Nigerian roots even while this slips away from him, symbolised by his father's failing health. There is a tension created through looking backwards, as Ellams reflects on and represents his past, and the growing up narrative which pushes time forward. Thus, we witness Ellams' transformation in time and in culture, the processes which have severed him from his roots even while he seeks to reclaim them. This ambivalence encapsulates the liminality of diasporic identity: feeling simultaneously 'of there' and 'of here' and 'of neither' of those places.

The evolution of the diasporic self is forged across national landscapes. The space given to his childhood years in Nigeria and the friendships he made underlines how formative the time spent in Nigeria was. The representations of his life experiences in Nigeria provides a counter-balance to his experiences in Ireland and England. They enable him to represent and therefore demonstrate his Nigerianness to the audience and provide the context and foundation for the process of cultural amalgamation he experiences on leaving:

> I left the green of Ireland singed with Celtic fire and
> a mismatched accent: the straight speak of Africans,
> stiff lip cockney and the thrust of Southern Dublin,
> arrived in London more scatterbrained than ever!
>
> *(p. 22)*

The sense of being scattered, which recalls the Greek meaning of the term diaspora (scattering of seeds), becomes embodied though his accent and the way in which he articulates himself. This hybrid identity is echoed in the bricolage of images on the piece of paper hanging above the stage. They signify a visual map of the multiple cultures that have defined his life experiences and act as a mnemonic for the story as it is told. The traces of different cultures and lands are also embodied in Ellams' performance. Through re-enactment, Ellams performs himself at different stages of his development. Through changes in physicality, vocal pitch and accent, we witness a personal transformation from boy to man and from Nigerian to Nigerian British. His journey provides him with multiple cultural strands which he knits together to fashion a unique diasporic identity characterised by in-between-ness. Having lived in Nigeria, England and Ireland he imitates the different accents to comic effect. Similarly, his lived experience and cultural knowledge as someone of the 1.5 generation is fed into his language. Surprising word combinations render unusual mental images in a celebration of cross-pollination and fusion. Thus, when he describes kissing his high-school love Donna he states:

> we kiss as though Shango [Yoruba god of thunder] flung small sweetened lightning bolts between us like firework-flavoured mangoes [. . .] I was caught between wild stallions and electric mangoes.
>
> *(p. 23)*

The oral tradition of storytelling from which the trickster tales derive informs Ellams' performance style which relies more on the spoken word than visual theatrical effects. During the solo performance attention is drawn to the performer's voice and to the physical demands of delivering the text. The performance demands that the intercultural imagery of the complex word combinations become vocalised. Ellams impressively controls the rhythm of the poetry and his ability to articulate the complex language and word juxtapositions over the duration of the performance event. His virtuoso delivery renders his tongue as much a trickster as his tale.

The trickster is characterised differently in continental African and New World contexts. Shaped by the experience of slavery and racism, trickster tales transported to the Americas from West Africa during the Middle Passage emphasised the trickster's potential to subvert authority from within and ability for self-preservation. Similarly, following Ellams' move to the UK we witness the young trickster flourish in different ways as he responds to his change in circumstances. On discovering that, unlike in Nigeria, British schools don't practice corporal punishment, Ellams exploits the situation and its possibilities for naughtiness. The trickster in him also gives him the wherewithal with which to counter racism. At school in London, he describes 'the first time I'm called a *nig nog*' (p. 15) and he portrays Dublin as 'a world more alien than London was, so far from Nigeria, I was the only Black boy in school' (p. 21). But being a trickster empowers him to revel in his difference as 'half-boy, half-blur, Nigerian thick-accented black attack' (p. 16) providing him with the apparatus to challenge the system: 'My grandfather's fleet feet and my father's contempt for authority catapult me across the swirling new world' (p. 16). Henry Louis Gates, Jr. argues that the recurrence of the trickster archetype in African origin cultures in the 'New World' renders it a 'repeated theme or topos' and is proof of 'shared belief systems maintained for well over three centuries' (1988, pp. 4–5). The trickster tales which were changed to suit their new contexts nevertheless 'continued to function both as meaningful units of New World belief systems and as traces of their origins' (pp. 4–5). *The 14th Tale* recalls this Old to New World creolisation of the trickster archetype as Ellams narrates his transformation that is simultaneously Nigerian and Nigerian British. In doing so he performs his Nigerian roots and subtle diasporic allegiances.

The 14th Tale does not resemble the politically charged words of many of Britain's (and other globally celebrated) black performance poets. Neither does it explore issues of race and racism in the same way as other black British playwrights, especially those working within a similar solo poetic/dramatic performance or 'monodrama' (see Osborne, 2008) mode. *The 14th Tale* is a more inward-looking exploration of Ellams' personal Nigerian British diasporic condition. Arguably, however, the play subverts dominant approaches by challenging assumptions and rejecting any 'burden of representation' (Hall, 1988). At the start of *The 14th Tale* Ellams' clothes are covered in a red substance which the stage directions insist must give '*the impression of blood*' (2009, p. 7). It is only towards the very end of the play that we learn that it is, in fact, red paint (he had been playing a trick on a girl who had jilted him by putting red paint in her shower head). This ultimate act of trickery is to make us think that his play will include a dangerous encounter, probably involving knife-crime. In doing so he deliberately challenges audience assumptions about black British dramas as well as his fellow contemporary playwrights' focus on such themes. The cheeky rejection of expected representations articulates his 1.5 generation status as being in-between categories and categorisations, a theme explored more fully in his second play.

Untitled, also directed by Thierry Lawson, opened at the Bristol Old Vic and toured nationally. It was also performed at London's Soho Theatre. *Untitled* resembles a traditional piece of drama more than *The 14th Tale* in its presentation of a fictional narrative involving two characters and its use of costume and set. Like *The 14th Tale*, *Untitled* is a one-man play written and delivered in a style which blends storytelling with performance poetry. *Untitled* draws on a wide variety of source texts from traditional Nigerian folk tales, modern Nigerian and other world literature:

> I stole from Chinua Achebe and Ben Okri, celebrated Nigerian writers. Their novels 'Things Fall Apart' and 'The Famished Road' inspired parts of Untitled as did Salman Rushdie, Neil Gaiman, Terry Pratchett, Nii Parkes, Roger Robinson, Major Jackson, Jay Bernard, Kayo Chingonyi, Kwame Dawes, Jacob Sam-La Rose, Niall O'Sullivan, Mos Def, Talib Kweli, Saul Williams, Tracy Chapman, Sekou Sundiata, John Keats . . . the list goes on.
> *(qtd in Austin, 2010)*

Ellams is both a diasporan and a twin. Two fundamental aspects of his identity are based on binaries. He describes the genesis of thought for his play:

> I was born with the first seed of the play: I have a twin sister. [. . .] Now, way back when, twins were seen as evil portents in parts of Nigeria. When they were born they were destroyed instantly, sometimes with their mother. Things have changed, twins are celebrated now. There is even a twin worshiping cult that sees us as spiritually powerful, tricksters, gifts from God, two halves of the same soul. And finally, I believe Nigeria's identity to be twinned; split between its indigenous population and its far reaching diasporic communities.
>
> *(qtd in Austin, 2010)*

Untitled is about two identical twin brothers X and Y who are separated at birth and raised in Nigeria and London respectively. The play operates on a symbolic level as an articulation of the complexities of diasporic identity. The notion of the dual or twin provides the conceptual apparatus for Ellams' exploration of diaspora. The play is divided into two acts and presents twin protagonists X and Y in two locations. By constructing the play around binaries Ellams deconstructs diaspora into its constitutive parts of home and host-land. Although fictional, the play contains autobiographical elements which makes it possible to find slippages between the protagonists' and writer's experiences. Through his performance of *Untitled*, Ellams explores his personal relationship to ideas of 'home'.

The play begins with a naming ceremony in which the new-born twins (born on 1 October, Nigeria's Independence Day) are taken to the forest to be named by their parents. During this rite of passage, Ellams (who plays multiple characters in the play including the narrator) tells us that in Nigeria there is the belief that a name's meaning will define the child's future. However, although Y received a name (we never find out what this is in the play), when it was X's turn he cried and rejected his name. Perceived as an ill omen, X's un-naming causes his parents to fight and separate. X remained in Nigeria with his father and Y was taken to live in Britain with his mother. The remainder of the first act depicts X's childhood.

X revels in his namelessness and the freedom it allows him to define himself. However, the village interprets his lack of a name as the reason for his refusal to conform to their traditional way of life. Eventually, he is banished from the village by the elders and given a term of seven days to find a name or be killed. Defiant, X refuses to conform to either the villagers or the gods. The act ends with him being struck by lightning.

The second act begins in London and describes a week in Y's life working for an advertising agency. When Y is taken ill with a sudden fever, he is urgently called to his mother's flat where she tells him to return to Nigeria and find his brother. Arriving in Lagos, Y discovers X buried beneath a pile of leaves. He drags him, almost dead, from the earth. At their touch, they share each other's memories, a connection which brings X back to life.

Untitled is a coming of age story about twins who, despite being raised in different environments, find each other through a deep-seated psychic connection. However, the play operates on a more symbolic level beyond the apparent narrative. *Untitled* explores the diasporic psyche as split in two, producing a 'double consciousness' (Du Bois, 1903/2015, p. 5). However, unlike Du Bois' use of the term which described the psychological condition of being caught between being 'an American, a Negro; two souls, two thoughts' (p. 5), *Untitled* is not presented as a dialectic between being Nigerian and British or black and British. Rather, the play dramatises Ellams' experience of being 1.5 generation Nigerian British. His specific diasporic condition manifests itself in an acute double consciousness, caught between the dialectic of being Nigerian and Nigerian British.

As opposed to being three-dimensional characters, the twins represent the psyche of the diasporic individual split between home and host-land, with X and Y represented as insider and outsider respectively until their unification in the end. The individual is at once at home in Nigeria (X) and not (Y) and likewise he is at home in the UK (Y) and not (X). This double consciousness is echoed in the play's performance in which Ellams plays both characters. In doing so, Ellams performs his own diasporic in-between-ness, switching in accent and physicality between X and Y. Acting as X he exhibits his Nigerianness and transforming in front of the audience (he puts on a shirt and tie at the start of the second act) he performs his Nigerian Britishness through Y. When Y saves X they, and consequently Ellams who plays both roles, become one.

The textual representation of Nigeria (in contrast to contemporary Britain in act two) is deeply reminiscent of the pre-colonial Nigeria portrayed in the first half of Achebe's 1958 novel *Things Fall Apart*. The lack of modern references, characters from village life (including elders, drummers, a medicine man) and the language of the piece with its storytelling style, poetic, proverb-laden text and evocative vocabulary (mango trees, koala nuts, cassava and cocoyams) combine to evoke a very 'Achebian' imagery and atmosphere.

This earthy and fecund depiction is contrasted in the second act with the 'concrete jungle' of London in which the elaborate assonant language and story-telling style of the first act is replaced by a diarized structure and a clipped monosyllabic linguistic delivery. Likewise, the experiences of X and Y could not be more different. In Nigeria, X grows up in a world marked by traditional values and beliefs. He trains as a drummer and then a healer and lives in a world where humans and spirits interact. Y, on the other hand, works in corporate London in advertising and lives in a world of mobile phone technology and high-rise buildings.

It is tempting to see Ellams' portrayal of the homeland in terms of a typically diasporan nostalgic re-imagining. Similarly, given the significance of the twins' birth on Nigeria's Independence Day, it is also tempting to view the piece as an Afrocentric polemic, pitting the values and traditions of pre-colonial Nigeria in opposition to those of the West. However, X's experiences growing up in Nigeria are marked by his conflict with the conservative society. The significance of the twins' birthday has more to do with the notion of independence from restrictive notions of nationalism, authenticity and borders than it does with African nationalism. X is portrayed as a rebel to conservative tradition. By rejecting his name, X refuses to be defined by social norms. It is his position outside of traditional customs that allows him to find new rhythms as a drummer and express himself creatively. X's rebellion signifies a culture clash; however, this clash is not between child and parent, first and second-generation, but between diasporan and homeland. X, in other words, represents a pre- or latent diasporan wanting to escape the confines of Nigeria. Conversely, Y returns to the homeland and feels a deep connection and simultaneous sense of un-belonging: 'I stand a stranger in my mother's land, feeling the voice of its flora beneath' (2010, p. 65). Together, X and Y represent the conflicting sense of having intimate knowledge of the homeland and yet feeling disconnected from it. They embody a diasporic paradox of understanding and identifying with a culture while simultaneously rejecting it. It is this profound ambivalence which characterises their diasporic experience.

That is not to say the play is not politically engaged. The piece does not articulate the need to preserve traditional Nigerian culture. Instead its critique is levelled at those in the homeland who see diasporans as somehow diluted versions of themselves, the indigenous inhabitants still living there, and those in the host-land who see diasporans as representative of indigenous authenticity. The play alludes to the relationship that exists between immigrants and their children with their original homeland communities. Ellams' somewhat romantic depiction of Nigeria, steeped in tradition and conservative values, highlights the diasporic sense of exclusion from belonging to the homeland. The gradual erosion of markers of authenticity which underwrite national belonging, such as the ability to 'perform' certain cultural traditions or speak the language, highlight the dissonance between the diaspora living in the West and their 'people' living in continental Africa. The play's tagline is 'If we let our children name themselves, will they author their own destinies?' Ultimately, the play is about the freedom to choose your own identity and, therefore, your own destiny. According to Hall:

> Diaspora does not refer us to those scattered tribes whose identity can only be secured in relation to some sacred homeland to which they must at all costs return [. . .] The diaspora experience [. . .] is defined not by essence or purity, but by the recognition of a necessary hetero-geneity and diversity.
>
> *(1990, p. 235)*

Therein lies the work's 'resistance': By locating him/herself between places with an allegiance that exists both beyond and within the nation, the diaspo-ran's transnational identification challenges restrictive notions of belonging, identity and culture held by those in both home and host-lands.

Ellams' borrowings from a diverse range of genres and cultures, while maintaining a close connection to, and interaction with, the cultures of his Nigerian homeland, combine to produce an aesthetic which is distinguished by its Afropolitan transnationalism. In relation to black British plays in this book, what is striking is that Ellams' plays discussed here do not explicitly speak to wider social or political concerns as they intersect with issues of race. Given that he cites Nigerian storytelling and hip-hop traditions as inspiration, and given that among many black artists in the UK and USA performance poetry has distinguished itself as counter hegemonic, the absence of race politics could be seen as remarkable. Osita Okagbue defines the key char-acteristics of African storytelling as being audience participation (chanting, call and response), its flexible form (improvisation) and formulaic structure (opening with a song or address to the audience and closing with a summary of the tale's moral point) (1997, p. 127). Black performance poetry traditions and hip-hop genealogies are often traced back to and located within African oral traditions. Beth-Sarah Wright claims that:

> What we recognize as performance poetry today derives from the structure and roles of the griot of western Africa [. . .] But the

contemporary cultural variations do not reflect direct recreations, but represent repetitions of the original 'with a difference'.

(Wright, 2000, pp. 285–286)

The same characteristics of African storytelling identified by Okagbue are often used to authenticate the genre by locating its position within a continuum of African tradition that emphasises historical preservation and community cohesion. Arguably, Ellams moves away from the participatory and communal elements that define traditional notions of 'African' storytelling and, by extension, black performance poetry. He describes his journey from performance poet to playwright:

> I write dense poems, try to pack them with imagery to always keep a mind turning and listening. This means that my work thrives in quiet places and in sobriety. Sometime in 2007, in a big headed kinda way, I got tired of presenting work of the latter description to audiences intoxicated or in an environment of easy distractions. For this reason, I wished to work in solitary confinement, in a blank space where light and sound could be controlled. Theatre gives exactly that opportunity.
>
> *(Ellams, 2011)*

Furthermore, his combination of Nigerian, black diasporic and (white) Western sources also suggests an approach which foregrounds a postmodern and globalised identity and identification. In *Black T-Shirt Collection* [2012, Bristol Old Vic] Ellams expands his focus to interrogate wider issues, including islamophobia, homophobia and global capitalism. The play, also a solo performance, follows two foster brothers who flee Nigeria and travel around the world setting up their T-shirt brand. In *Black T-Shirt Collection* Ellams explores social issues with a global resonance and of direct relevance to the country of his birth and the wider African continent. Nevertheless, preoccupation with themes of displacement and diaspora recur. Ellams' website states that *Black T-Shirt Collection* 'drew on Inua's own experiences of religious tensions in Nigeria to tell a story about the universal longing for a place to call home' (Ellams, 2016). Ellams' plays complicate dualistic notions of diaspora by blurring distinctions between homeland and host-land, giving dramatic form to his 1.5 generation Nigerian British experiences. The combination of African (origin) and Western performance modes and artistic influences in his works support and echo his thematic and ontological concerns rather than providing a critique of Western hegemonic discourses. Ultimately, his plays reject polemic in favour of foregrounding an exploration of the (middle-class) self before the 'community'.

Note

1 *The 14th Tale* was commissioned by the Battersea Arts Centre after a showcase in which Ellams dramatised a selection of poems from his first collection of poetry, *Thirteen Fairy Negro Tales* (2005). As a performance poet, Ellams has performed at a number of UK festivals and venues, including The Royal Albert Hall and The Southbank Centre.

Works cited

Austin, M. 2010. Inua Ellams Q & A. *Theatre Bristol.* [Online]. 21 September. [Accessed 24 June 2015]. Available from: http://theatrebristol.net/showcase/inua-ellams-q-a

Dent, S. 2008. Poetry that doesn't toe a party line. *The Guardian.* [Online]. 7 October. [Accessed 3 February 2011]. Available from: https://www.theguardian.com/books/booksblog/2008/oct/07/radical.poetry

Du Bois, W. E. B. 2015. *The souls of black folk.* New Haven, CT: Yale University Press. (Original work published 1903).

Ellams, I. 2005. *Thirteen fairy negro tales.* London: Mouthmark.

———. 2009. *The 14th tale.* London: Flipped Eye.

———. 2010. *Untitled.* London: Oberon.

———. 2011. Biography. [Online]. [Accessed http://phaze05.com/]

———. 2016. Welcome. [Online]. [Accessed 21 October 2016]. Available from: http://www.inuaellams.com/#about

Gates Jr., H. L. 1988. *The signifying monkey: A theory of African-American literary criticism.* New York: Oxford University Press.

Hall, S. 1988. New ethnicities. In: Mercer, K. ed., *Black film, British cinema: ICA documents 7.* London: Institute of Contemporary Arts, pp. 27–31.

———. 1990. Cultural identity and diaspora. In: Rutherford, J. ed., *Identity: Community, culture, difference.* London: Lawrence & Wishart, pp. 222–237.

Okagbue, O. 1997. The strange and the familiar: Intercultural exchange between African and Caribbean theatre. *Theatre Research International.* 22(2), pp. 120–129.

Osborne, D. 2008. Lemn Sissay's life's source: An interview and commentary. In: Osborne, D. ed., *Hidden gems.* London: Oberon, pp. 318–326.

Pelton, R. D. 1980. *The Trickster in West Africa: A study of mythic irony and sacred delight.* Berkeley: University of California Press.

Wright, B.-S. 2000. Dub poet lekka mi: An exploration of performance poetry, power and identity politics in black Britain. In: Owusu, K. ed., *Black British culture and society: A text-reader.* London: Routledge, pp. 271–288.

9

EMPATHY IN DIASPORA

debbie tucker green's *stoning mary*, *generations* and *truth and reconciliation*

In this chapter, debbie tucker green's *stoning mary* [2005, Royal Court Theatre], *generations* [2007, Young Vic] and *truth and reconciliation* [2011, Royal Court Theatre] are discussed in relation to the notion of the African diaspora and against the wider backdrop of what Butler refers to as 'race logic' that connects 'Africa and its descendants' (2010, p. 23). As a black British playwright of Caribbean heritage, tucker green's engagement with Africa in these plays prompts questions about her relationship with the notion of the African/Black diaspora and the 'ancestral' homeland and how this informs the content and style of her dramas. In particular, this chapter is concerned with examining how tucker green's plays about Africa articulate a collective yet differentiated experience or, as Richards puts it, a central issue of diaspora, how they build 'affective bonds within the context of historical differences' (2010, p. 201).

Since 2003 with the staging of *dirty butterfly* [2003, Soho Theatre] followed by *born bad* [2003, Hampstead Theatre],[1] for which she won the Laurence Olivier Award for Most Promising Newcomer, tucker green's work has been staged in high-profile venues to critical acclaim.[2] Alongside having written over ten plays for stage she has also written for radio, television and film.[3] tucker green's work has been praised (and criticised) for its thematic boldness and innovative style. Her exploration of topical issues, dramatised through personal relationships in plays that often foreground women's experiences, has earned her a reputation as a political, ethical and experimental contemporary British dramatist (see, for example, Goddard, 2015; Osborne, 2015). Her pieces are encased in a short play format. This has led some reviewers to remark on her ability to create a powerful effect in a short time and others to suggest that she does not allow space to fully explore complex issues. Furthermore, her treatment – which favours exposition over action – could be described as theatrically conservative. Her plays are so word-heavy that some reviewers have suggested tucker green's works are more akin to performed poetry than plays and are better suited to radio than to theatre (see, for example, Billington, 2005; Johns, 2003; Spencer, 2011).

Yet tucker green's treatment of bold and provocative subjects suggests anything but vagueness or emotional detachment on her part. Her treatment of issues such as knife crime in *random* [2008, Royal Court Theatre], sex tourism in *trade* [2005, Swan Theatre] and capital punishment in *hang* [2015, Royal Court Theatre] demonstrate a commitment to representing experiences of those who are marginalised and/or victims of abuse, exploitation or extreme conflict. tucker green's style and subject matter has elicited comparisons with a number of white British playwrights such as Harold Pinter, Caryl Churchill and the 'in-yer-face' (Sierz, 2001) writers of the 1990s such as Sarah Kane and Mark Ravenhill. For Ken Urban, what tucker green and the New Brutalists share in common is writing which, through Artaudian cruelty, 'seeks possibilities in an ethical nihilism' and 'challenges the cynicism and opportunism of the historical moment' (2008, p. 53). However, the comparison of her work to white British playwrights is an association tucker green refutes:

> Critics have likened Tucker Green's [*sic*] work to that of the late Sarah Kane. You can see why: her plays are urgent, angry accounts of the way we live now. [. . .] Tucker Green [*sic*], however, is having none of it. 'I just don't see it,' she sighs. 'I think it says more about critics' reference points than my work. The influences for me are people like the Jamaican poet Louise Bennett – and music, particularly songwriters such as Jill Scott and Lauryn Hill'.
>
> *(Gardner, 2005)*

tucker green also cites Ntozake Shange and her choreopoem technique as inspiration and Osborne notes similarities with Suzan-Lori Parks' work (2015). For tucker green, her stylistic, aesthetic and thematic influences are primarily rooted in the African/black diaspora and fundamentally shaped by her race and gender:

> Obviously I'm a black woman, so I know the conversations I've had with my friends. With Zimbabwe, we were like 'You know what, if

> it was them, they'd make sure it was on the news, they would make
> sure it was flagged up 24/7 if it was white people'. So that's from my
> standpoint, but obviously my standpoint is different to somebody else's
> standpoint, maybe a white person's standpoint.
>
> *(qtd in Peacock, 2008, p. 60)*

Existing criticism has explored the content and form of tucker green's work in
relation to feminist and human rights concerns (see, for example, Aston, 2011;
Goddard, 2015, pp. 69–94 and 121–154; Osborne, 2015). Analysing the mainstream critical reception of tucker green's work, Osborne (2007) argues that
tucker green destabilises the critics' paradigms of what theatre should be, while
also revealing their inability to discuss her work within a framework which does
not subscribe to white male Western orthodoxy. Goddard insists 'it is equally
imperative to understand black women's work within traditions of black cultural production, and tucker green locates her main inspirations as coming from
black music, poetry and performance' (2007, p. 185). However, work remains to
be done in terms of mapping the influence of black cultural traditions on tucker
green's plays and analysing them using non-Western critical frameworks. tucker
green's work, both stylistically and thematically, draws on the creative influences
and political legacy of the African diaspora. Locating her work in this space
yields insight into her writing style and aesthetic approach.

On the one hand, tucker green's claimed debt to Caribbean and especially
African American women artists prompts an analysis of her work within the
context of the USA or Caribbean. As a result of the Afrocentric movement
in African American art, especially since the 1970s, an African connection
mediated through black America is discernible in tucker green's stylistic
approach. In particular, as discussed below, notions of 'African' orature and
ritual emerge through her poetic style and structural repetitions respectively.
However, on the other hand, mythical or pre-colonial romantic representations do not feature in her work. Instead, she engages with very specific
and contemporary African issues, concerns and places. This yields a complex
relationship with Africa that is both direct and indirect in terms of how it
is represented in her plays as well as how Africa and notions of the African
diaspora inform her work stylistically.

stoning mary

stoning mary, directed by Marianne Elliot in 2005, was the first play by a black
British woman writer to premiere in the Royal Court Theatre's main house.

The play challenges its audience to think about how their feelings for 'others' are shaped at the intersection of race, gender and class against a media saturated backdrop in an increasingly globalised world. The play is divided into sections each focusing on a set of seemingly discrete characters and storylines. The first, 'The AIDS Genocide', portrays HUSBAND and WIFE who are locked in a perpetual battle over a single bottle of antiretrovirals. They are shadowed by two EGO characters who verbalise the couple's inner thoughts. The second, 'The Child Soldier', features a mother and father and their child soldier son, who was kidnapped but briefly returns to visit his family. The scenes featuring this couple focus on their bickering over which of them loves their son most. The last scenario, 'Stoning Mary', is about Mary, the only character with a name in the play; she has been sentenced to death by stoning for murder. In prison she is visited by her older sister. It is only at the end of the play that a connection between the scenes emerges. We learn that Mary has been sentenced to death for killing the child soldier in retribution for him killing her parents, the husband and wife with HIV. The combined issues of AIDS, child soldiers and death by stoning locate the play somewhere in Africa. However, tucker green stipulates in her stage directions that 'All characters are white' and that 'the play is set in the country it is performed in' (2005, p. 2). When the play premiered at the Royal Court in London it featured an all-white cast who wore contemporary British fashion and spoke with English accents.

tucker green's impetus to write the play was in response to the way in which particular issues are racially prioritised in the media:

> with Stoning Mary I was interested in questioning what we don't see and hear. The stories of people who would be in the headlines every day if what was happening to them was happening to white people. It happens all the time. Look at Rwanda. It just fell out of the news. Or Zimbabwe. We're always hearing what is happening to the white farmers but what about the black political activists who are also being killed? Where are the news stories about them?
>
> *(qtd in Gardner, 2005)*

In a challenge to the media's failure to represent Africa's racially and economically marginalised communities, tucker green's play brings the plight of AIDS victims, child soldiers and those who face death by stoning to a mainstream British stage. In order to underline her point, she inverts the audience's assumptions of what victims in the so-called 'developing world' look and sound like. In doing so she poses a question to the Royal Court's audience: how does your relationship to these atrocities change when the victims are white and English?

The 'shock' of seeing and hearing white people with English accents represented as victims of issues associated with non-white people in low-income African countries provocatively draws attention to racialised empathy bias. Some scientific research would suggest this to be true, that a person observing someone of their same race in pain results in a greater 'neural empathic response' (Cao, Contreras-Huerta, McFadyen and Cunnington, 2015, p. 69). But there are also historical socio-cultural factors at play that condition such a response. Theorists such as Edward Said (1978, 1993) and Frantz Fanon (1963, 1967) have illustrated how, in order to limit empathy and thus justify and facilitate enslavement and colonisation, representational discourses 'othered' and dehumanised non-white people. In *stoning mary* tucker green draws attention to this process and legacy through counter-discursive representations.

The play does not plunge the audience into an emotional experience during which they feel empathy for the people depicted because they are white and speak with English accents. Peacock argues that 'the intention is not to distance the audience, but by altering their perspective and thereby forcing them to read the situations portrayed in terms of their own environment, to generate empathy' (2008, p. 60). But, it is difficult to believe what is presented is or even could be England. Watching white people with Estuary accents (associated with people from South East England) brandishing machetes or being sentenced to death by stoning is jarring and, at the time of performance, incongruous within a British context. Such a scenario would be shocking and emotional if the realism of the piece allowed us to accept such events could occur in the UK. However, the audience remains aware that they are watching what is more of a provocation than a 'fourth wall' drama. The fact that tucker green's device of re-locating the play's African issues to England became the major focus of every press review reveals the extent to which a Brechtian distancing effect was achieved. Arguably, this 'alienation' allowed for a critical engagement with the play's discourses on representation and social responsibility. This is not to say that the play is reducible to a simple polemic. tucker green's characters and scenes are involving, yet never completely absorbing, creating a tension which yields a critical viewing position. The audience members, in other words, are not positioned as empathisers but are made conscious of their capacity (or not) for empathy and the conditions which structure such an emotional response.

The various scenes depict characters whose lives have been devastated by circumstances beyond their control. MUM and DAD reminisce about happier times with their son before he was kidnapped. Since the event, however, their relationship has soured and the father blames his wife for their loss. HUSBAND and WIFE are forced to fight each other for their own survival because their economic position only allows them to be able to afford medication for one. MARY is stoned to death in the end for killing the CHILD SOLDIER who killed her parents; the last image of the play is MUM who 'picks up the first stone' (p. 73). The cycle of violence continues. tucker green does not romanticise her characters who, for the most part, are depicted as violent and self-serving. When OLDER SISTER visits MARY in prison she does so begrudgingly and criticises her sister's appearance in a manner which reveals her resentment for the attention MARY has received for killing the child soldier. The result is a complex portrait of the desires, fears and obstacles faced by people living in such circumstances structured by poverty, war and dictatorship.

Before each scene begins, its title is projected onto the set in a bright white light. For example, the first scene begins with the projection: 'The AIDS Genocide. The Prescription' (p. 3). These titles, reminiscent of newspaper headlines, frame each scene. The tension created by the titles, and the scenes of human suffering which follow, highlight the media's often sensationalist, superficial and monolithic portrayal of Africa. The wider political point this raises is one of social responsibility. As Urban points out:

> In a real sense, tucker green's play envisions the consequences of Blair's widely reported statement made to the World Economic Forum in January 2005. There, Blair told his audience, 'If what was happening in Africa today was happening in any other part of the world, there would be such a scandal and clamour that governments would be falling over themselves to act in response'.
>
> *(2008, p. 52)*

tucker green highlights that this lack of responsibility is rooted primarily in racism. However, she also draws attention to other barriers which prevent the individual from engaging with the politics of global solidarity, which must necessarily transgress not only racial divides but also ethnic, economic and national borders. In particular, she takes women to task as recipients of oppression who refuse to see or act beyond the confines of their own racial/ social/ethnic/economic positionalities. When Mary finds out from her sister that only twelve people signed the petition for her release, and fewer than ten marched for her, she launches into a monologue which attacks women ('bitches') who do not support each other:

Mary: So what happened to the womanist bitches?/. . . The feminist bitches?/. . . The professional bitches./What happened to them?/ What about the burn their bra bitches?/The black bitches/the root-sical bitches/the white the brown bitches/the right-on bitches/what about *them*?

(2005, pp. 61–62)

In *stoning mary* tucker green speaks to a diverse audience. Although the play is geared towards inverting images of poverty, disease, and violence associated with non-white people, the play also raises questions for a black British audience and their situation within the West and relationship to developing countries, the so-called 'third world'. For all women, Mary is an example. At the end she asserts herself and says defiantly: 'Least I done something. I done something –/I did' (p. 63).

The relationships between each set of characters add to the play's overall message in microcosm. Each pairing of characters reveals a relationship of antagonism, disloyalty and selfishness. It is this ego – which finds physical representation in the husband and wife ego-characters, and again in those of the older sister and her boyfriend at the end of the play – which impairs symbiotic and loving relationships. These relationships reinforce tucker green's message of society's failure to see through the eyes of the other. By using white actors to play characters typically associated with black Africans, the play literally brings the 'third' world into the body of the 'first' and the global into the local: we are them and they are us it implies. The set, an azure playing space surrounded by rocks, reiterates this idea. It represents the sky, which connects and unites the globe. It is on this globalised stage that tucker green's drama unfolds. The play's genesis and performance, like the other 'African' dramas discussed in this section, stems from and can be located within tucker green's sense of African diasporic identification and responsibility.

generations

In *generations*, directed by Sacha Wares, tucker green continues her exploration of urgent African themes.[4] With a running time of under thirty minutes, *generations* is a simple yet poignant play about the devastations of AIDS in South Africa. It presents a family of three generations preparing a meal. The family banter with each other about who taught who to cook and how each couple came together. As the play progresses family members leave: first the younger sister, then the elder sister and her boyfriend, followed by the father, and then the mother, until just the grandparents remain. With each character's 'death' the dialogue between the family begins again and is repeated, becoming shorter as the family numbers dwindle.

The play's staging at the Young Vic in 2007 accentuated the emotional impact of the piece by immersing the audience in a participatory and sensuous experience. The space was transformed into a kitchen in a South African township. The floor was covered in red earth (typical of soil in some parts of South Africa) and the audience sat around the playing space on up-turned drinks crates. In the centre was the kitchen, with pots on the stove and the smell of stew in the air. The cast of seven actors were supported by members of the African Voices choir who were positioned throughout the audience and which added to the communal feeling of the experience. The singing added a highly emotional soundtrack which amplified the poignancy of the drama. As the audience entered the space the choir sang a dirge comprising a list of names, which represented the many South Africans who have died from AIDS. As each character left the stage, they joined the choir and their names were sung and added to the list of the deceased. The play ended with the choir singing the South African national anthem.

Generations does not utter the word 'AIDS', though disease is mentioned in the programme. This 'silence' (see Abram, 2014) emphasises the stigma associated with the disease in Africa, where AIDS-related deaths often continue to be misattributed to other causes. By focusing on the family the play dramatically portrays the effects of the disease on a personal level; the incorporation of the choir adds to this a national level. As one reviewer noted: 'The statistics are rendered human and the tragedy of an entire continent made personal in Debbie Tucker Green's [*sic*] devastating play' (Gardner, 2007). Unlike *stoning mary*, *generations* does not distance the audience. Instead, its poignant repetitiveness and immersive elements prompt quiet reflection and meditation.

The personal drama is presented through the ritual of cooking. As the family members discuss methods of preparation, boast about personal skills and joke about how they met their partners, tucker green highlights the meal as the nucleus of family: it is through cooking we see a family come together and share their stories and skills with the next generation. The tragedy, tucker green suggests, is not just the breakdown of families in terms of people; the loss of memories, history, traditions and skills are also at stake. By placing the two rituals of cooking and funerals (signified by the choir) together, the former associated with life, the latter with death, tucker green underlines the dark irony of AIDS itself as a deadly virus transmitted through the act of creation.

Presenting complex emotional issues and character interactions through the form of a pared-down ritual is a hallmark of tucker green's dramaturgy. The repetitive sections of dialogue in *generations*, which begin again with each family member's passing, resemble the prescribed order of events which characterises ritual practices. According to Osita Okagbue, two key elements that have shaped the dramatic structure of African and Caribbean plays are 'the relationships between the living and the dead' and a 'cyclic view of life (an expansive universe that is in perpetual flux and thus demands an expansive mode of perception and expression)' (1997, p. 122). Okagbue attributes these to an 'African cosmological system' (p. 122). The belief in a shared cosmological system is intrinsic to Afrocentric conceptualisations of the African diaspora. (As previously argued, African American activists and artists in particular have played a prominent role in shaping this discourse and giving form to it through dramatic representations. Both elements of this cosmological system can also be traced in the dramatic structuring of Kwei-Armah and Adebayo's plays, as discussed in earlier chapters). These elements are also present in *generations* (and throughout tucker green's work). The choir becomes symbolic of the world of the dead, and the play's ritualistic dramatic structure and focus on the ritual of cooking and how culinary culture is passed on from generation to generation both tap into the notion of the 'cyclic view of life'. However, tucker green does not borrow elements of ritual practices from specific cultures, nor does she present a romantic, cobbled together idea of an 'African' ritual drawn from a range of sources. Instead, she avoids cultural appropriation or misrepresentation while still engaging with and communicating an African diasporic world-view by using the ritual of the everyday. The result is a distinctly contemporary African diasporic ritual theatre.

Okagbue also identifies the common use of what he refers to as the 'ritual-dream form' in African and Caribbean plays. These plays, by writers such as Soyinka and Walcott, frequently employ a dream-like structure which disrupts time/space unities and linear plots, and rely on a more circular, episodic structure and use of symbols. The audience's understanding of these plays 'works more through a process of cumulative association rather than as a linear continuum of events' (p. 124). Like a dream, the disjointed sequences find order as a whole on later reflection. tucker green's plays speak to these traditions. In terms of structure, her works often comprise fragmented scenes which only tie together at the very end, or which provide key information slowly and often without a full explanation. Scenes of banality are balanced with moments of explicit lucidity which act as exposés as a piece comes to a close. It is in these moments that the themes come into focus most sharply and provide a glimpse into the writer's aims. For the rest of the play, the actions of the characters and the 'politics' of the piece are left deliberately opaque. Thus, although *generations* explores AIDS, the subject matter is never stated, and the characters are never given the opportunity to articulate their emotions. Instead, the piece operates more impressionistically, producing a feeling rather than a discussion of loss and the social implications of AIDS. Through the repetitive dialogue and circular action, meaning is made not by linear progression but rather by this 'process of cumulative association'. It is only at the end of the piece that, when considered as a whole, one may reflect on its full implications. The cooking ritual also acquires its symbolic meaning through repetition, signifying home, nourishment, and the passing on of traditions and skills. In each cycle a family member disappears. The food is uneaten and preparation begins again. In the process, issues of waste, futility, and the impact of the regression the disease is causing in society are underlined. Thus, the natural order of death is reversed.

truth and reconciliation

Using the form of South Africa's Truth and Reconciliation Commission (TRC),[5] *truth and reconciliation* stages the interaction of victims and perpetrators of crimes against humanity. The play's staging in 2011 at the Royal Court's smaller Theatre Upstairs also marked tucker green's début as a theatre director. The play is made up of disconnected and interwoven vignettes set in five countries which share a common experience of prolonged conflict and trauma: Bosnia, South Africa, Northern Ireland, Rwanda and Zimbabwe. In each vignette, through the meetings of victims and perpetrators (and, in the South African case, the refusal of the perpetrator to meet a victim's family), tucker green explores whether the truth can ever be unearthed and if indeed it will lead to reconciliation.

In South Africa, a family of three generations waits in a TRC court for the man who killed MAMA's daughter twenty-two years previously. In a *Gacaca* court in Rwanda, Stella confronts the man who killed her husband. In Bosnia, two war criminals try to shift the blame for acts they committed when confronted by their victim, a pregnant woman. In Zimbabwe, a husband berates his wife for speaking openly against the government; in a later scene the wife has disappeared and the husband accuses a woman of being involved in her disappearance. In Northern Ireland, two mothers who have lost their sons clash over who should take responsibility for their sons' actions. The scenes set in Bosnia and Northern Ireland are brief, and more attention is paid to the African narratives. These lesser developed scenes seem somewhat tokenistic; they are used as an expansive device to highlight the wider, global context of conflict and to disallow any easy racial 'third world' stereotyping. However, the emotional complexity of the African characters and emotional weight of their scenes render tucker green's principal focus clear.

The play presents a negative view of the ability to discover the truth and the possibility of reconciliation. Characteristically for tucker green, the play explores the pain of the victims mainly from the perspective of women, who are either direct recipients of violence (Bosnia), family members of a victim (South Africa, Rwanda) or perceived as perpetrators (Zimbabwe, Northern Ireland). Characters are nameless and specificities kept to a minimum. 'Truth' is presented as something that is deliberately withheld, framed by power and self-serving interests. Men, in particular, are constructed as gatekeepers of truth who try to prevent women from speaking out against injustice (Zimbabwe), prevent them from learning the truth (Rwanda), or try to mediate what is and is not allowed to be spoken about (Northern Ireland). The nature of truth as highly subjective and illusive is reiterated by tucker green's often ambiguous portrayal of character and situation. In her plays, characters are frequently given generic names such as 'mum' or 'wife' and descriptions beyond gender and race are virtually absent from stage directions. Biography, psychological motivation and inter-character relationships are left to the actors to establish through their interaction with the other performers. Typically, tucker green fluctuates between allowing characters to extrapolate issues and explore their dreadful detail, or limiting their observations and interactions to the seemingly irrelevant. The technique provides a poignant sub-textual approach where the emotional power is located at the interstice of what is said and what is withheld. In *truth and reconciliation* tucker green deliberately resists clarifying who people are and why they are there, forcing the audience to decipher who is a victim or perpetrator, and the nature of the crime:

Woman: The fact that you. . .

> *She watches him.*
> The fact that you –

Husband: the 'fact'?
Woman: The fact that you are sitting there.
Husband: the 'facts' –

Woman: says to me –
Husband: the 'facts' to you – you stand there and talk of 'facts' to me?

(2011, p. 51)

The repetitive language and oblique character interactions further highlight how language is used to avoid truth, providing a means to circumvent the facts.

tucker green's writing style (evident in all her plays) is based on everyday conversation with its overlaps, repetitions, unfinished phrases and silences. Her plays are prefaced with instructions for the delivery of the text: an oblique indicates when dialogue is to overlap; names without dialogue refer to an 'active silence' between characters; bracketed words refer to a character's intention and are 'not to be spoken' (p. 3). The result in performance is a textual delivery that wavers between the naturalistic and the stylised and which produces a hyperreal, sometimes poetic, often hypnotic effect. The result is a ritualisation of language. Simple words take on added weight through their repetition and become 'heard' by the audience in a different way. The notion of conversations as ritual also comes into focus during a performance, reiterating the ways in which repeating words or refraining from saying something has the power to comfort, coerce or conceal.

As with *generations*, tucker green delivers her thematic exploration through a performed everyday ritual. The interactions between characters hinge on the ritual of meetings. The seemingly banal convention of offering someone a seat and allowing them to speak first is a motif repeated throughout the play with such frequency that it becomes ritualised. The effect is a deconstruction of the everyday which reveals the power-dynamics at play that govern human interaction. To sit down (or not) is to hand over (or withhold) power to (from) the person standing. Furthermore, where one sits is made to be an indicator of one's guilt or innocence. In Zimbabwe when HUSBAND confronts WOMAN whom he accuses of being behind his wife's disappearance she refuses to sit opposite him in the designated chair of the guilty party. Instead, she accuses him of ultimately being responsible for his wife's abduction by not behaving like a 'proper' man and preventing his wife from becoming involved in political activities, and offers him the 'guilty chair'. In the court in South Africa the grandmother vainly tries to coax her daughter to sit down with the rest of the family as a sign of solidarity for when the perpetrator arrives. However, she refuses, saying 'not before one of *them* sits down in front of me on their hard chair first' (p. 44).

The audience sits on the same hard chairs in a circle around the playing area. Each audience member is confronted by a person opposite them, replicating the power dynamic in the play that hinges around a confrontational separation of 'them' and 'us', innocent and guilty. This seating arrangement echoes a major theme of the piece: the divide between the living and the dead. Once again this aspect of African cosmology can be located in tucker green's play structure and, in this case as the director of the piece, its staging choices. tucker green dramatises this 'African' world-view by incorporating two spirit characters in the play. Indeed, only the African characters are visited by spirits, and in performance the scenes where the spirits appear to the living are not framed as surprising but are played as if such an experience is expected and quotidian. Mama's murdered daughter visits the policeman who shot her, and Rwandan widow Stella's husband Moses appears to his killer. These spirits resemble the African ancestors who are spirits of the community's deceased. Because of their maintained interest in and contact with the community, they occupy a position between the living and the dead. In the play, the spirit characters are there to assist their families. Their role is not to achieve reconciliation between themselves and their perpetrators but rather to secure the well-being of the living and to seek vengeance for their murders. The ghost of Moses tells his Hutu murderer that, 'We are not honourable dead . . . we are not forgiving' (p. 72) and that he will continue to haunt him until he tells Stella the truth. It is only through the interaction between the living and the dead that victims engage directly with perpetrators, reiterating the appalling truth that these truths are literally buried forever.

tucker green's stated reasons for choosing certain subject matters, casting stipulations and the way in which, as a writer and, in some cases, director, she structures the experience of her plays, indicates her identification with Africa as a real and as an imagined diasporic space. At play is a tension in her work that balances the mythic and homogenous with the precise and the lived. Thematically, Africa is not represented in an imagined pre-European contact time/space. Instead, pressing African issues are explored and, apart from *stoning mary*, specific countries are represented (Rwanda, South Africa Zimbabwe). Her representations are considered and careful. The critic writing for *The Independent* saw tucker green's *stoning mary* to be perpetuating homogenised Western representations: 'by clumping together these different situations [HIV, death by stoning, child soldiers], Tucker Green [*sic*] seems to imply a generic Africa; a dark continent' (Hanks, 2005). However, by casting the play with all white actors, tucker green was making the point that the West represents Africa by 'clumping together' African issues and portraying the continent as homogeneous. Stylistically, her approach is influenced by and draws on African American-inspired Afrocentrism via the artists she cites as having an impact on her work. As a result, her work echoes and can be discussed through a black/African diasporic cosmological system. Yet she navigates representing essentialist beliefs. Afrocentric features – time as circular, the close relationship between the living and the dead – underpin the work but the evolution of this belief system is suggested through her reinterpretation and modernisation of the African ritual drama format. This is something some reviewers find difficult to accept. For instance, one reviewer stated of *stoning mary* that 'in the end, it feels like a staged poem: what I'd really like to see Tucker Green [*sic*] do is combine her verbal gifts with song and dance to create a real piece of total theatre' (Billington, 2005). For Billington the play was disappointing in that it did not conform to his assumptions of African (and black) theatrical aesthetics. Yet tucker green's challenge to race-based assumptions and expectations lies in her ability to express empathy with the challenges faced by many people living in African countries while not attempting to appropriate or belong to Africa. This negotiation of collectiveness yet difference suggests an ethnical engagement whereby tucker green draws on Africa's diasporic myth for artistic inspiration while representing some of the particular challenges facing contemporary African people and nations.

Notes

1 *Born Bad* has also been staged in the USA, at the off-Broadway Soho Rep in New York in 2011.
2 In 1999 tucker green's first play *She Three* (unpublished) was shortlisted for the Alfred Fagon Award. It was later developed and staged under the title *Two Women* in 2000 at the Soho Theatre as part of a lunchtime programme to showcase new writing (see Osborne, 2015, pp. 161–162).
3 tucker green adapted her play *random* into a film for television which she also directed. It was broadcast on Channel 4 in 2011 and earned her a BAFTA for Best Single Drama. Her first feature film, *Second Coming*, which she wrote and directed, was released in 2014.
4 *generations* premiered at the National Theatre in June 2005 as part of a series of short 'G8 plays' commissioned to explore some of the global issues scheduled to be discussed at the G8 Summit which was being held in Scotland in July of that year.
5 From 1996 to 1998, the South African TRC heard evidence from thousands of testimonies of the atrocities of apartheid from both victims and perpetrators. In the play, the form of South Africa's TRC is used as a conceit to explore the meetings of victims and perpetrators from a range of national contexts. Rwanda has held a similar process, run through its Gacaca Court system. However, Zimbabwe, Bosnia and Northern Ireland have not yet undergone truth and reconciliation processes.

Works cited

Abram, N. 2014. Staging the unsayable: debbie tucker green's political theatre. *Journal of Contemporary Drama in English.* 2(12), pp. 113–130.

Aston, E. 2011. debbie tucker green. In: Middeke, M., Schnierer, P., and Sierz, A. eds., *The Methuen drama guide to contemporary British playwrights.* London: Methuen Drama, pp. 183–202.

Billington, M. 2005. Stoning Mary. *The Guardian.* [Online]. 6 April. [Accessed 21 October 2016]. Available from: https://www.theguardian.com/stage/2005/apr/06/theatre1

Butler, K. 2010. Clio and the griot: The African diaspora in the discipline of history. In: Olaniyan, T., and Sweet, J. H. eds., *The African diaspora and the disciplines.* Bloomington: Indiana University Press, pp. 21–52.

Cao, Y., Contreras-Huerta, L. S., McFadyen, J., and Cunnington, R. 2015. Racial bias in neural response to others' pain is reduced with other-race contact. *Cortex.* 70, pp. 68–78. [Accessed 4 March 2016]. Available from: http://www.sciencedirect.com/science/article/pii/S0010945215000672

Fanon, F. 1963. *The wretched of the earth.* New York: Grove Press.

———. 1967. *Black skin, white masks.* London: Pluto.

Gardner, L. 2005. 'I was messing about'. *The Guardian.* [Online]. 30 March. [Accessed 18 July 2011]. Available from: https://www.theguardian.com/stage/2005/mar/30/theatre

———. 2007. Generations, Young Vic, London. *The Guardian.* [Online]. 1 March. [Accessed 2 March 2014]. Available from: https://www.theguardian.com/stage/2007/mar/01/theatre2

Goddard, L. 2007. *Staging black feminisms: Identity, politics, performance.* Basingstoke, UK: Palgrave Macmillan.

———. 2015. *Contemporary black British playwrights: Margins to mainstream.* Basingstoke, UK: Palgrave Macmillan.

Hanks, R. 2005. Stoning Mary, Royal Court, London. *The Independent.* [Online]. 12 April. [Accessed 5 September 2008]. Available from: http://www.independent.co.uk/arts-entertainment/theatre-dance/reviews/stoning-mary-royal-court-london-485356.html

Johns, I. 2003. Dirty butterfly. *The Times.* 6 March, p. 19.

Okagbue, O. 1997. The strange and the familiar: Intercultural exchange between African and Caribbean theatre. *Theatre Research International.* 22(2), pp. 120–129.

Osborne, D. 2007. Not 'in-yer-face' but what lies beneath: Experiential and aesthetic inroads in the drama of debbie tucker green and Dona Daley. In: Arana, R. V. ed., *'Black' British aesthetics today.* Newcastle upon Tyne, UK: Cambridge Scholars, pp. 222–242.

———. 2015. Resisting the standard and displaying her colours: Debbie tucker green at British drama's vanguard. In: Brewer, M., Goddard, L., and Osborne, D. eds., *Modern and contemporary black British drama.* London: Palgrave Macmillan, pp. 161–177.

Peacock, D., Keith. 2008. Black British drama and the politics of identity. In: Holdsworth, N., and Luckhurst, M. eds., *A concise companion to contemporary British and Irish drama*. Oxford: Blackwell, pp. 48–65.

Richards, S. 2010. 'Function at the junction'? African diaspora studies and theatre studies. In: Olaniyan, T., and Sweet, J. H. eds., *The African diaspora and the disciplines*. Bloomington: Indiana University Press, pp. 193–212.

Said, E. 1978. *Orientalism*. New York: Vintage.

———. 1993. *Culture and imperialism*. New York: Vintage.

Sierz, A. 2001. *In-yer-face theatre: British drama today*. London: Faber and Faber.

Spencer, C. 2011. Truth and Reconcilliation, Royal Court, Theatre Upstairs. *The Telegraph*. [Online]. 7 September [Accessed 15 April 2015]. Available from: http://www.telegraph.co.uk/culture/theatre/theatre-reviews/8746373/Truth-and-Reconciliation-Royal-Court-Theatre-Upstairs-review.html

tucker green, d. 2005. *Stoning mary*. London: Nick Hern.

———. 2011. *Truth and reconciliation*. London: Nick Hern.

Urban, K. 2008. Cruel Britannia. In: D'Monté, R., and Saunders, G. eds., *Cool Britannia?: British political drama in the 1990s*. Basingstoke, UK: Palgrave Macmillan, pp. 38–55.

CONCLUSION

This book has highlighted how interactions between, and identification with, the USA and countries and cultures in Africa and the Caribbean have shaped black British drama since the 1970s. Networks underwritten by race-based solidarity have emerged from and in response to experiences of racism. The sustenance of these ties speaks to racism's legacy and, regrettably, to the persistence of racial inequality. In post-war Britain, black peoples' experiences of marginalisation, un-belonging and rejection from the 'imagined community' (Anderson, 1991) of the nation provide the principal context for tracing transnational influences in black British drama. Racism has affected black playwrights' ability to access British theatres and, in particular, mainstream stages. It has influenced their thematic explorations and stylistic experiments. Experiences of racism have led playwrights to seek inspiration from wider cultural contexts and identify with and speak to a range of international concerns. And, although many of the plays in this study reveal black British playwrights engaging thematically with their local contexts, transnational influences can still be traced in their form and style. If a black British dramatic tradition exists, it is located not in but *through* the nation – in the *trans*-nation.

The transnational frameworks employed in this book have highlighted how black British plays since the 1970s draw attention to the ways in which globalisation has brought about shifts in patterns of migration, settlement and the ways in which identity, national belonging and citizenship are perceived and practiced. The large number of plays surveyed and analysed in this book suggest that migration has been, and remains, a key organising principle of black British dramas. Transnational social and cultural ties and representations are to be expected in plays by and representative of first-generation immigrants. In terms of first-generation playwrights from the Caribbean, numerous examples throughout this book have highlighted their engagement with their homeland and/or the theme of migration. Plays by writers such as Michael Abbensetts and Mustapha Matura document the emergence of a 'West-Indians-in-Britain culture' (Page, 1980, p. 99) and chart the evolution of Britishness and black Britishness. However, second-generation Caribbean British writers producing work in the 1990s and early 2000s also draw on their parental homeland cultures, histories and myths for thematic and stylistic inspiration. Their continued bond and involvement with the Caribbean reiterates that when processes of acculturation are hindered, diasporic ties are strengthened. Plays set in and between the Caribbean reflect a playwrights own positioning in-between their and their parents' birth places. These types of plays often feature characters in search of, or coming to terms with, their ancestral origins. In cases where plays are set in the UK, particularly the urban dramas of the 2000s, migration continues to inform content and structure. In these plays, migration themes are often expressed in the relationships between the different generations of characters as defined by their age, the time when they came to the UK and the country from which they came. Their representation, often accompanied on stage by a multicultural 'soundtrack' of different accents, underlines the diversity of black British peoples' genealogies, which encompass different histories, cultures and geographies. Kwame Kwei-Armah's *Elmina's Kitchen* is one of many examples of a black British play that, despite being set locally, is inflected by transnational ties and situated within global currents: by naming the London café where the play is set (and where the young Ashley is shot and killed at the end) after a Ghanaian slave trading post, Kwei-Armah harrowingly stitches together West Africa and Britain; framing the relationship within the context of 400 years of racial trauma.

The increase in immigrants from African countries to the UK since the 1990s and emergence of African British, particularly Nigerian British, playwrights has disrupted narratives that claim contemporary black British plays have moved away from exploring identity through migration and diaspora. Representations of diasporic identity and identification have not abated in black British plays. Indeed, they have become increasingly complex. Plays by African British playwrights re-complicate notions of Britishness and linear narratives of black

British acculturation and indigenisation. In particular, works by middle-class and 'Afropolitan' first and 1.5 generation playwrights reflect and often represent their own experiences of acute in-between-ness and '*multi-locationality*' (Brah, 1996, p. 197).

Contemporary Black British plays draw attention to the current state of the nation and how the social and theatre landscapes have changed since the 1950s. Since then, Britain has gradually evolved into a multiracial and, arguably, a multicultural society. The success of British multiculturalism is highly contentious – especially in light of, among other events, the 7 July 2005 London bombings, the 2005 Birmingham riots, the death of Mark Duggan, the 2011 England riots and 'Brexit'. It is not the intention to paint an overly optimistic picture. Nevertheless, a number of black British playwrights and practitioners no longer find themselves in the same position of invisibility highlighted by Naseem Khans' report, *The Arts Britain Ignores* (1976). By the time the new wave of African British playwrights emerged on the theatre scene in the 1990s and particularly in the 2000s, precedents had been set by playwrights such as Kwame Kwei-Armah, debbie tucker green and Roy Williams in terms of mainstream access and recognition. However, it also meant that the overwhelmingly white and middle-class Establishment of British theatre producers, commissioners and artistic directors had a precedent of what 'sold'. The prevalence of urban stories of crime and/or racism on British stages has been noted by playwrights, scholars and cultural critics and is echoed throughout this book. Arguably, this appears to have had quite an impact on the types of black British plays that eventually reach full production.

Yet, contemporary plays by second-generation African British playwrights do not engage with race politics in the same way as contemporary works by older second-generation Caribbean British playwrights who grew up in the 1970s and 1980s. The ways in which plays by this latter cohort recalibrate notions of white-only conceptions of Britishness and British drama has been a central area of enquiry of this book. In particular, this book has highlighted how new African British dramas draw attention to these creolising processes but often extend their consideration to the evolution of *black* Britishness. Plays by African British writers such as Bola Agbaje and Inua Ellams point to the difficulty some new African arrivals have in terms of fitting into a black British identity framed by Caribbeanness, the anti-racist struggles of the 1970s and 1980s and working-class experiences. Arrival in this 'diaspora space' (Brah, 1996, p. 208) requires negotiating established notions of Britishness *and* black Britishness. It also requires a negotiation of expectations of what a black British play should be about or look like.

Plays such as *Detaining Justice* and *Gone Too Far!* by Bola Agbaje represent conflicts between characters from African and Caribbean backgrounds. The representation of these antagonisms complicates the idea that white racism alone strengthens diasporic ties with the parental homeland. In *Gone Too Far!* Agbaje explores how intra-racial hostilities drive cultural retention and the main-tenance of homeland nationalism. (This theme reflects her personal experiences. In contrast to Kwei-Armah's experience of racism growing up, which drove him to discover himself as a diasporic African, Agbaje's experiences prompted an attempt to assimilate Caribbean culture before rejecting this and undergoing a process of re-discovering her Nigerian roots). Yet, in plays that explore intra-racial relationships, including *Gone Too Far!,* playwrights often point to the his-tory of slavery as a reason for underlying ethnic antagonisms. Thus, these works reiterate that historical white/racism underwrites contemporary intra-racial hos-tilities. In many plays, divisions between black people based on national and ethnic particularism frequently signify how counter-productive such belief sys-tems are in the global struggle against racial oppression. Roy Williams makes this point in *Sucker Punch*. Just before the boxing match between Leon (black British) and Troy (naturalised black American), Leon's father tells him:

Squid: You don't understand, you can't win, neither of you. Why you think all them white people are gonna be there watching you tomorrow night? Ca they love you?

Leon: They do.

Squid: Yer fart. Ca they love nuttin better than see two black men beat up on each other. They too afraid to do it themselves, so they get you to do it.

(2010, pp. 76–77)

Black British Drama: A Transnational Story highlights that experiences of margin-alisation and racism have not just strengthened diasporic ties vertically – between the parental homeland and Britain or from first-generation to second. These experiences have also led to lateral diasporic ties – identification with black cultures from elsewhere. As Michelle Wright explains:

Unlike a vertical diaspora, in which identities are *inherited* and then per-formed or subverted but regardless reify their origin, a lateral diaspora pushes the subject to understand him or herself outside of those iden-tities we are handed passively and more towards identities that reflect one's own movements and aspirations.

(2013, p. 228)

This book demonstrates the significant way in which identification with African American politics, art and popular culture has influenced black British identity and dramatic representations. Kwei-Armah, speaking on a radio documentary about the impact of the television series *Roots* on his career, remarks on 'the power of the narrative' to fashion identity: 'narratives have shaped my life' he states, 'it's no wonder that I'm in theatre. It's no wonder that I'm a writer' (qtd in *Raising the bar*, 2015). African American narratives from plays, books, films and television shows have inspired many playwrights and are woven into a number of black British plays. Both Mojisola Adebayo's and Kwei-Armah's explorations of black British experiences and identity through the USA are linked to their own experiences of un-belonging growing up in Britain in the 1970s and 1980s. Similarly, they both cite *Roots* as inspirational to their work and sense of identity and articulate the African diaspora as a 'home'. That this displacement has led to identification with, and adaptation of, African American culture is hardly surprising given its visibility, accessibility and the way in which black America has traditionally dominated African diasporic and Afrocentric discourses. Thus, black British drama's African Americanisation is a result of race-based identification and globalisation processes. Technological advancements which have facilitated exposure to other cultures underline that transnationalism is not an experience restricted to cosmopolitan elites. Kwei-Armah acknowledges the power of the narrative; clearly the power of television as a medium has played an important part in bringing African American culture to the UK and facilitating diasporic networks of identification. However, the results are never carbon copies of American works but rather speak to them in a tradition of 'Signifiyin(g)' (Gates Jr., 1988).

Plays staged in the UK from Africa, the Caribbean and the USA that explore black experiences have been an important means by which black British playwrights find exposure to ideas. The influence of August Wilson and Ntozake Shange are particularly discernible across a number of plays. Chikura's humorous opening to *The Epic Adventures of Nhamo the Manyika Warrior and his Sexy Wife Chipo* in which the narrator character implores Chinua Achebe, Wole Soyinka and Richard Pryor (Chikura, 2013, p. 3) for assistance with writing his drama playfully highlights how imagination is not hampered by geographic or generic constraints. The diverse cultural references and allusions to popular culture that litter the texts of, for instance, Mojisola Adebayo and Inua Ellams, reiterate that stories come from stories. The art of storytelling in a postmodern, globalised world is pastiche. In this contemporary context, inspiration is never (if it ever was) only localised.

The array of transnational generic influences evident in black British plays reiterates the need for flexible critical frameworks to discuss the complex cultural significations that occur at the level of their content and form. While African Americanisation, creolisation and diaspora provide this flexibility, there is still work to be done in exploring these interactions and their implications. Black British theatre companies have played a vital role in nurturing new playwrights as well as programming international work and exposing audiences to plays from the USA and countries in Africa and the Caribbean. Where possible, the important programming work carried out by these companies has been signalled throughout this book; however, the contribution of black British theatre companies to nurture transnational artistic networks requires further scholarly attention. Black British theatre tends to be fixed on a given producing location because it does not generally transfer or get re-produced internationally. Some plays have been produced abroad, including Adebayo's *Moj of the Antarctic* (tour of countries in southern Africa), Kwei-Armah's *Elmina's Kitchen* (USA), tucker green's *generations* (USA) and Williams' *Sucker Punch* (USA). An analysis of their international production and reception is beyond the scope of this book but signals further interesting areas of focus. Likewise, international touring companies such as Collective Artistes and Two Gents Productions that work between Nigeria, the UK and the USA and the UK and Zimbabwe respectively signify other areas of theatre production that merit a transnational approach.[1]

Gilroy writes that diaspora 'disrupts the fundamental power of territory to determine identity by breaking the simple sequence of explanatory links between place, location and consciousness' (2000, p. 123). This book has been organised into three sections in order to track how black British drama interacts with a range of geographic, cultural and political spaces. Such separation, however, was only ever intended as a heuristic device. In other words, cultures are not discreet: black British drama engages with all three (and other) spaces of the USA, the Caribbean and Africa in complex ways. When examining black British plays, we are confronted by texts that are 'rooted' within and 'routed' (Gilroy, 1993) through the nation. Creolisation theory in particular is helpful for thinking about culture as process; moving beyond conceptions of cultures as separable units. In turn, this highlights the ways in which the representation of creolised cultures and the process of creolisation can undermine essentialist belief systems structured around notions of purity and the authentic. Black British plays that explore inter- and intra-racial conflicts frequently speak to the need for tolerance. Roy Williams' plays, for instance, reflect on the damages wrought by binary discourses of culture, ethnicity and race. It is at the juncture, and subsequent negotiation, of the terrain inhabited by black Britons and the 'indigenous' white population that Williams draws his rich material. Williams states that 'life in a multicultural society is one big grey area – and I want to see shades of grey when I go to the theatre' (2004). For Williams, the conventional multicultural understanding of Britain as made of people from a range of cultural backgrounds living side by side is unrealistically bounded and neat – in fact Britishness is creolised and amorphous. In this way he centres black British as being essentially British and vice versa. This is not to say that his plays are a celebration of 'optimism'.[2] On the contrary, the prevailing tragedy in Williams' dramas arise when these 'grey areas' of cultural miscegenation are contested by white and black people alike in the name of ethnic and racial purity.

Arguably, through the process of rehearsal and performance, Williams' and many other black British plays enable inter-ethnic and intra-racial interactions, between actors, actors and audience members and audience members alike. In this space, capable of articulating a politics of tolerance and culture of solidarity in and through performance, anti-racism and multiculturalism become embodied. Similarly, transnationalism can become embodied in performance too. The diverse backgrounds of people involved in all aspects of production of many black British plays highlight the cultural complexity of many theatrical performances occurring on the contemporary British stage. For instance, the 'mash-up' of cultural influences that define the style of *The Epic Adventures of Nhamo the Manyika Warrior and his Sexy Wife Chipo* is echoed in the company's make up. The Zimbabwean-born Chikura immigrated to the UK in 2002. Lucian Msamati, the director, grew up in Zimbabwe but was born in Britain to middle-class East African parents. (At the time of the production he was the artistic director of the African British theatre company Tiata Fahodzi). Of the cast of four, two were born in the UK, one in the USA (but also lived in Zimbabwe and England) and the other in Rwanda (as well as the DRC, Kenya, Spain, Belgium and England). The play was staged at the Tricycle, located in the ethnically diverse area of Brent in London where large numbers of people from African and Caribbean backgrounds live. In this light, black British drama not only merits a transnational approach, it is a transnational practice in itself.

Erika Fischer-Lichte proposes the notion of 'interweaving' (2014, p. 11) as a way in which to think through such complex interactions (in this case companies made up of different nationalities). Of particular interest is Fischer-Lichte's identification of the potential for a *'utopian dimension'* (p. 11) to materialise from such collaborations in performance, whereby: 'new forms of social coexistence may be tried out, or they simply emerge' (p. 11). As a result, she argues, 'processes of interweaving performance cultures can and quite often do provide an experimental framework for experiencing the utopian potential of culturally diverse and globalised societies by realising an aesthetic which gives shape to unprecedented collaborative politics in society' (p. 11). Many black British playwrights who have persistently explored issues of inter-racial, inter-ethnic and inter- and transnational interactions have, for a long time, contributed to such utopian imaginings on Britain's stages. Through performance their works can also provide a framework that challenges reductive and essentialist racial and cultural discourses and initiate a space in which to imagine social alternatives. This book has focused on plays and playwriting. The issues raised by Fischer-Lichte in terms of exploring the political potential between artists and audiences generated during performance, and how they structure an affective experience with regard to issues of race and representation, (trans)nationality and (un)belonging are particularly compelling. Hopefully, this book begins this conversation.

The perpetual interplay between the collective and the individual, solidarity and difference emerges from a transnational perspective. By drawing attention to influence and interaction, *Black British Drama* highlights networks of kinship and circuits along which ideas and practices travel and are reconfigured. On one level, this contributes to our understanding of 'black' as a political category, which has enabled a sense of diasporic and transnational solidarity and how this has impacted on dramatic representations. On the other hand, a transnational perspective registers the implications of belonging to multiple spaces on notions of individual and collective identity and how this is reflected in and influences arts practices. Furthermore, as demographics have changed (alongside the development of technologies that facilitate travel, both literal and virtual) so too have definitions of black British and black British drama. To analyse black British drama transnationally is not to see it as something fixed or in isolation or as a discrete entity forged within a single social/cultural/political/geographical area; but in terms of a practice that emerges within and as a result of connections to the spaces of (among others) the USA, the Caribbean and Africa.

Recent events since the research was undertaken for this book, such as the refugee crisis and the referendum in the UK to leave the European Union, might suggest that the power of the nation state to structure experience is strengthening. Certainly in the wake of the vote to leave the European Union a number of incidents of racism have been reported in the media. In this context, it could be argued that the need for the nation as an analytic paradigm is more urgent than ever. Although too early to tell, these events will have implications for black theatre, and black drama will no doubt register these interactions. Transnational approaches, however, are, as this book has demonstrated, no less attuned to the nation and the material ways in which racism shapes black British drama. Stuart Hall writing in 1997 uncannily predicts recent events in his assessment of how nation states will react to globalisation:

> when the era of nation-states in globalization begins to decline, one can see a regression to a very defensive and highly dangerous form of national identity which is driven by a very aggressive form of racism.
> *(Hall, 1991, p. 26)*

If a resurgence in nationalism accompanied by xenophobia and racism is the future, we can expect black British ties with other global black communities to strengthen. In that context, transnational analytic frameworks for analysing black British culture will become even more relevant. Furthermore, understanding the ways in which black British plays are positioned within and speak to wider cultural and political currents highlights the key role black British dramatists fulfil in presenting alternative stories and modes of belonging. These have the potential to enable a deeper understanding of our contemporary globalised condition and to represent 'imagined communities' that are both diverse and tolerant.

Notes

1 For studies that have begun to examine some of these complexities, see Osborne (2010) who discusses Lennie James' experience working in New Zealand on his play *The Sons of Charlie Paora* and Pearce (2016) who discusses *Two Gentlemen of Verona* by Two Gents Productions at Shakespeare's Globe, London.
2 See Suzanne Scafe for a critique of the 'tendency towards optimism in critical readings of Black British culture' (2007, p. 71). She finds Williams' works to be characterised by 'models of 'social antagonism', exclusion and unbelonging', and are, she argues, a useful way in which to 'interrogate this wave of optimism' prevalent in the work of contemporary critics and theorists (p. 72).

Works cited

Anderson, B. 1991. *Imagined communities: Reflections on the origin and spread of nationalism.* Revised edition. London: Verso.
Brah, A. 1996. *Cartographies of diaspora: Contesting identities.* London: Routledge.

Chikura, D. 2013. *The epic adventure of Nhamo the Manyika warrior and his sexy wife Chipo*. London: Bloomsbury.

Fischer-Lichte, E. 2014. Introduction: Interweaving performance cultures – rethinking 'intercultural theatre': Towards an experience and theory of performance beyond postcolonialism. In: Fischer-Lichte, E., Jost, T., and Jain, S. I. eds., *The politics of interweaving performance cultures: Beyond postcolonialism*. New York: Routledge, pp. 1–24.

Gates Jr., H. L. 1988. *The signifying monkey: A theory of African-American literary criticism*. New York: Oxford University Press.

Gilroy, P. 1993. *The black Atlantic: Modernity and double consciousness*. London: Verso.

———. 2000. *Against race: Imagining political culture beyond the color line*. Cambridge, MA: Harvard University Press.

Hall, S. 1991. The local and the global: Globalization and ethnicity. In: King, A. ed., *Culture, globalization and the world system: Contemporary conditions for the representation of identity*. Basingstoke, UK: Macmillan, pp. 19–40.

Khan, N. 1976. *The arts Britain ignores: The arts of ethnic minorities in Britain*. London: Arts Council of Great Britain.

Osborne, D. 2010. 'I ain't British though/Yes you are. You're as English as I am': Staging belonging and unbelonging in black British drama today. In: Lindner, U., Mohring, M., Stein, M., and Stroh, S. eds., *Hybrid cultures – nervous states: Britain and Germany in a (post)colonial world*. Amsterdam: Rodopi, pp. 203–227.

Page, M. 1980. West Indian playwrights in Britain. *Canadian Drama*. 6(1), pp. 90–101.

Pearce, M. 2016. 'Why then the world's mine oyster/which I with sword will open': Africa, diaspora, Shakespeare: Cross-cultural encounters on the global stage. In: Jarrett-Macauley, D. ed., *Shakespeare, race and performance: The diverse bard*. London: Routledge, pp. 65–79.

Raising the bar: 100 years of black British theatre and screen – episode 1 – the big time. 2015. [Radio programme]. BBC Radio 4. 9 November, 13:45.

Scafe, S. 2007. Displacing the centre: Home and belonging in the drama of Roy Williams. In: Anim-Addo, J., and Scafe, S. eds., *I am black/white/yellow: An introduction to the black body in Europe*. London: Mango, pp. 71–87.

Williams, R. 2004. Shades of black: Time for racial myths on our screens and stages to be retired, says Roy Williams. *The Guardian*. 29 April. p. 15. Available from: http://www.guardian.co.uk/stage/2004/apr/29/theatre.race

———. 2010. *Sucker punch*. London: Methuen.

Wright, M. M. 2013. Middle passage blackness and its diasporic discontents: The case for a post-war epistemology. In: Rosenhaft, E., and Aitken, R. eds., *Africa in Europe: Studies in transnational practice in the long twentieth century*. Liverpool: Liverpool University Press, pp. 217–233.

INDEX